GOOD MORNING
MIDNIGHT

GOOD MORNING
MIDNIGHT

Life and Death in the Wild

CHIP BROWN

RIVERHEAD BOOKS

a member of Penguin Putnam Inc.

New York

2003

Riverhead Books
a member of
Penguin Putnam Inc.
375 Hudson Street
New York, NY 10014

A list of credits and permissions appears on page 301.

Library of Congress Cataloging-in-Publication Data

Brown, Chip.
Good morning midnight : life and death in the wild /
Chip Brown.
p. cm. *27854/80 5/03*
ISBN 1-57322-236-4 (acid-free paper)
1. Waterman, Guy—Death and burial.
2. Mountaineers—United States—Biography. 3. Suicide
victims—United States—Biography. I. Title.
GV199.92.W37 B76 2003   2002030695
796.52'2'092—dc21
[B]

Printed in the United States of America

1 3 5 7 9 10 8 6 4 2

This book is printed on acid-free paper. ∞

BOOK DESIGN BY AMANDA DEWEY

For my father, Sandy Brown,
and for Ollie, my son

CONTENTS

✳

GOOD MORNING
MIDNIGHT

1.

THE WILDERNESS
OF THE DEAD

✳

Out of his eyes, I saw the last light glide.
Here among the light of the lording sky
An old blind man is with me where I go
Walking in the meadows of his son's eye
On whom a world of ills came down like snow.

DYLAN THOMAS, *Elegy*

... the stark reality of death, that half-dreaded, half-invited angel ever brooding in the shadows of the climber's world.

GUY WATERMAN, *A Fine Kind of Madness*

B Y FRIDAY MORNING he'd been gone five nights in the killing cold. The climbers who had come to hunt for him had no hope of finding him alive. With only a general idea of his whereabouts but precise knowledge of his intentions, the best they could expect was to confirm his death and recover his body. They weren't certain they could manage even that. Visibility was deteriorating. The forecast called for new snow to blanket northern New Hampshire by the weekend. State search-and-rescue officials who had flown over Franconia Ridge in a helicopter Thursday had seen no sign of his faded navy blue jacket or battered blue pack, nothing in the monochrome landscape of rimed rock and drifted snow that even hinted at the outlines of a man. And now, with new snow pending, with wind churning the dark firs along the tributaries of the Pemigewasset River and roiling the spindrift on the treeless reaches of Mt. Lafayette, the possibility loomed that if the body of Guy Waterman were not located by this afternoon, it might not be found until the whole mountain melted off in the spring.

Making up the morning's party were five experienced climbers and outdoorsmen. Four of the men—Doug Mayer, Jon Martinson, John Dunn, Mike Young—were old friends of Waterman's. They had hauled many casualties out of the wilderness. Mayer estimated he'd been on fifty search and rescue crews in the past decade, and Martinson still remembered his very first rescue, when he'd reversed tradition and gone to the aid of a distressed Saint Bernard. But none of the men had ever set out to find a man they knew so well or cared so much about.

Mayer had gotten the sad news Thursday in Boston, where he worked as a writer for the public radio show "Car Talk." He had driven straight home to Randolph, New Hampshire. When the flyover turned up nothing, he persuaded state Fish and Game officials to let him organize a private ground search. It was hard for Mayer to explain his devotion to Waterman except to say that in recent years he realized Waterman had helped fill a void left by the death of his father. He'd read all of Waterman's books; he'd embraced the principles Waterman had advanced in defense of wilderness; he'd even been instrumental in getting Waterman a job as a winter caretaker of some mountain huts in the Presidential Range, the first steady gig Waterman had had since he'd quit writing speeches for the president of General Electric, in 1973.

Mayer's friendship with Waterman was anchored in the adventures they'd shared. One diamond day in October a few years earlier, they'd scrambled onto Franconia Ridge via the Gargoyle slabs and visited the cairn Waterman had built in 1981 in memory of his son John. Mayer was wiry and fit, and in his early thirties at the time, but whenever they teamed up he was amazed to find himself having to hustle to keep up with the old guy, a Social Security pensioner no less! Waterman and Mayer planned most of their trips by mail. They'd been exchanging letters regularly for more than a decade. Doug was always thinking of things he wanted to tell Guy, and anticipating the prompt reply that would arrive typed on Waterman's manual Olivetti or written out in his neat small hand, the "G" in Guy shaped like a fishhook. Waterman's homestead stationery was any blank paper he could recycle—cardboard candle-box liners, the back side of renewal notices from the Society for American Baseball Research, the glue-free portion of labels he had carefully detached from forty-six-ounce cans of Grand Union pineapple juice. One of his notes to Mayer was scribbled on the back of a Sidwell Friends alumni fund solicitation letter written by a breathless classmate under the assumption that the decades since 1950 had been as good to Waterman as they had been to him. "Dear Guy, we've been alumni for more than forty years. I'm not sure that it's great to have been around that long, but it sure beats the alternative!"

Well, maybe not. Waterman's last letter had been waiting in Mayer's mailbox when he got home Thursday. It was written in first person plural, the somewhat stilted voice Waterman had always employed to speak for himself and his wife, Laura, but which seemed especially tortured and roundabout now that he had to speak for himself about an intention that was his alone: "On a less cheery note, one of us wants to mention what perhaps he has hinted at in conversations over the past couple years. If you hear he's off to the mountains in killer weather, he hopes you may respect that it's his considered preference, and thus not sad news . . ." Driving through the Notch that Friday morning, Mayer had found himself weeping in the shadow of less cheery notes, pinned to his friend's "considered preference" by the lyrics of a suddenly poignant Lucinda Williams song coming from his CD player: "Did an angel/Whisper in your ear/and take away your fear/in those long/last moments . . ."

Surrogate father, surrogate son: the same dynamic defined Jon Martinson's and John Dunn's relations with Waterman. Martinson lived just down the road from Mayer in Randolph; he'd gone to Doug's house Thursday night to help plan the recovery effort. He was forty-nine, the oldest member of the group. He and Waterman had met in the mid 1970s, and had become friends bushwhacking on a bitterly cold day in January 1980. They were embarked on a long route of Waterman's devising, which went from the Hancocks to Mt. Carrigain by way of a gap Waterman referred to ever after as Martinson's Notch. Martinson was panting and muttering under his breath while Waterman whistled Gaelic melodies. Sometimes the elder man would come bounding back from the front to sing of the wonders ahead. His enthusiasm was a force of nature; the worse the weather—the harder the wind, the deeper the snow, the more brutal the temperature, the happier he seemed. It was as if nothing could be better than to be pitted against adverse terrain in awful conditions. Martinson had once lived in Pinkham Notch, and when winter trips brought Waterman into the area, he would always bunk at Martinson's house, careful to bring his car battery into the kitchen for the night to keep it from freezing.

John Dunn had known Waterman even longer. They'd met in 1975 when Dunn was enrolled in the winter mountaineering course Waterman taught. Dunn was now a physician in Jeffersonville, Vermont. Waterman had been the best man at his wedding, and Dunn had named his daughter Laura after Waterman's wife, hoping the older man would see the gesture as the gift of an honorary grandchild. When Dunn received the news, he'd put his big golden-haired dog, Brutus, into the backseat of his blue Honda and had driven two hours to East Corinth, not far from the New Hampshire border, and then slogged with Brutus another half an hour through the snowy woods to Waterman's homestead. He was the first of many friends who would call on Laura Waterman over the next week, a stream of bereaved people bearing baskets of fruit, pea soup, and pints of Ben and Jerry's ice cream. He stayed two hours, drinking tea and tearfully reminiscing in the kerosene lamplight of Waterman's small cabin. Laura relayed what she knew of her husband's plans. Then Dunn and Brutus hiked out in the dark and headed east to Randolph to join Mayer and Martinson in preparing for Friday's mission.

The fourth member, Mike Young, lived in Hanover, New Hampshire. Like Dunn, he was a physician; and like the three other men, he had been aware of the father-son overtones in his friendship with Waterman. He had asked Waterman to be the godfather of his thirteen-year-old daughter, Jessie. Just the summer before, on a sweltering day, he and Jessie had hiked up onto Franconia Ridge. Once when Jessie was little, Waterman had joined them on a trip to Arethusa Falls. He had brought three wooden elephants in his pack, mementos of his long-gone career as a hotshot Republican aide and speechwriter on Capitol Hill. As they were hiking out, he darted ahead, placing the elephants along the trail for Jessie to find. She raced from bend to bend, handing the elephants to her godfather for safekeeping, too entranced by the cornucopia to notice Waterman slyly rehiding the same three figurines.

Waterman's books and conversations had molded many of Young's convictions about the importance of wilderness. He shared Waterman's ethos of self-reliance, his reluctance to accept help, his disdain for intrusions like helicopters, cell phones, trail signs, or lurid unnatural colors that might undermine the integrity of wild places. It pained Young to think the values Waterman had prized in life might be compromised by the spectacle of his death if the search for his body turned into a circus. He and the others were sure Waterman would have dreaded becoming the object of a massive man-hunt by professional rescuers traipsing around in blaze-orange jumpsuits and ten-fouring each other with walkie-talkies. They were privately relieved on Thursday when the helicopter returned without his body. Despite the stormy forecast and a touch of the flu, Young was prepared to go look for Waterman, by himself if necessary. He agreed to drive up early Friday morning with his dog, Jamie, and rendezvous with Mayer and the others at the Old Bridle Path trailhead.

The fifth member of the group was Mike Pelchat. Mayer had invited him along on the grounds that his expertise as the head of the Cannon Mountain ski patrol and a leader of the local Androscoggin Valley Search and Rescue organization might be useful. Pelchat was the only man in the party who had no intimate history with Waterman—and thus was the only one free not to wonder helplessly what he might have said or done to change the old man's mind.

The search party assembled shortly after eight A.M. in the parking lot where the Old Bridle Path enters the woods west of Mt. Lafayette. Waterman's green Subaru was parked across the highway at the foot of the great ice-laced cliff of Cannon's east face. It was a somber day, under somber skies, in a season that makes mountain trailheads seem immeasurably more wild and inhospitable. Nights fall swiftly come winter in New Hampshire. Most of the backcountry huts are shuttered. The mountains are clamped in an immense mineral silence that makes the pastoral gaiety of summer seem as fey and foolish as a dream.

The men dressed outside their cars, pulling on boots and gaiters and parkas. They loaded their packs with snowshoes, crampons, ice axes and, in the event they were benighted on the return, headlamps. Mayer brought a thermos of hot chocolate; Pelchat and Mayer had UHF two-way radios. The one item they would not have been carrying were they headed out for the lark of a winter climb was the portable litter, a red plastic two-piece sled.

Snow was falling when they filed into the woods around 8:30. They were seven in all, counting the dogs. The mile-high summit of Lafayette lay 3,600 feet above, shrouded in blowing snow and cloud. Down among the evergreens and the leafless birch and beech, the air was almost still. They kicked through the cover of fresh snow, and knocked soft bombs of powder from laden branches. Where the trail was packed, the footing was good. Where it wasn't, they sank to their knees in a sort of clownish genuflection.

At the outset, the men conversed among themselves, catching up on travels and exchanging stories of adventures they'd had with Waterman. They had not been under way long when Pelchat posed a question that was on the minds of many people who had known Waterman only by reputation: how thoughtful could the man have really been if he'd been willing to subject his friends to the risk of retrieving his body? Mayer could see Mike Young wince in irritation. Mayer shook his head. That wasn't right, he said. He tried to explain to Pelchat. Waterman wouldn't have wanted or expected them to risk themselves on his behalf. What they were doing this morning was of their own initiative, a way of . . . how to put it? Of paying tribute.

Young was easily the strongest mountaineer in the group—his climbing résumé included the second winter ascent of Mt. McKinley, in Alaska, via the daunting Cassin Ridge, in temperatures of fifty below zero—but he uncharacteristically found himself falling behind the others. His thoughts were a tangle of improbable fantasies: maybe Waterman was alive; maybe they would arrive in time to save him. How many ways had Waterman hinted this day would come? Young faulted himself for not having tried harder to help Waterman. He couldn't ever remember feeling too weak to carry his own gear, but now, as he moved up the Old Bridle Path, laboring with the flu and the burden of what he might have done, he asked Mayer to take some of his weight.

As the trail grew steeper, the conversations ebbed; the men moved upward in the hush of stone and snow. Something sacred in the silence made the occasional crackle of static from Pelchat's radio seem a profane intrusion. (Mayer had switched his off.) By midmorning, the climbers were clear of Dead Ass Bend and were plodding over the Agonies, the three steep sections that try the legs of the trail crews who carry supplies to backcountry huts in summer. The gulf of Walker Ravine yawned to the east. To the west lay the Cannon cliffs and the Great Stone Face, the famous rock formation Hawthorne had immortalized in a short story about the governing power of ideals.

When they reached the Greenleaf Hut, they stopped to strap on their snowshoes. The shelter was boarded up for the winter. The lake it overlooked was a frozen pan of snow ringed by dwarf spruce. Mayer with all his careful preparations was exasperated to discover he had forgotten his snowshoes. But he did not have to flounder in the drifts for long: where the trees quit and the upper flanks of the mountain were exposed to the brunt of the wind, the snow was like concrete. The men fastened on their crampons and began to pick their way through a bitter mist. It was about twenty degrees, winds gusting to thirty miles per hour, visibility one hundred feet or so. Decent conditions, actually, given what things could be like—the sort of weather, Mayer noted with relief, in which you could stop to rest without immediately shivering.

The trail up the last thousand feet zigzagged between tall rock cairns plastered with hoarfrost. Dunn was touched to see the dogs, Brutus and Jamie, move steadily up into the storm, trusting the judgment of their masters. Around noon, men and dogs reached the summit: Mt. Lafayette, 5,260 feet, highest of the peaks along Franconia Ridge.

On the off chance that Waterman had deviated from his plan, they searched the stone foundation of an old summit house, a vestige of the days when people could ride horses up the Old Bridle Path and pass a night atop the mountain indoors. Nothing. The authorities had asked Mayer to carry a camera and, in the event Waterman's body was located, to document the scene of what would be officially designated "an unattended death." Mayer discussed the request with the others. They agreed that photographs seemed pointless and intrusive, and that the camera would be disabled by a puzzling, weather-related malfunction.

They fanned out along the ridge, five ghostly men and two dogs walking toward the north peak of Lafayette. As it would not be easy to shout over the wind, they kept within sight of each other, hunting behind large boulders and combing shallow, drift-filled concavities. Martinson followed a contour on the west flank below the divide; Mayer was higher up on his right; Pelchat was positioned on the crest of the ridge itself. Young and Dunn took lines on the eastern slope, where in good weather they could have gazed across the forest of the Pemigewasset Wilderness to the ramparts of the Presidential Range.

After ten minutes, having descended scarcely more than a hundred yards along the ridge trail, Pelchat whistled out: "I've found him." The others hurried toward the spot where he had stopped. Jon Martinson knew the search was over when he saw Mayer and Pelchat halted in the mist. Mayer watched Martinson come up, struck by how old Jon looked all of a sudden, as if the now ineluctable fact of Waterman's death and the demise of all their fugitive hopes had ravaged his face. No one said anything. For several minutes they stood in a half circle in what seemed to Pelchat to be a state of shock. They wiped their eyes. They put their arms around each other and held on.

Waterman was lying on his side in an alcove of rocks ten feet from where the trail made a sharp turn. The site was screened from the south by a large boulder and opened to the north on commanding views of the upper Connecticut River Valley. Waterman's knees were slightly bent. His hands, in beige leather overmitts with gray knit liners, were clasped against his chest. Snow had drifted over his torso, but his legs were visible, crampons still strapped to his boots—plastic double boots Mike Young had given him in hopes of getting him out climbing again. He was wearing wind pants, a faded navy blue wind shell over a shirt and sweater, and on his head, a blue wool balaclava. In his left hip pocket was a white handkerchief. His ice axe, feathered with hoarfrost, was staked in the ground like a headstone. Its long antique wooden shaft was etched with the initials of his father, Alan T. Waterman, who had carried it to the summit of the Matterhorn in 1928.

As Dunn knelt beside the body to clear away the snow, Brutus sauntered over and sniffed Waterman's face. Waterman had always slipped the dog biscuits during the holidays and tousled the fur on his neck. With men, Waterman mostly confined himself to shaking hands, but dogs he embraced unreservedly, squatting down to greet them nose to nose. Waterman's last published book, a collection of mountaineering articles and stories called *A Fine Kind of Madness,* was dedicated to his seven favorite dogs—Brutus among them. He had completed the book a month before he died.

But Brutus could detect nothing familiar, and he shambled off, leaving Dunn to finish brushing the snow from Waterman's face. Can one see clearly at such a moment—see beyond the semblance of one's self that is revealed in what one reads in the face of someone else? Five men look at one man and see fifty faces. Years of doctoring had exposed Dunn to many lifeless bodies, but now, having undone the work of the wind, he stepped back in dismay as if confronted for the first time by the wilderness of the dead. The man he knew was gone; his friend was gone; Waterman was gone. What remained was an effigy wrought of ice, rigid as a statue. Pain in Dunn gave way to reverent awe. To Pelchat's disinterested eye, the victim appeared to have drifted off to sleep, the end coming quickly enough to produce no evidence of paradoxical undressing, that phenomenon of late-stage hypothermia in which a false sensation of warmth caused by the evacuation of blood back to the extremities prompts a person to disrobe. Martinson, for his part, saw a faint enigmatic smile on Waterman's face that put him in mind of the Mona Lisa. Young was struck by what seemed the mask of suffering fixed there, and again reproached himself for falling short as a friend. When Mayer managed a moment alone with the body, he knelt on the ground and caressed his friend's fatherly face, absurdly worried by what seemed a spot of frostbite forming on the granite cheek.

The men built a cairn on the boulder that backed the spot where Waterman had come to rest. When they had finished paying their respects, they turned to the practical task of evacuating a corpse. They removed the crampons from Waterman's boots. To free his backpack from his frozen arms, they had to hack off one of the shoulder straps with an ice axe. "It was very *Pulp Fiction,*" Martinson would recall later with a rueful laugh. The pack contained two frozen half-filled water bottles, four flashlights, two tins of salmon, a can opener, two clocks, and two small stuffed animals from the menagerie that inhabited the bed Waterman had shared with his wife—a snow leopard called Killy and a tiger named Ben. Mayer unrolled a blue nylon bivouac sack. The climbers worked the bag around the body. A tartan cap fell out of Waterman's shirt; Dunn put it in his pocket. After the bag was cinched, the bundle was lashed to the litter. The whole dismal business took less than half an hour. When everyone was ready to go, Mayer paused to take a long final look so that he might never forget the site of Waterman's last camp.

And then the party started down, two men in the lead, hauling the sled, two trailing to brake it from behind wherever the terrain was especially steep. The fifth man helped out where needed, and they all took turns at each position, trading places as they tired.

"It was a mountaineer's version of a funeral procession," Dunn would say later. "We were pulling him along quietly on the sled, like it was a casket, each of us lost in our thoughts about the meaning of his life. It was as if he were still with us, as if there were six of us."

Down the way they had come, rewinding their route across the upper mountain to the drifts at tree line, pulling past the shuttered hut and icebound pond, then down along the ridge, and into the forest. Martinson remembered a summer day in July eight years before when he and Waterman had been up on Lafayette repairing sections of the trail and were chased off by a savage thunderstorm, Waterman galloping down the Old

Bridle Path brandishing an umbrella above him, his zeal to stay dry vying with his fear of getting toasted by a lightning bolt. Down the way they had come not just that morning but season after season, year after year, descending as much through the strata of memory as through landscape, immersed in times that were gone forever now, blithe days spent with the old man unclogging watercourses or repairing switchbacks or just fooling around on the rock tower known as the Gargoyle, where Waterman loved to make a showy little leap across a heart-stopping abyss. Even when the crew grew weary, worn out by the sled and the weight of the day, they were still braced by a strange joy, the defiant, animal happiness of being alive, kindling their faces in the cold.

The light was fading when the procession emerged from the woods around 4:30. "It was painful to reach the road," Dunn would later say. "It was painful because it broke the spell."

A while later, a hearse arrived to take the body to the Littleton Regional Hospital. An autopsy was performed in the morgue that evening by Dr. Richard Monroe, the medical examiner for northern Grafton County. It was his duty to pronounce the cause and manner of Waterman's death. For the record, the cause was "advanced hypothermia due to environmental exposure." The manner was suicide.

2.

A Peculiar Response

✳

Please don't tell me it all adds up in the end.
I'm sick of that one.

JOHN ASHBERY,
Variations on "La Folia"

Every few years there occurs a particular incident that especially trans-fixes public attention, and the story becomes widely told and retold, with fascination far exceeding that of dozens of other accidents and fa-talities, some of them in the same mountains or involving more people. Some particular ingredients of drama or pathos strike a peculiar re-sponse of sympathy or fascination, perhaps morbidity, perhaps a feeling that some special blend of heroism and fatalism was involved.

GUY WATERMAN, *Forest and Crag*

HERE WERE THE FACTS at the end, the last measurements of a man: a sixty-seven-year-old bearded Caucasian, five feet five inches tall, weight one hundred forty pounds, eyes gray, died on February 6, 2000, of advanced hypothermia due to environmental exposure. The im-mediate cause of death—the "efficient cause"—was a subzero winter night on a New Hampshire mountain. But of course the chilly empiricism of a coroner's report cannot address the deeper reasons and more mean-ingful causes. It can't shed any light on what could bring someone to such a place on such a night.

And what is this "peculiar response" noted by Waterman himself, this desire to know more than can be weighed and measured in a morgue? What is it if not a kind of faith in the ultimate sense and comprehensibil-ity of life—faith that there are deeper reasons and more meaningful causes and that, indeed, the twists of a life can be explained? Or do we delve into a gray-eyed stranger's death for the more fearful reason that we want distraction from the dread of our own—want something to help us tame it, drain it of its terror, make it less wild, less the last ineradicable blank spot on the map?

It's a commonplace that death makes family of us all, but it's just as true that nothing imposes a more drastic and absolute isolation. It may well be that the pity even a stranger's story can evoke arises from what in each of us seems a profoundly private struggle to assert our singularity against the egalitarianism of nature—nature, which does not prefer sentiments to stones, and spends its trillions of lives as casually as rain. Maybe this "peculiar response," this desire to know more than *gray eyes, sixty-seven, five five,* is a measure of our yearning to defend what seems unique and real and doomed about ourselves and the people we love. Maybe it's a measure of our yearning to circumvent the untenable terms of an existence in which everything is vanishing even as it appears. Burying the dead is the most paradoxical of arts. They seem to go not into the ground but into memory—into the strange afterlife of stories that enable us to let them go because they still seem near.

Imagine a winter afternoon in East Corinth, Vermont, a little postcard village strung along the Tabor Valley branch of the Waits River in the east central portion of the state. A village that is home to a few hundred people—dairy farmers, cheese makers, odd-lot loggers, maple sugar men, and come summer, a tribe of city refugees with soft hands and nice-looking cars. On the afternoon in view, Main Street was lined with banks of snow as white as the foursquare houses and the clapboard Congregational church in the center of town. It was a Thursday, the seventeenth of February. Cars were parked all the way back to the second bridge out of town, and, in the other direction, past the general store and the post office, where Laura Waterman had stopped the week before to report her husband's suicide, knowing with what dispatch the news would spread from there.

Now nearly three hundred mourners sat in the pews of the Congregational church. As they waited for the service to begin, piano music was spinning out of a tape player. The careful plans the deceased had made for his funeral included a set of songs he wished to be heard performing posthumously—Scott Joplin rags, lovely waltzes, and pop songs from long ago. On the altar a spray of pine boughs framed a hat—the plaid woolen tam-o'-shanter Guy Waterman seldom went anywhere without, the hat he used to wear at a jaunty slant in the style of those tough Scottish mountaineers who would return from a near-death experience on the local crags saying how refreshed they were, how they had had a spot of trouble at the crux but it was nothing too bad, shame about McPherson losing all his fingers though . . . Waterman liked to be seen in a certain way, and the tam bespoke the showman in him. But he could be witty about his stagecraft. Someone once asked him, "Why do you wear that hat? Are you Scottish?"

"Not as Scottish as I pretend to be," he'd said.

Over the next two hours, the church resounded with hymns, prayers, and passages of Scripture—affirmations of an order Waterman did not believe in. Which is not to say he would not have taken comfort in the poetry of the 23rd Psalm when the congregation stood to recite it: *He maketh me to lie down in green pastures. . . .* Or that he would not have been moved when his niece Laura Cooley stepped forward to read Milton's "Song on May Morning," or when Mike Young presented an excerpt from one of Waterman's five books, *Backwoods Ethics,* or when Jon Martinson declaimed the stern, antipastoral lines in Elinor Wylie's poem "Wild Peaches":

> *Down to the Puritan marrow of my bones*
> *There's something in this richness that I hate.*
> *I love the look, austere, immaculate,*
> *Of landscapes drawn in pearly monotones.*
> *There's something in my blood that owns*
> *Bare hills, cold silver on a sky of slate . . .*

Close friends could only imagine how touched he would have been to hear Danuta Jacob sing "Over the Rainbow," a song that always reminded him of his middle son, Johnny. Waterman had accompanied Danuta on the piano at a local cabaret show just three weeks before his death—his last performance. She was still shocked, having assumed their concert was the beginning of an exuberant collaboration, not a swan song.

After the benediction, the tape machine was turned on again and Waterman could be heard playing four of the pieces nearest his heart. A transcription of Hayden's Opus 54 quartet in G major, the violin part of which he had played as a teenager at the Greenwood Music Camp. Joplin's "Maple Leaf Rag," whose magical melody he had strolled through for decades. Then an old Scottish ballad, "Lament for the MacLean of Ardgour," which had been performed on bagpipes at the funeral of his distinguished father. And finally, one last hymn—"Just a Closer Walk with Thee," which was one of Laura's favorites and which he had always treated as an up-tempo jazz tune.

At an apple-juice-and-coffee reception in the church basement, the mourners sifted their memories of a singular man, glad to recall how sometimes in camp he would roust tentmates with "The Star-Spangled Banner" at five A.M., warbling in his high, reedy voice, wearing his tam and one of those old woolen shirts and the cherished drab orange duct-tape-swathed wind pants that had belonged to his son Johnny. What a remarkable résumé he had compiled in the backcountry of the Northeast, climbing all the classic routes on rock and ice in the Adirondacks, on Cannon Mountain, in Huntington Ravine. His life outdoors was written in his hands: knobby, callused, rock-scored, earth-stained hands that were as attuned to the textures of quartzite and the grain of oak logs as to the syncopations of Jelly Roll Morton. He'd damaged most of his knuckles planting his antiquated 1970s Chouinard ice axe in frozen waterfalls. But at sixty-seven he had been fitter than men half his age, and when it came to bushwhacking through fierce thickets of dwarf spruce, he was unrivaled. As a hiker, he had achieved the epic feat of becoming the first person in the White Mountains to make winter ascents from all four points of the compass of all the forty-eight peaks over 4,000 feet.

For many in the church basement that afternoon, it was hard to imagine how such a vital man could consign himself to the grave. Waterman's death was not entirely unforeseen. Yet somehow all the hints he'd dropped—the not-so-veiled allusions to the house he and Laura were building in town as "Laura's house"; the intimations that he, the youngest of the five Waterman siblings, would probably be the first to go; even his cheerful request of Doug Mayer to come by with a broadcast-quality tape recorder so Waterman could lay down a soundtrack for his funeral—had only sharpened the general sense of shock. Knowing what might happen had not made it any easier to understand.

Most of the mourners had never met anybody who lived a more deliberate life than Waterman, or who had thought so carefully and self-consciously about what was necessary to make the days worthwhile. Or who seemed to see so deeply into others, and yet, on the evidence of his end, was unable to see into himself. Many of them could only guess at the extent of his suffering, which he kept veiled, or referred to impersonally by means of metaphors and literary allusions. Waterman had a prodigious memory and a phenomenal store of references at the ready. He could recite the first eight books of Milton's *Paradise Lost,* nearly six hours of poetry, with his eyes closed. His predominant tendency was to transform the raw stuff of daily life into analyzable packets of data. He was almost never without a sheaf of index cards, which he carried in his breast pocket and would produce to check what was next on his daily schedule or to jot down some small milestone, the first warbler of the spring or the names of the dogs and climbers with whom he had reached such and such a summit in such and such conditions. Every time he hiked a new trail, he'd jot down its notable bends and switchbacks, adding to the map of New England paths he carried in his head. He religiously recorded snow depths, daily temperature readings, number of quarts of ice cream consumed. He counted every blueberry picked in his berry patch, tallying annual harvests that, to choose a year, exceeded 43,000 in 1998. People who helped out sometimes got distracted by conversation and found themselves apologizing for forgetting how many blueberries they had put in their pail. "That's okay," Waterman would say, "I was counting for you." He kept track of every bucket of sap drawn from the maples in his sugar bush. He knew the number of hand-carved pegs used in the construction of the guest cabin on his homestead. On and on, an endless welter of notations, penciled figures, totaled sums. To some of his friends, all the note-taking and data-gathering seemed symptomatic of a not-so-healthy obsessiveness. A compulsive drive for order. And yet by the same token many considered the behavior as a mark of his character, his delight for the patterns that could be uncovered in compilations of data and his intense relation to nature, his aptitude for *noticing*.

The town librarian, Janine Moore, remembered the time Waterman had come into the East Corinth library, where he and Laura volunteered three days a week, and asked if he could photocopy the side of a log Laura had found in the woods. When the page emerged from the photocopier, Moore was astonished to see what looked like a perfect lithograph of a prairie—the trees, the grass, everything but the sod-roofed house.

"What does this look like?" Waterman asked.

"A prairie!" Moore said, still unable to see in the wood what had been made so plainly visible on the paper.

"That's what I think too."

The difference was that Waterman could see it in the wood. He'd always been a man of scrupulous attention to details, his considered preferences having been fashioned in the ethos of a Wasp family in which the emphasis was on education and achievement, self-effacement and service. "Christian morality without Christian metaphysics," as his nephew Dane Waterman characterized it. Waterman had organized the latter part of his life around the ideal of self-reliance. Not a man who liked to whine or ask for help, or who had any patience for the pigeonholes of a therapeutic culture. He shut down his drinking unaided, by force of will. What would seem to have been his classic symptoms of depression he preferred to call "black moods." Problems to other people were demons to him— demons that might be sketched in literary metaphors and conquered, if they were conquerable, by Yankee will and hard work, the fortifying effects of great books, and the company of dogs. Waterman maintained a calendar for which he selected a "quote of the day"—some apt or uplifting bit of literary Prozac. Having determined that one should live by principles, he took the time to articulate a set for himself; he typed them up and let them guide his life, and eventually he savaged himself for honoring them in the breach. He had little use for church or organized religion but unhesitatingly embraced the concept of the soul—seeing it not as a fragment of what was immortal in human life but as the essence of a free and autonomous being, what was expressed when one had mastered one's self in the here and now. As he often liked to say, in one of the many lines he had on call from *Paradise Lost:* "Better to reign in hell than serve in heaven."

So the congregation in the white village church dispersed. Four months after the service, Laura Waterman arranged for her husband's ashes to be scattered at Barra, the homestead she and Waterman had lived on for twenty-seven years. Barra was named for one of the Scottish Hebrides where Waterman's family had roots, and it was mostly family who attended this time, brothers and sisters, Waterman's one surviving son, nieces and nephews. A few friends who hadn't been able to make the service in February were invited, and there were dogs, of course. The little crowd roved the woods, flinging the dust of the man at the maples in his sugar bush—trees for which everyone felt a tender and unusual familiarity because Waterman had carefully tracked the flow of their sap for two decades and had bestowed on each a name, variously commemorating famous mountains, great poems, literary characters, and guys who played baseball for the Washington Senators in 1912. Ash on the bark, ash on the ground, ash in the stream where the absent master had filled his buckets with water and hauled them to the cabin by hand. Ash in the garden. Ash in the blueberry patch, where bolted to a rock a simple plaque read "Guy Waterman 1932–2000." Ash down by the path, where a tree he called the "Gabriel birch" once stood sentinel at the entrance to his homestead, like the angel at the gate of Eden.

Later, friends helped Laura Waterman box up the life she had shared with her husband. They packed the heavy cartons out to the road on their backs: boxes filled with climbing journals, and books, and loose-leaf binders holding lists and notes, sketches for cabin furniture, jazz and baseball article ideas, worthy quotes from Byron and Milton and Wordsworth. And photo albums—a time-lapse collection of pictures showing Waterman as a young Capitol Hill aide next to Richard Nixon and as a bearded, sap-stained geezer fresh from an ascent of a tall pine tree; as a young boy, age two and a half, sawing wood in the family forest in North Haven, Connecticut, and as a soon-to-be pensioner reunited with his brothers and sisters in 1989. Pictures of his sons in their gawky-proud high-school-portrait phase; of Johnny, the beloved middle son alone on Mt. Hunter in Alaska, defying the void in a landmark ascent still considered one of the greatest crazy-genius feats of mountaineering. Pictures of Waterman's father, Alan, the pipe-puffing physicist and founding director of the National Science Foundation for whom a mountain in Antarctica and a crater on the moon are named. Pictures from Waterman's second wedding, when he and Laura paraded under an arcade of ice axes and spent their honeymoon night in a tent on a ledge halfway up a cliff in the Shawangunk Mountains.

Into the boxes went the flood of letters Laura Waterman had received since her husband's death, upwards of a thousand from old climbing partners, jazz buddies, schoolboy pals, inspired hikers, grateful conservationists, colleagues from Capitol Hill; letters even from perfect strangers moved by the story of a man's life as it had been sketched in newspaper obits—all moved by some feeling for the pathos and drama of his death, the way it invited them, perhaps, to brood on the division of pathology and spirit in their own lives.

At the very center of the pathos and drama, of course, was the act of suicide. That a man's death is self-inflicted can add immeasurable angst to the feelings of grief and loss afflicting those who loved him. And even for a casual obit reader there is often an extra measure of mystery in a suicide report. When a person's life is stopped from without by accident or disease, there is nothing to redress—we are obliged to yield to mute Fate and accept that it is not for us to know why. But when life is stopped from within by a god-like self that could presumably communicate and explain its reasons, what in the first case was necessity here appears to be the perversity of choice, and hence seems endlessly contestable. We suddenly feel that it is for us to know why life has to end, that we are owed an explanation—that indeed, at some level, if people are knowable at all, there *has to be* an explanation.

As Gil Murray wrote to Laura Waterman:

I keep arguing with Guy. Why didn't he continue the climb toward our final mysterious summit? Why didn't he savor the adventure ahead? Why wasn't he excited by the challenge of growing old? He was so creative; we create our lives out of the stuff at hand. He had so much stuff. I guess he was too intent on measuring it all instead of reveling in the mad glory, the randomness and all the surprise. It seems as if he saw it all as a log or a record and not a dance with an indeterminate ending. He must have been afraid of being marked or graded instead of pursuing one's own joy—unfathomable and indescribable by others. I think about you. Can you take what you want of him with you? Can you let go of the perplexity, anger, and sadness, and find the spontaneity he might have had could he have escaped his construct?

But of course Waterman died of his own most lethal construct. Whatever life the man who kills himself has before he becomes a suicide, he exists afterward as the invention of a storyteller, a composite remembered and, in effect, reconceived by people who knew him or found something unforgettable about him. If he appears in such accounts to march expeditiously into the death trap of his genes or to founder ineluctably on some dire childhood misapprehension, it is only because hindsight creates the illusion of inevitability. Hindsight swaps the end for the beginning, and lends the false causality and momentum of a plot to what is the banal, meandering, un-story-like way people actually make choices in the face of an unknowable future.

Where do these ghosts come from that have always hovered over the stories and shaped the myths of suicide? Part of the answer surely has to do with the mind's long-standing estrangement from the body, and the dualism that is second nature to us now. We may have conquered the phobias that induced the ancient Greeks to sever the hand that killed itself, or that persuaded some European societies to remove the self-murdered man through a window and then burn the frame, or that once dictated in England that suicides be staked through the heart and interred at crossroads to keep the restive spirit from harassing its old haunts. But the emotions that engendered these cruelties are still in play, and whisper in the trees at night. Moreover, the wraiths of suicide that don't arise from superstition may well come from what can genuinely seem ghostlike in a suicide narrative. There is something elusive and haunted at the center of many accounts of self-inflicted death, a sense that a life is finished but not resolved, that its events are unchangeable yet still in flux. The suicide's story often seems suspended in moral ambiguity, entreating us either to make sense of its senselessness or to take up the harder job of refuting its ominous logic. What but a ghost could be a better figure for a life that not only vanishes into its last act but implies a momentous hidden history in the instant of its oblivion?

When I was first traveling in New England to interview people who knew Guy Waterman, I found myself treading gingerly around the question of whether the significance of Waterman's life depended on the circumstances of his death. Many of his friends had been offended by the morbid emphasis of accounts in newspapers and magazines. Something about the attention his death attracted struck them as unseemly, distorted, more than a little voyeuristic. How easy it was to focus on a man's flaws and ignore his virtues when conventional wisdom and tribal morality assumed that only someone who despised himself would take his own life. To his friends and family, he was a climbing partner, a teacher, a historian, a maple sugar man, an author, a pianist, a baseball scholar, a poet, a confidant. He was someone who beguiled them with homemade birthday cards and spirited quizzes about presidents and favorite Shakespeare characters. But to strangers caught up in his story, he was little more than an interesting death. His life was compelling only insofar as it had prepared him for his death.

The heartlessness of this detached and impersonal view was driven home to me one day when, six months after Waterman's death, I went to see one of his friends, a former Columbia professor named Louis Cornell. Cornell lived on a farm in West Fairlee, Vermont, not far from the Connecticut River. He invited me to sit in his living room, where the walls were floor-to-ceiling books, among them his own biography of Rudyard Kipling, entitled *Kipling in India.* He was a dapper man with an urbane manner; he had met Waterman climbing at the Shawangunks, in New York State, in 1969. They had corresponded for years. Cornell had read some of Waterman's works in draft, and had given him useful advice and criticism.

"Would you even be sitting here if Guy had died quietly in his sleep?" Cornell asked before I could open my notebook.

Or say suicide could not have been averted, would I be troubling him for an interview had Waterman employed a statistically more common method and killed himself with a shotgun? Or a rope, a razor, an overdose of sleeping pills? What if he'd shunted in the exhaust from the tailpipe of his car—the four-wheel-drive Subaru being his one major concession to twentieth-century conveniences? What if he'd forgone the dramatic location of a mountaintop and had sat down in the snow behind his outhouse? Would there have been a story to write? Would his death warrant long articles, much less a book? More to the point, would the riddles of his life have been any less challenging or profound had he died in a manner less noteworthy?

It was a painful catechism, because the answer in every case was inarguably no. The very noteworthiness of Waterman's death was why people were taking note. Had he died in some more prosaic way he wouldn't have gotten half the ink. He wouldn't have been as good a story. Not only was there was no getting around the centrality of his death, there was no getting around the aesthetics of it. And suddenly, sitting in that genteel living room, confronted with Cornell's grief for the life of his lost friend, the clinical sensibility of journalism seemed awfully ghoulish. What could be more unseemly, not to say invasive, than the sort of effort I was embarked on? I stammered out one of the lame rationales my profession often invokes to justify its behavior, this one having to do with the public nature of Waterman's death—as if Waterman, having decided to freeze himself in a U.S. National Forest, had committed an intrinsically public act and thus forfeited any right to privacy. And couldn't you say his death was by some measures a self-dramatizing performance—an extreme way of drawing attention to himself?

Cornell was kind enough not to laugh in my face. Nor did he belabor his cross-examination. Much as he missed his friend, he shared with him the affliction of a literary sensibility and understood the symbolism of a night on top of a mountain in the teeth of a New England winter. He was sure those considerations had been resonating in Waterman's thoughts, Waterman being too much a student of mountains not to appreciate their long history of service to people who have lost their way and want some answers from the universe. As well as anyone, Cornell grasped the aesthetic elements that distinguished Waterman's death from those of the roughly thirty thousand other people who killed themselves that same year in the United States. Bereaved as he was, he could not fault an outsider, a journalist or anyone else, for being drawn to the artfulness of Waterman's final project, not when the art of it had possessed him too.

Cornell and I talked for several hours about Waterman's book-soaked life, his love of literary characters, his penchant for uplifting apothegms, his calendar with his quote of the day, the record he kept of the 269 books he'd read aloud with Laura, his prodigious feat of memorizing two-thirds of *Paradise Lost*. And the paradoxes that encircled him. "I couldn't believe that Guy, who was brave as a lion under most circumstances, was afraid of flying," Cornell said. Although Waterman was steeped in literature, Cornell pointed out that in some crucial ways he was not really "a literary man." "He used language well but completely without flair," Cornell said. "He loved literature. He loved reading. But he wanted to be that kind of person more than his temperament and his intellect allowed him to be. It was as if he had a nostalgia for literature, a yearning for it."

That might account for the sense one got from Waterman's writing of a voice dogged by an almost willful superficiality. To be sure, it was a merry voice, concise and well organized and eager to please, entertaining in its way, adept at spinning "tales," but ultimately a voice handicapped, if not trivialized, by its determination to keep emotions at bay. Waterman had learned his craft perfecting reports and speeches; he was a skillful ghost writer, good at putting words in the mouths of corporate executives and politicians. Once shown a draft of a profile about him that would appear in *Backpacker* magazine, the old ghost couldn't resist revamping the ending, and deferentially proposed it as a template for the writer's revision. He himself wrote quickly, and acknowledged (but didn't explain) that he had little interest in revising. It was only later in life that Waterman turned to composing poetry as a way of engaging—albeit obliquely—emotions beyond the range of his prose. He left an unpublished autobiography called *Prospero's Options*. It was succinctly written and expeditiously organized. But the author chose to belabor tedious Senate Republican history of the late 1950s and only glance at the themes that had consumed his life—the broken contracts of fatherhood, loss and grief, chronic depression, and the temptations of death.

"He didn't want to enter those rooms," Cornell said. "He was raised not to burden other people with his complaints. He came from a culture of reticence. He was courteous to a fault. That courteousness among other things prevented him from burdening people with his feelings. I never heard a complaint from him about depression or an overt expression of grief about his kids. Whether he suffered from depression isn't the issue. If he did, you'd say give him the pill and get it over with. But the question of depression doesn't strike to the root of the matter. What could there have been that was so frightening to a brave man? What was he defending himself against? Even Guy's commitment to traditional ways came out of a series of refusals. No power tools. No electricity. When he was climbing he refused to wear a harness—he would tie a bowline around his waist. He built a life that was so structured he couldn't take it off. He erected an armature against chance, and once you start constructing something like that you have no choice about what you add on to it.

"He didn't like surprises. There wasn't room for serendipity. There wasn't room for loss. He set himself up in a way. Mike Young and I both told him 'You can count on us for money if you need it.' He was touched by the offer but very reluctant to take any step that would show vulnerability, or have that kind of interchange with someone. Everybody wants a degree of independence, but there comes a point where your need for independence interferes with your ability to love, your ability to know the richness in other people. You can't know the richness of other people if you don't make some concession to their needs. He had a way of moving on—of quitting an organization, of moving past a friendship. You have to ask yourself, where does concern for yourself turn into hardness and cruelty? I've often wondered what would have happened if I'd taken him by the lapels and said, 'Come clean, Guy, what's really going on here?'"

The question hung between us for a while as Cornell gazed out at the pastures ripening in the summer sun. He shrugged.

"It wouldn't have made any difference," he said.

Toward the end of our conversation, I remembered the letter of condolence Cornell had written to Laura Waterman two weeks after her husband's death. He had alluded to a tribute Laura had published in a local paper in which she had mentioned Waterman's lifelong enthusiasm for the literary characters Ahab, Satan, and Prometheus. Despite Waterman's affinities for the mixed company of that trio, Cornell declared that Guy reminded him of someone else:

"He wasn't cruel like Satan, or monomaniacal like Ahab, though he did want to help mankind, like Prometheus, at great cost to himself. I thought instead of Hamlet. To me, Hamlet has never been the wishy-washy intellectual that the Romantics wanted to make him; rather a Renaissance prince, a formidable swordsman, a brilliant and witty mind addicted to word play, but afflicted with depression, a questing imagination haunted by self-doubt and tempted by the thought of death—by far the most interesting of Shakespeare's tragic heroes, the only one you could imagine talking to. I thought of Guy's friends carrying his bier down the mountain as Fortinbras' soldiers carry Hamlet off the stage, and Horatio's wonderful lines of farewell kept running through my mind.

"It's the tragic dimension to this story that makes it interesting," Cornell was saying. "Very few people can have the kind of death that Guy had. To call it a suicide is almost wrong. It doesn't fall into the pattern of feeling miserable and blowing your brains out. There is a mystical quality to the deliberateness of it, the intentional manner of it. As if it were part of his life. Guy was the most intentional person I've ever known. He never did anything without intent. In a way, he created his death as he created his life. And he did it with considerable style. In this sense, his death was like a successful work of art. It fulfilled the requirements of tragedy— which is a representation of suffering that communicates the suffering and gives a cathartic pleasure. He gave us a mirror in which we could see our own tendencies. If he hadn't died in the way he did, his story wouldn't have been as interesting. He would have been another eccentric. A worthy man. A lovable man. We would miss him—but we wouldn't all be talking about him."

That was it exactly. The point wasn't that Waterman's life was meaningful only as a prelude to his death. The point was the two were mated. They shared the yin-yang reciprocity in which the shape of one determines the shape of the other. Their correspondence lent the allure of a story to even the most cursory outlines of Waterman's biography. Each additional fact drew you deeper into the story, as the curve of a river draws the fisherman upstream from bend to bend.

I began to sense something else at work, which was the need for people who loved the man to emphasize this correspondence above everything else and to turn it into the leitmotif of Waterman's motivation. If he could be transformed into a kind of artist, and his last act a piece of art, it might be possible not just to ignore the darker aspects of his death but even to redeem them. Redeem the nihilism inherent in his despair. Redeem the selfishness. Redeem all those decidedly unheroic qualities that were braided together with what indeed seemed noble, even heroic, attributes.

It does not take away from the beauty and depth of the correspondence between his life and death to say Waterman's decision can be seen in an unflattering light. In some respects it was morally craven, born of a self-involvement that flew in the face of his social conscience and of a grief for his lost sons that, however profound, began to seem disproportionate, even fetishized, as if it were an elaborate way of maintaining pity for himself. Certainly it bespoke a cruel indifference to his wife, of whom he was otherwise so solicitous.

One could argue that Waterman's decision illustrated the philosopher David Novaks' psychological description of suicide as "egocentric narcissism in its most radical manifestation . . . the most desperate human attempt to be a complete universe unto oneself." In his book *Suicide and Morality,* Novaks makes the diagnosis of a distended egotism in the character of the person who attempts to take his own life, and the remedy he optimistically proposes lies in teaching the suicidal person "to see and accept his own limitations so that he can affirm a world outside himself; only thus can he be helped to draw vitality once again from natural inclination, to converse with other persons, and to be silent in the face of what he cannot know, which for some is to wait for God."

Waterman's death encapsulated all the paradoxes of his character. He himself had embraced the idea that he was a welter of contradictions, and he invoked the figures of Ariel and Caliban from Shakespeare's *Tempest* to symbolize the division of dark and light within himself. That morning in July, Lou Cornell was trying to get a rope around the waist of a ghost, like so many other of Waterman's friends who were struggling to reconcile his contradictions. Cornell could view Guy's death as Waterman wished the world to see it—a choice born of great deliberation, fully consonant with the principles of autonomy and independence to which his life had been pledged. Perhaps it was as some of Waterman's most protective defenders were wont to idealize it: an act of self-fulfillment.

On the other hand, the inconvenient fact was that the man had killed himself. And so Cornell went 'round the mulberry bush with everyone else, grappling with the way stories can devour lives and the way a point of aesthetics can make the horror of a death inseparable from its beauty. One moment you might find yourself contemplating the heroic autonomy of a mountaineer who sat down to freeze in the snow, admiring a man who closed out his life on his own terms. Another moment you were helplessly attuned to the cri de coeur implicit in the act, pained not only by what seemed the magnitude of a friend's suffering but also by your doubts about it, misgivings fostered by the hollow note in the man's rationalizations, the blind spots in his thinking, the salient frailties like his preoccupation with appearances. Much like the mountaineers who'd combed Mt. Lafayette for the body, Cornell found himself brooding about Waterman's reluctance to ask for help. Was it a malign side effect of the rock climber's creed by which holding on to the rope or grabbing a piton is considered "bad form," a sign of weakness that compromises the purity of the ascent? Had Waterman gotten himself boxed into the code of the Hard Man, who takes the biggest risk at the sharp end of the rope and lives or dies by his own ability to extricate himself from difficulties?

How could anyone have "helped" when it had never been Waterman's nature to ask for help, when everything in his life was structured to ensure his autonomy? Waterman could barely be persuaded to see a doctor when he wasn't feeling well. If you wanted to broach the subject of mental health, if you dared speak the forbidden word *depression*, forget it. Yes, he acknowledged having his "demons"—but he was adamant that they were not to be driven off with pills or the aid of therapists. They were to be borne stoically. They were to be owned, almost as a point of pride, as if they were part of who he was, the necessary dissonant notes of human complexity. He owned his demons until the end, when they owned him. If, in fact, they did.

Who can say beyond a doubt whether Waterman's choice to die on a winter night high in the mountains was the action of a noble figure who withdrew before old age made him a burden to society, or the action of a tragic figure doomed by his code and by his nature never to find the strength to be weak: the strength to ask for help, the strength to be a burden, the strength to understand that ultimately we know ourselves in the compassion of others.

When I got up to leave Lou Cornell's farmhouse, I was no clearer about the meaning of Waterman's life and death, but I knew more about the hold they had, the story-ness of what had happened. The correspondence they exemplified. The challenge they posed to the morality of the tribe. *He gave us a mirror . . .* I wanted to explore what the psychoanalyst author Adam Phillips once called "the conflict between knowing what a life is and the sense that a life contains within it something that makes such knowing impossible." Waterman's story would be an amalgam of elegy, meditation, and wilderness adventure: the story of a man who, in the American tradition, took himself to the woods to restore his fractured soul with the tonic of wildness and lived there in league with the seasons, loving wild Nature with a rare and distinguished intensity—but who in the end was unable to find the will or balance or grace to let the gift of his life run its course.

3.

THEATER OF THE SPIRITS

✳

The Lamb just says, I AM!
He frisks and whisks, *He* can.
He jumps all over. Who
Are *you*? You're jumping too!

THEODORE ROETHKE,
The Lamb

Hawee's ice axe has arrived safely. Many thanks for sending it. . . . I plan
to use it as my regular walking stick in winter around here, but it's hard
to get used to how tall it is.

GUY WATERMAN, *letter to his brother Alan, April 4, 1997*

I N THE LAST YEARS of his life, Waterman wondered if he had
not spent the better part of his days trying to re-create the idyll of
his boyhood in the woods of a small farm in North Haven, Connecticut.
"The Farm," as the family called it, had been purchased by Waterman's
father in 1929 from a Swedish family that was quitting the East for California. The two-story white clapboard house with pine-green shutters
and a four-hundred-foot-long driveway was surrounded by ten acres of
orchards, hayfields, and wood lots. The small barn came with a cider press
and an old horse named Dolly. There were cats and chickens and dogs.
Gardens, grapevines, a cold spring, a swamp, and best of all, a brook that
traversed north of the house through steep, fifty-foot banks shaded by
hemlocks and the dappled canopies of beech and maple trees. The under-
story teemed with jack-in-the-pulpits and skunk cabbage and lady's slip-
pers and enormous ferns; after spring rains, legions of mushrooms would
bewitch the dusky ravine known as the Fairy Glen. Although the Farm

was only eight miles from downtown New Haven, where Professor Waterman taught physics at Yale, it seemed a world apart, a kind of Connecticut Shangri-la exempt from the privations of the Great Depression and far from the portents of the Second World War, and impossible, really, to separate from the enchantment of childhood itself, part place, part time, part the memory of that theater of the spirits where Mother is forever calling you home from the woods with a silver whistle and Father is ushering you to bed with a lullaby on the grand piano.

It was said that of all the Waterman kids—Alan Jr., Neil, Barbara, Anne, and Guy—baby Guy, born three years after the family moved to the Farm, looked most like his father. Both were of modest height, with trim, athletic builds. Both shared the same strong jaw and foursquare face, the same inquisitive eyes and agile, birdlike movements. The son also inherited his father's formidable intelligence, ability to organize, love of the woods, and gift for music, especially for playing the piano. All the Waterman children were musical, but Guy was good enough to be playing professionally in Washington, D.C., jazz clubs before he was old enough to drink or vote. He had relative pitch—meaning he could identify any note if given another to compare it with. As his sister Barbara Waterman Carney, better known in the family as Bobbie, recalled: "When he was four, he'd be playing with his toys and trucks and I'd be practicing the piano, and if I hit a wrong note, he'd look up at me with an arched eyebrow. It drove me nuts."

Waterman's father was blessed with perfect pitch. He could play by ear and sight-read anything, instantly transposing the key to one more favorable to singers. He also was an accomplished violist who performed with a string quartet; he had a special feeling for Brahms. In truth, he could get passable sounds from almost any instrument he touched. On more than one occasion when he was the director of the National Science Foundation, or NSF, in the supposedly buttoned-down era of postwar Washington, he kicked off staff assemblies wearing a kilt and skirling a fanfare on the bagpipes. Vannevar Bush, the former president of the Carnegie Foundation whose report "Science—The Endless Frontier" laid the groundwork for the NSF, once described Waterman as "a quiet individual, a real scholar, and decidedly effective in a quiet way, for everyone likes him and trusts him." And Detlev W. Bronk, the former president of the National Academy of Sciences who served as the chairman of the NSF's board for fourteen years, called him "obviously kind and gentle, obviously firm and exacting, obviously a Scotsman persistent in the fulfillment of his duties, and a damned good-looking guy as well."

Alan T. Waterman had been born in Cornwall-on-Hudson, New York, and raised in Northampton, Massachusetts, the son of a physics professor who taught at Smith College for thirty-three years. As he once said drolly, his desire to pursue his father's vocation "met no resistance at home." He got his undergraduate degree at Princeton, and then completed his doctorate there in 1916, studying under the British Nobel laureate Sir Owen W. Richardson. A year later, at his first teaching job at the University of Cincinnati, he met a witty, soft-spoken, brown-haired twenty-three-year-old scholar named Mary Mallon, who was working as an instructor in the economics department. She was the oldest of eight children, daughter of a prominent Irish lawyer and judge in Cincinnati named Guy Mallon, who was a close friend of the Taft family. Four of Mary's five brothers went to Yale (the family's "black sheep" went to Williams); she and her two sisters graduated from Vassar. Like her future husband, Mary was elected Phi Beta Kappa. She wasn't uninterested in physics—in letters she sometimes made reference to Heisenberg's uncertainty principle, and after her marriage to Waterman she wrote a scientifically literate poem about entropy called "A Physicist's Wife Looks at the Future"—but her heart lay with history and literature. She was a suffragette, and fearsomely well read. "She could read the Koran in Arabic," recalled her daughter Barbara. "She was an intellectual snob."

The couple were married in August 1917.

"My mother, when she was in the mood, could be a brilliant conversationalist," her oldest son, Alan Jr., recalled in a letter I received after his brother's death; he was living in California, where he'd spent much of his career teaching atmospheric physics at Stanford.

She tended to be a champion of lost causes like Bonnie Prince Charlie and the Arabs. One strange attitude, in a way, was her aversion to sentimentality. She could feel, and appreciate, true sentiment, but she drew the line at trivial dripping. Another aversion she had was to growing old. As far back as I can remember, she would say, "Before I get old, I hope I get hit by a Mack truck." It wasn't meant to be taken literally, of course, but the general drift was clear. In later years she would say, "There is no need for a hell. Old age is it." It's possible that some of this dread of aging may have rubbed off on Guy.

Mary had started a club for the lonely wives of the scientists serving in the Office of Naval Research and continued the tradition when Alan assumed the reins of the National Science Foundation. The club convened once a month for twelve years at the Watermans' house. At official capital gatherings she almost always wore a small black toque, and if the occasion were especially fancy she might spiff the hat up with a sprig of fresh ivy. She kept her hair long, usually coiled in a bun, and did not cut it until her husband died. She was always unimpressed by Washington pomp. The writer Diana Trilling, who was introduced to her at a Kennedy administration party at the White House in April 1962, described the encounter three decades later in *The New Yorker* magazine: "And then a little lady, just a wee thing, and the most enchanting-looking person, was being introduced to me—she looked to be about eighty-five, and her name was Mrs. Waterman. . . . She said to me, 'Oh, Mrs. Trilling, you're literary. Is there anyone here I'm supposed to know?' She had a charming, birdlike way of speaking, and I said, 'Well, I haven't seen many writers, but that's Katherine Anne Porter over there in the white brocade dress and the white hair and the white pearls.' 'Am I supposed to know her?' Mrs. Waterman inquired. 'Because I don't want to.'"

When the Watermans moved to the Farm after twelve years of marriage, they found themselves overseeing a menagerie of two boys in puberty, two girls sailing toward it, a beloved collie–German shepherd mix named Donny, a brown-and-white cocker spaniel named Robby, a horse—Dolly—whom they'd been promised wouldn't live another year but hung on for thirteen, plus a flock of chickens and an ever-shifting number of cats who were always being strafed by agitated barn swallows. Mary shopped by phone for groceries; someone usually came in to do the cooking and help clean the house. Alan Jr. and Neil had tagged their father with the nickname "Hawee," which stuck so well that Mary found herself eventually succumbing to "Mawee." She assigned the children's chores and took on the duties of family disciplinarian and enforcer of manners. Elbows lingered on the table at their owner's peril. But the main emphasis in the house was on education. As Anne Waterman Cooley recalled, "I was afraid if I got less than an A in physics I'd be disowned."

Neither parent would have known what to make of the view that science and art were two cultures with no common language. Well before the children were old enough to be ferried off to school in Hawee's old Ford, family conversation had exposed them to the latest developments in science and to sophisticated literary themes. Hawee, a pipe smoker, would emerge from the fragrant haze of his den to explain the to-and-fro of the tides or to demonstrate the effects of gravity with the aid of a large globe on the living room table. On a shelf below the globe lay the treasured *Britannica*, into whose volumes the kids would delve on rainy days while drying their socks on the covered radiator. On winter evenings before bedtime the children gathered on the Persian carpet by the fire while Mary read aloud, often from the works of Sir Walter Scott—*Ivanhoe* and *Lady of the Lake* and *Marmion*. A child's lack of interest in books could concern her enough to arrange an appointment with a pediatric shrink. In Mary's view, it was essential that children learn to entertain themselves with the resources of their imaginations and not rely on movies or the radio. Imagination within limits, of course. Anne and Bobbie put on plays in a remodeled chicken coop, but Mary trimmed most of the racy wooing from their production of *A Midsummer-Night's Dream*.

Apart from his music, Hawee's chief passion was for the Maine woods. Yale's academic schedule (and his wife's indulgence) gave him the liberty each summer to mount month-long canoeing expeditions through the waterways of the northern forests, usually beginning at Moosehead

Lake, and ending with a run down the Allagash River to its confluence with the St. John. When Alan Jr. and Neil were old enough, he brought them along. As befitted a man named Waterman, Alan senior could handle the era's wood-and-canvas canoes in all kinds of conditions. He was a skillful camp cook and adept at backwoods orienteering. He eventually

obtained a license as a Maine guide, a qualification that his daughter Anne said meant more to him than the Presidential Medal of Freedom he was awarded in 1963.

Every Sunday, no matter what the weather, Hawee brought the camp life of the Maine backcountry to North Haven. The Watermans were agnostics, with little interest in church—the Sunday picnic was the closest they came to a religious observance. Neither Mary nor any other woman was allowed to lift a finger. The picnic site lay in a clearing in the forest down by the brook. Hawee and the boys, aided by a complement of regular male guests, would cut and split firewood with long-handled axes and get a blaze roaring in the fireplace. They would strip the tarpaulin off the picnic table and benches, unpack the wooden crate containing tin utensils, metal mugs, and a miscellany of old plates, then set to work baking cornbread and powder biscuits, and fixing the main course, which was usually a large kettle of stew. Cocoa and coffee were served in blue-and-white enamel pitchers. After lunch, the men scrubbed the dishes, and loaded the plates and cups into a wooden box, which they hauled back up the steep banks of the brook on a kind of rope-rigged cable car. Chores over, the games began, a veritable Olympiad of baseball, volleyball, touch football, whatever the sport in season, all waged on a grass field cropped close by

Dolly. Life on the Farm never lacked for competition. If a quorum were unavailable for team sports, a game could be found on the lumpy home-made croquet or tennis courts. The Sunday picnic contests lasted long into the afternoon, often till four P.M., when Mary would encourage the players to abandon their rivalries by bringing out tea.

Little Guy, born May 1, 1932, and named for his mother's father, arrived in time to taste but not take the full measure of life on the Farm. "He hasn't any coat and he hasn't any collar, but he sure has a holler," his mother reported to his sisters. Mary was thirty-nine, Alan forty—old for parents of a newborn in those days. Guy was fourteen years younger than big brother Alan Jr.; six and half years removed from his nearest sibling, Anne. Years later, he remarked in his unpublished autobiography that his decade on the Farm left him with the paradoxical feeling of being at once part of a big boisterous family and an only child. The house was relatively isolated. It was hard for him to find playmates. When his siblings went off to school, he was obliged to amuse himself. By the time he was ready to explore the Maine woods, the war had curtailed his father's expeditions. All those early years alone, Waterman believed, contributed to what he called his "life-long high tolerance for solitude." He emerged as a self-sufficient, highly imaginative boy, a boy who gave names to his mittens, and who was distressed if you closed a gate too quickly on his fraternity of invisible  friends, and who was sure the four little doors in his room that led to the storage space under the eaves were portals of the "night demons." He loved to wander the banks of the brook, navigating toppled tree trunks and tangled roots. Faded sepia snapshots show him at age one riding on

Dolly, sheltered in the arms of big brother Alan. A year later he appears in a stocking cap, contemplating a large buck saw in the groove of a half-cut log, an oddly rapt expression on his face, as if he'd had some presentiment of the mammoth role logs, saws, and hand-cut firewood would play in his future.

In December 1934, when Guy was two and a half, a baby sister was born: Mary, named after her mother. Sad to say, she was not to be Guy's longed-for playmate. She was born with Down's syndrome and in February 1935, she died, probably of heart failure. Miss as he might sometimes a wedding anniversary, Hawee never forgot the day of his infant daughter's death and unfailingly marked it with a bouquet of pink roses for his wife. Many years later, after her own death, in June 1980, an elegy Mary Waterman wrote for her lost child was discovered among her papers:

Can we lose that we never had
Or weep for what was never here?
Oh little, little, little one,
There's none more dear.

Oh little, wished for, darling child
Tiny, tiny, and so sweet,
How would we know our hopes were wild
Our victory, defeat?

The other children true and brave
Must each go on his gallant way;
But little, little, darling one,
You shall stay.

So the Farm years unfurled, with much in evidence from the beginning—not the provenance of a suicide but the small inflections of character, the hints of tendencies and preferences that would be amplified in the time to come. In a chronology he once drew up for his second wife, Waterman dated the inauguration of his conscious life to age five, when he remembered himself being footloose in the enchanted forest, playing Tarzan in a deerskin loincloth. Also lodged among his earliest memories was the boggling contraption that arrived to spray the family's apple trees with pesticide. He climbed his first mountain in the summer of '36—Mt. Carmel, "the Sleeping Giant," north of New Haven. He was dressed in shorts and white socks, and waited just shy of the 739-foot summit for big brother Alan to catch up.

Waterman's first encounter with the sort of merciless weather that would become one of his transcendent pleasures was the hurricane of 1938, when torrential rains and winds clawed the fall's crop of apples off their boughs, uprooted the orchard trees, and wracked the peace of the Fairy Glen with the crack and boom of shattering wood. The storm, which blitzed New England with winds in excess of one hundred miles per hour, was the most devastating hurricane in the region's recorded history. It passed over the Farm shortly before four P.M. Hawee, on his way home from Yale, had to stop the car and chop the road free of downed branches with his axe. The power went out, and the family took up camp life. Candle and lantern shadows danced on the pale yellow walls of the dining room. School was canceled for two weeks. The boys helped their father haul in drinking water from the spring.

Toward the end of the 1930s, nothing seemed further from life on the Farm than the tensions in Europe. Even when war broke out in 1939, the conflict remained a distant abstraction until a pair of young refugees turned up on the doorstep of the Farm. They were known as the English twins, Christopher and Theodore Braunholtz. They were fraternal twins, but had lookalike toothy smiles and similar high cheekbones. Their parents, professors at Oxford, had been anxious to distance the boys from the Battle of Britain, and had arranged for them to board with the Watermans on the Farm until the bombs stopped falling and it seemed safe to resume life in England. The twins were two and a half years older than Guy when they crossed the Atlantic in the summer of 1940; however traumatic the upheaval in their own lives, their arrival at the Farm brought a most welcome change in his. The boys stayed four years, and as Waterman recalled in his autobiography, Ted and Kiffy (as Christopher was known) became "more like brothers to me than my brothers." Here suddenly were boon companions with whom to plunge into the intricacies of baseball, and to climb the Tarzan red maple, and to help prepare the Farm's own vintage of grape juice. They joined the outings to the Yale Bowl to watch the contests against Dartmouth or Princeton, huddled under a canoe tarpaulin to ward off the rain. Mary bundled them off to the beach club on Long Island Sound and to Niagara Falls on a summer trip with Guy and Guy's sisters, and Guy's stuffed gorilla. Guy and Kiffy became particularly close; they thought nothing of spending hours together on a rainy afternoon, devising a language for baboons.

From the outset, Mary made it clear that she intended to treat the twins as she treated her own children. They observed the same strict bedtimes. They were shuttled off to music lessons—Guy played the violin, Kiffy the flute, Ted the piano. They were assigned household chores. Homework essays had to be completed Saturday morning before they could fly to the brook. The twins joined the family games of bridge, cribbage, and Scrabble. Mary recorded the progress of all three young boys in weekly letters to the Braunholtzes in England, filling the parents in on the twins' health and activities, and mentioning Guy's along the way. The letters were descriptive for the most part, offering wonderfully detailed portraits of life in a university culture in the last year before America entered the war, before penicillin was widely available or much of anything effective could be done to treat polio or scarlet fever. To read through them is to page through a thousand small moments saved from oblivion, a vanished world of home-delivered milk and fresh cream skimmed off the top, of hangdogging it over to Miss Darling's dancing class in a blue suit, of bowl haircuts and playing Jesus in the 1940 Christmas pageant and traveling by the night train to visit Grandma in Cincinnati.

The first week of January 1941, for instance—Guy would have been eight, the twins eleven—Mary reported:

> Guy woke me up two days ago with "Methinks it is a fair day, God wot." (It was pouring rain!) He and the twins repaired to the costume trunk, and now Guy goes about in scarlet cape and hose

as Will Scarlet. Ted is Robin Hood in a Lincoln green doubleton and cape, and Kiffy has a brown cassock as Friar Tuck but says he needs a pillow too! God wot the good yeoman would boggle at the boys' idea of jerkin and hose! As soon as it cleared, they journeyed up the brook with homemade bows and returned to report twenty of the king's deer slain and a stag often.

There were times, however, when Mary found herself in a more analytical mood. A little later in January 1941, she took the occasion of a letter to the Braunholtzes to reflect not just on the cultural dislocation of her young English wards but on the emotional tenor of her own family and the Waterman-Mallon style of childrearing, which the presence of the twins had thrown into relief:

Another lack on our part bothers me more. We are not at all a demonstrative family. We have our full share of family affection I am sure, and do feel absolutely devoted to the twins, but we do not make outward show. I really can't say when I last kissed either of the girls, for instance. Guy becomes cuddly now and then when we are alone together, but not often. I suppose it must seem coldhearted to the twins if they are accustomed to more demonstration. . . . We are interested in their interests; we are eager to share in their problems and enthusiasms, and I am convinced they are quite sure of that and do bring them to us. . . . And of course we are just as cold (?) to Guy and the girls as to the twins—in manner and as far as "petting" goes. Am I being very unintelligible about this? I can't get it into words without exaggerating it. We are a normal, outspoken, healthy family, but we don't kiss good morning and good night. Perhaps that says it all.

A month later, she confided to the Braunholtzes that

Sometimes watching the children I think how awfully characteristic of their whole selves one small part of them can be. The tip of Guy's nose—classic and straight with but the tiniest and yet unmistakable tilt toward the skies; Ted's sturdy square hands, which seem always stretched out in an offer of friendship and helpfulness. With Kiffy it is the delicate modeling of his temple with the blue vein showing, at least his left one, which I see at table—it seems significant of his sensitive secret life. Perhaps that is only sentimentality, but I do think children are such defenseless beings—not only your poor bombed Londoners but all children—even in the happiest of homes. Their whole moral climate is made by their elders (not their betters) and they are constantly being pushed and shoved and shaped. The hope of the world of course lies in their ability to retain their own essential being in spite of all we, their elders, do to them. (In our blindness, we call it "for" them.) That's one reason it does seem to me necessary that they all—Kiffy included—learn to take the daily routines in stride and save their physical and moral energy for the thing that is essentially themselves.

Was it just small physical traits that could intimate the character of the whole self? In an April letter, a week before Guy's ninth birthday, Mary assured the Braunholtz parents that, go on as she might about the twins' growing pains, she didn't lack for concerns about her own children. Guy, for instance, had been displaying "a deplorable tendency to self-pity." He had come to her moaning, "I know nobody likes me, but I can't blame you, for I don't even like myself." Is the tilt of a boy's mind any less of a constitutional endowment than the tip of his nose? Can one small puzzle piece of the psyche accurately convey the picture of the whole?

It's tempting to impute the motivation of self-pity to a grown man's suicide if as a boy he has been observed by his mother as having a "deplorable tendency" for it. Who, after all, can resist the logic and symmetry of *As in the child, so in the man*? But we should be cautious given how often the facts that rush to the fore are the ones that fit our preconceptions. It was Waterman himself, in his autobiography, who posed the idea that the homestead he'd carved from the hills of east central Vermont might have been an attempt to replicate the idyll of his boyhood on the Farm. Were it so, it was a folly in any case. No one can return to the same woods with the same mind. How could the adventure and excitement of terra nova ever beckon as luminously as it did in that boyhood year of 1941? Imagine the spring days flooding with light. Mother rising at seven to make her bed. Ted tending his chickens. Guy conjuring armies from a handful of marbles as news of the war comes rustling through the radio. Father trooping out to feed and water Dolly in the barn—Dolly, who would be crippled by a stroke later that year and have to be put down, her body carved up and carted off by fox farmers because it was too big to bury in the stony ground.

One day in the latter part of May, Hawee called out that the *Bismarck* had been sunk. Guy began to weep.

"But that was a German boat!" said Kiffy, indignantly.

"I don't care—I can't stand people getting drowned," Guy said.

And then Kiffy began to cry.

"We don't sit ghoulishly over the radio—as some do here—but of course the children do get the main events on time," Mary wrote to the Braunholtzes. "On the whole, the twins are less concerned over the news than they were when they came to us—and their British confidence is quite unshaken. Guy is distressed by it all and very much confused in his mind with his school history and the newspapers."

The Watermans, parents and children, studied the Russian lines on war maps brought to the house by Mary Waterman's brother Neil—Neil Mallon, who had been Prescott Bush's roommate at Yale and went on to make a fortune in the oil business and generously supported a lot of his impoverished intellectual relations, including nephew Guy, whose college tuition he helped defray. (Neil Mallon also gave the future president George Bush his start in the oil business.) As July rolled into August, Mary, who had been air-mailing her letters, risked sending them by ship again; German U-boat attacks seemed to have let up. Guy and Kiffy were inseparable, a regular pair of Lewis and Clarks pushing deeper into the woods around the Farm.

All this wilderness is safe for them—no roads to cross, and they can't lose themselves, for all they have to do is follow the stream down to our brook. [They] have ventured further into it this month than ever before—further, they are convinced, than any man has ever trod. (Neil and Alan tactfully have kept silent about their thorough knowledge of the whole region.) We have not urged exploration before because we found with the other children that to find it a completely unexpected extent and mystery was much more thrilling than to be told to go up and explore. Of course it is not really wilderness—it has been cut over for firewood by generations of farmers, but it is really a lovely little glen with some big hemlocks, many ferns, and wildflowers. And to Kiffy and Guy, it has been everything from Sherwood Forest to the banks of the Congo.

In the fall, the three boys circled around Mary to listen to *The Last of the Mohicans*—Guy's choice, but he wouldn't admit it was too complicated and gory for his taste, his mother said. For her part, she was irritated by Cooper's long-winded sentimentality and his depiction of women, and found herself trimming the text as she went along. In the orchard, the apples were ripening, but baskets to put them in were hard to come by. Three days before the Japanese attack on Pearl Harbor, she wrote: "News this morning about Japan looks nasty." And three days after, when the country was plunged into war, she told the Braunholtzes: "Guy is still simply horrified. He has a deep-seated but very conscious hatred of all violence. Also, he is quite frankly worried about his own little skin. He didn't know whether to be relieved or not when I told him that statistically speaking he still had a much greater chance of being killed by an automobile than by a bomb. Then I had to show him the Safe Driver Awards that Hawee and I had [received] for the last years." Alan Jr. volunteered for enemy airplane spotter duty, taking up a post in a woodshed on the highest point in New Haven. Six months later, Hawee took a leave of absence from Yale to become director of field operations for the federal Office of Scientific Research and Development, where he and his staff were later credited with, among other things, refining the accuracy of the B-29 bombing missions and demonstrating the effectiveness of radar.

And with America's entry into the war, suddenly life on the Farm was done, suddenly the Watermans were packing up their belongings and heading east for a house in Cambridge, Massachusetts. They threw a party for all their New Haven friends, a party Guy always remembered. And then, like that, he was looking out of the car and the Farm was receding in the window; the barn, the brook, the woods, the enchanted childhood, all of it falling away in the window; a part of him as tell-tale as the tip of his nose vanishing into the theater of the spirits, an innocence of which he knew nothing, an essence unwittingly relinquished, which he was not able to see until years later, and even then was not certain what it was exactly, or when it had gone, or whether the loss of it could be recouped. In his autobiography, he raised the question of what was dawning that day: "I wonder," he asked, "if I looked at those woods with a special light as we pulled away." But by then he was lost to the whisk of a boy's delight, and it was too late for the answer to matter.

4.

BEWILDERED

✳

What I was when first
I came among these hills; when like a roe
I bounded o'er the mountains, by the sides
Of the deep rivers, and the lonely streams,
Wherever nature led: more like a man
Flying from something that he dreads than one
Who sought the things he loved. . . .

WILLIAM WORDSWORTH,
Tintern Abbey

What makes man *man* is his potential ability to conquer both himself and his environment. We are each inevitably and terribly and forever personally responsible for everything we do. . . . This is a tough philosophy. But it is the *only* one—as proved through the ages—by which man can turn his personal hopes into reality through individual incentive and deserved rewards he can win and keep.

GUY WATERMAN, speech for a General Electric executive

NOW COMES A PERIOD of conflict and turmoil that might be ascribed simply to the wild weather of adolescence and the passing rebellion of teenage years had it not been so packed with drama and consequence—had it not been resolved so rashly and in such seeming ignorance of its origins, virtually guaranteeing that it would resurface years later in predictably more damaging and self-destructive forms. His "war," Waterman called it in an apt if battle-weary metaphor. His war with the adult world. His war with the "forces of respectability," which is to say his militant disdain for the upper-middle-class world of privilege and expectation, for lily white prep schools and Ivy League entitlements, for the prejudice and hypocrisy behind the public face of Establishment values. When he was filled with the zeal of youth, he saw the enemy as outside himself—snobby preppies, ineffective shrinks, the cross-burning bigots he encountered at a summer camp in South Carolina, even his own poor liberal parents, who were scrambling to rein in a fractious child. But age eventually made Waterman understand his greatest adversary was within: the seesaw of his temperament, whose demonic ups and downs were symbolized for him in the figures of Ariel and Caliban.

"I believe that there have been these two strains in conflict within me," he wrote in his autobiography.

A dark, defiant combativeness, which leads eventually to a destructiveness, breeding an impassioned resentment of real or imagined affronts; and a clear-sky acceptance of respectability, of genuine adherence to high standards of public and private morality and responsibility. These impulses are probably in conflict within everyone, but in me the swings, the vehemence of the contrasts, seem remarkable.

Waterman was nine when Pearl Harbor lowered the curtain on the Farm, thirteen when the peace was finally won. The five years that followed marked a swift and wrenching passage from one woods to another. He was often engulfed by what he called his "arousable fire." Boyhood loneliness gave way to a misfit's more complex sense of social alienation, and something he interestingly identified later as his tendency toward "morbid self-pity." Waterman discovered his craving for the spotlight, and it didn't matter initially whether he got attention by playing the piano at parties or by getting pie-eyed on beer and bourbon. Perhaps some of his thirst for attention can be attributed to the absence of his father, who was increasingly drawn into war work, first at the Massachusetts Institute of Technology, where the naval research program was headquartered, then later in Washington, D.C., where, in August 1946, he became the deputy chief and chief scientist of the newly created Office of Naval Research.

In the summers of that period, Hawee managed to sneak away to Maine only for abbreviated canoeing trips. Guy went along on four altogether, but the last-born boy missed out on those epic sojourns his brothers had enjoyed—missed out on the luxury of an unhurried Huck Finn summer and the long arc of days in the boundless north woods: heightened days adrift under a great sky; days of packing up for the portage by horse-drawn sledge between Caucomgomoc and Allagash lakes; of poling through Chase's Rapids, where one of your brothers had once wrecked a canoe; of watching the red-haired guide Bill Arthur mend a broken gunwale with a splint of white cedar; of living so close to rain and wind and clouds and sun you wondered how anyone could ever stand being shut up in a house. Weeks and weeks of hearing the loons cry as you pitched the canvas tent by another lake, and prepared your mattress from boughs of fresh-cut spruce, and lingered around a snapping fire as the summer dusk deepened into night, stirred beyond words by the sound of your father and his woodsy pals all singing "Now the Day Is Over" and "To the Tables Down at Mory's" and the shivery pagan verses of the "Dartmouth Winter Song," "For the fire has a spirit in the embers. / 'Tis a god and our fathers knew his name."

"One of the saddest things about my life was that Guy didn't know my father as well as the rest of us did," his sister Bobbie recalled.

What Waterman did know, he viewed equivocally. As he wrote in the opening chapter of his autobiography:

> While I have no complaints about my parents, who were good to me and did their best, I do not feel that I was close to either one, not in the warm, loving way that I see in some others. The relationship that, for example, existed all their lives between [Bobbie] and my father never happened for me. I shouldn't overstate this point. Kiffy ... was certainly a good brother to me; my sisters were good sisters, and [Bobbie] especially was a source of warmth and affection always; and I had friends throughout junior high and high school, and indeed throughout life. But it seems to me that I see others who enjoy closer relationships than I do. I guess the closest I've come to that were some times with my three sons, especially one of them; and with my second wife, Laura.

In the last, despairing pages of the manuscript, which were completed shortly before his death, Waterman returned to the subject of his father, vacillating between idealization and a kind of wounded scorn:

> My father . . . stood for everything positive, a deep sense of public service, an "Olympian calm" (my sister Anne's apt phrase), always in control, upright and strong, though always gentle and reserved. If this sounds like hero worship, let me add that he was never, for me, a warm father or able to be close to me, or to help me with my childhood, teenage, or young adult problems. I do not revere his memory.

Is there a note here of that self-pity his mother found deplorable, or are these passages simply matter-of-fact appraisals of the world as it presented itself to him—just the way things were? Surely they ache with a longing for intimacy, or a fantasy of what intimacy might entail, but there is also a strange whiff of passivity in the sentiment—the plaint of an emotionally disabled man baffled by relationships that "happened" or "didn't happen," as if he had no role in their creation and upkeep. His reflections on his parents, his guilty criticism of his father, his general sense of social estrangement makes the way Waterman lost touch with his own sons, and his own subsequent shortcomings as a father, all the more confounding. One might expect a man who didn't revere the memory of his father to go out of his way to be for his sons what he believed his father had not been for him—a close, warm, involved guide through the straits of adolescence and young adulthood. Instead, Waterman seems to have raised the ante on what he evidently considered his father's legacy of benign neglect. But then all of these confessions Waterman offered about himself and his father were rendered in the last years of his life, when he was crushed by depression. Would he have told his story differently had he written it in better days? And if he had, who could determine which of the two masks was the truer face?

After the family's move from the Farm to Cambridge, in 1942, Waterman entered the sixth grade at the Shady Hill School. There he stayed for four years, scooting home at lunchtime for a glass of milk and a stack of sandwiches, which he wolfed down while his mother read Shakespeare aloud. He'd been following major league baseball since 1940, and that next summer—the summer of 1943—he took advantage of his proximity to Braves Field to escape into the fortunes of the Boston Braves. Typically, he retained the stats that defined his life as a fan, and when the time came to prepare his memoirs, he was able to report that the eleven-year-old boy attended fifty-three out of seventy-seven Braves home games. He published an article about those long-gone games in a baseball journal called *Nine*:

> For me and my ten- to twelve-year-old friends, there was magic in those wartime games. We'd stroll along the Charles River, throwing a baseball all the way, across the bridges, and along the wide sidewalks of Commonwealth Avenue to the field. We'd buy unreserved grandstand—for some reason never the Jury Box— and be sure to arrive in time for infield and batting practice. I dimly recall the former might include hijinks like phantom routines, especially if the Cubs or the Cards were in town. With the crowd so thin, the ushers would let us move closer to the field by the fifth or sixth inning, and even out on the field after the final out. I remember peering into the dugout once, after yet another loss, to see an unsmiling, unphilosophical [Casey] Stengel still sitting there, his broken leg in a cast and propped up on the bench, long after the players had disappeared into the showers.

In the spring of 1944, Ted and Kiffy Braunholtz sailed back to England. Bereft of the companionship of the English twins, Waterman diverted himself for countless solitary hours fielding a tennis ball that he tossed up onto the intricately angled roof of the family's house. He ventured about the city, traveling the Boston subway to the Common and Harvard Square. In the summer, he attended the Greenwood Music Camp, near Tanglewood, in the Berkshires, where he happily fell under the influence of the owner, Dwight Little, a paternal stand-in who did Guy the honor of assigning him special jobs like pruning the tops of the pines that were blocking an important view.

When the Waterman family moved to Washington, D.C., in September 1946, Guy was packed off to start his turbulent high school career at

Taft, a well-known prep school in Watertown, Connecticut. Taft's motto was "Not to be served, but to serve." Mary Waterman thought highly of the place because of the Taft family, from whose ranks had come not just governors, senators, and an American president but also the founder of the school. Alas, the transplant from Shady Hill didn't take. Waterman did well academically, but he was the smallest and youngest boy in his class, he didn't excel at sports, and he felt ostracized by Taft's social cliques. He was dismayed by what he called the "pervasive upper-class snobbishness and conspicuous anti-Semitism [and] anti-Negro prejudice[s]."

> Perhaps as a reaction against this [he wrote in his autobiography], perhaps through identifying with the downtrodden (which I felt myself to be there), or for whatever reasons, I acquired during these years a deep antipathy toward prejudice or racial injustice in all its varied forms. . . . I felt enormously guilty that I had no black friends. The steady stream of anti-Semitic jokes and wisecracks among the students at Taft was excruciatingly painful to me. I regard this feeling of mine not as an admirable display of social liberalism, but as clearly some kind of identification with other outcasts.

And in truth, when Waterman's politics began to emerge in his twenties, he moved consciously to the right, throwing in with conservative Republicans almost as a reaction against the expectations of the liberal university culture. Liberals struck him as more "arrogant" than compassionate. He voted for Eisenhower when most college students were wild about Stevenson. He viewed the government and unions as a bigger threat to personal freedom than corporations, and the interest he developed in economics made him skeptical of social programs and reckless Congressional spending. To be sure, many of the issues like environmental protection and abortion that now divide liberals and conservatives were not on the table in the late 1940s and 1950s, and Waterman did later acknowledge that he would dispute the agenda of today's "so-called conservatives." But even taking the tenor of the times into account, the contradictions of Waterman's political views seem sharp enough to support the conclusion that his rebellion against respectability had more to do with his insecurity about his place in his father's world than a desire to stand in defense of the downtrodden. What his politics seem ultimately to boil down to is the classic colonial motto "Don't Tread on Me," which is really a kind of antipolitics based on the defiance proclaimed in that favorite line of his from *Paradise Lost* about preferring to reign in hell rather than serve in heaven. The real animating force of his political views today looks like a species of New England libertarianism born of injuries to the autonomy of a hypersensitive adolescent.

I'm at risk here of pigeonholing Guy Waterman, and he would not be happy about that. As he wrote in his autobiography: "If there is one strain in my makeup that has always been uppermost, it is my passionate insistence on my own (and everyone's, if they want it) individuality. I will *not* be placed in any pigeonholes." Much of Waterman's character stemmed from what he called his "deep-rooted sense of the uniqueness of each individual." His convictions about the singularity of people shaped his politics and his sense of himself. More problematically, they shaped his sense of obligations to others. By the end of his life, they had shaped—to the point of impairing—a sensibility that was unwilling and perhaps unable to ask for help.

I will not *be placed in any pigeonholes.* Where did it come from, that defiant note? It's not as though anyone strives to attain the banality of a stereotype or would argue with an apple-pie tribute to the virtues of individuality. Something else is at work here. As Lou Cornell might have asked, What was Waterman afraid of? Was it the case of the man who overstresses his uniqueness in the secret fear that he's just an ordinary schlub—asserting his idiosyncrasy because he experiences it as under siege, or short of the standard expected of his family and his background?

In Waterman's case, the agony of being pigeonholed (if agony it was) seems to have been quintessentially adolescent, something one ought to outgrow when the uncertainties of a young self have been surmounted and one's mature identity coalesces. The novelist Milan Kundera once pointed out that people are ninety-nine percent alike and only one percent different, and while it's the one percent that intrigues us, it seems to me that more harm comes from our unwillingness to accept our overwhelming similarities than from our failure to appreciate the marginal differences. Mindful of the frigid ridge to which Waterman's philosophy led him in his final hour, you have to wonder if there wasn't something arrested and self-defeating in his pursuit of life free from the oppression of pigeonholes. You have to wonder if what he heard in the snap judgments of others were the more severe judgments of an unforgiving inner voice—if, in his emphatic determination to shed the preconceptions and categories we collectively impose on each other (and for better or worse learn to tolerate), he ended up pigeonholing himself.

About the only good thing that came out of Waterman's two years at Taft was his musical destiny. During his final summer at the Greenwood Music Camp, between his sophomore and junior years at Taft, he decided he'd been sawing away long enough at classical violin and it was time to concentrate on what he really liked, which was jazz piano. At Taft in the fall of 1947, he met a senior named Bob LaGuardia, who was switching from the piano to the clarinet and needed someone to accompany him.

"We were two against the school," LaGuardia recalled. "I just started talking to him to see if he was friendly, and things fell in line. It turned out he played the fiddle and the piano, and I said, "You gotta hear this!" I played him some old Jelly Roll Morton records. If you got an ear you can get a feel for what Jelly Roll Morton was doing. You don't have an ear, you say, 'It's old-fashioned crap.' Guy, he could hear it. I said, 'If you can hear it, you gotta play it.' When you're fifteen and seventeen years old, you worship the music that gets to your feelings, particularly if it's antimajoritarian stuff and everyone else is dancing to Glenn Miller."

LaGuardia had gotten demerits for banging jazz on the pianos reserved for the sonatas of Bach and Beethoven, so he dragged Waterman down to a beat-up keyboard in a practice room beneath the school auditorium, where the sacrilege of stomping out whorehouse music was tolerated. There, with LaGuardia on clarinet, Waterman began a rigorous tutelage in the basics of the New Orleans style, a form of jazz then enjoying a brief renaissance. The two preppies pored over tracks Jelly Roll Morton had laid down in the late 1930s for the General label. "Ditny Ramble." "Winin' Boy." "Sweet Substitute." They loped through choruses of "Muskrat Ramble" and "High Society," and absorbed the nuances of boogie-woogie and barrelhouse blues.

"I thought he and I were both bright," recalled LaGuardia, who today lives in New York City and is a musician and a writer. "I saw at the time he was closed up. I pushed him a lot. I remember thinking of him as half the size of me, and looking up at me with a face that could be frowning or smiling. [He] was waiting to see whether he could trust you. He wasn't going to mess around with anybody he couldn't trust. I had a real sense of a kid who shouldn't be left alone."

There was a rigidity in his playing that dogged him all his life, but Waterman nonetheless developed a genuine feel and facility for New Orleans–style jazz—both as music and as overlooked cultural history. The life depicted in the compositions, most of which were written by black musicians, brought many of his concerns about his background into focus, heightening his sense that Taft, like the Farm, was an enclave walled off from "the real world." The music, he said, "added to the sense of it being somehow wrong that I was from a relatively privileged family."

Waterman's parents were not blind to his distress at Taft. Seeing how unhappy he was in Connecticut, they brought him south and enrolled him at Sidwell Friends, a well-known Washington day school. Mindful of his social fragility, they arranged for him to repeat the eleventh grade even though he was academically qualified for the senior class. His mood improved immediately, but his warring spirit was unappeased. The real fireworks would come over the next two years. "I credit my parents with doing their best to help a troubled teenager, and cannot blame them for the explosion that was about to take place," he wrote in his autobiography,

seeming to contradict some of his earlier criticisms of them. More am-
bivalence, perhaps: he wavered between respect for what his parents had
patiently endured on his behalf and the sense that they might have done
more to nurture him in his years of crisis, particularly his father. More of
what, exactly, Waterman seemed unsure about—the shortcomings of his
father, so obvious to him as a son, were suddenly much harder to grasp
when he had sons of his own.

"Where people come from is a mystery to me," he acknowledged. "As
a parent, I felt responsible for how my kids turned out, but I don't have
the foggiest idea what my parents could have done to make my transition
out of the despondency of those Taft years any smoother."

Waterman the junior ended up hanging out with the senior class at
Sidwell. His skill at the keyboard gave him an identity he never had at
Taft and entrée into a new circle of fairly sophisticated friends. His talent
was announced one day when he was practicing on the piano in the gym
and a popular football player named Richard Stimson came bounding out
of the locker room in amazement. Stimson, a senior, played the drums; he
loved New Orleans jazz; the last thing he expected was to hear it being
rendered in its full-blown glory by a pint-sized sixteen-year-old at Sidwell
Friends. The next weekend, Stimson and some of his classmates hauled
Waterman to a bar called the Casablanca in the black part of Washington,
where a quintet led by a clarinetist named Country Thomas had a regular
gig playing New Orleans style. The preppies cajoled the band leader into
letting Waterman sit in. The pros were pretty impressed, too—in fact, a
year later, Country Thomas offered Waterman a two-day gig at Washington's Moose Club, his first professional job. From that night at the
Casablanca onward, Waterman's role was set. He was the cat at the piano.
"He played every day during coffee breaks and after lunch—there was a
piano in the lunch room," recalled Stimson, who went on to a career in the
insurance business and ended up marrying Waterman's first wife after she
and Waterman were divorced, thus becoming for the duration of that
marriage a stepfather to Waterman's sons.

Over the fall of 1948, the piano man steadily crept into favor with
himself. Had he been content just to play, he would have been fine. De-

spite his radical opinions, he was known as a good if occasionally provocative student in his English and history classes. Looking back on his high
school days in his autobiography, Waterman repeatedly declares his disdain for what he was then, saying that he was the sort of teenager he
would hate today—saying it with enough vehemence to make you wonder if he wasn't trying to highlight his adult virtues by flogging his teen
vices. At any rate, Waterman was not content just to be the cynosure on
the piano bench. At a party one weekend, he began to lay into the beer on
hand; although not his introduction to alcohol, the effect seemed especially marvelous to him.

> I proceeded to get quite drunk and to hold center stage on the
> piano, singing "Buddy Bolden's Blues" and other ancient jazz
> tunes and pounding out my barrelhouse piano. This was where
> I decided that my way to be accepted as an interesting personal-
> ity was to become the class drunk. From then on, I got good
> and drunk at every possible occasion where classmates got to-
> gether. . . . I set the stage for a serious problem with alcohol in the
> future.

That was also the party where he met Emily Morrison, a dark-haired
senior who had grown up in Washington and was tagged in the Sidwell
yearbook as someone who "loves ballads and camp songs, which she usually sings in her inimitable fashion at the slightest invitation (usually
around two A.M. at slumber parties)." She took an instant liking to the
school's budding jazz star and "interesting personality." Like Guy, she
came from an academic family, a stoic, rock-ribbed, emotionally hide-
bound New England clan whose ancestors stretched back to Puritans
who'd sailed over on the *Mayflower*. Her father, Harold, had a doctorate
in entomology from Harvard and worked at the U.S. Department of
Agriculture. Her mother, Emily Reed Morrison, had a master's in entomology from Radcliffe; she'd learned Russian in order to read the extensive Soviet research on bugs, but had sacrificed a career to have a family.
Emily and her twin sister, Harriet, were born twelve years after their

brother, Peter. (Having old parents—old by the standards of the day—was one of the things Emily believed she and Guy had in common.) "My mother was a quiet person whose goal was not to upset anybody or say too much," recalled Peter Morrison, who earned a Ph.D. in zoology from Harvard, and oversaw a research laboratory at the University of Alaska before retiring to the San Juan Islands, in Washington State. Harold Morrison is often remembered as a strict and daunting patriarch who dominated his wife and nearly everyone else in the family circle; children did not have the option of disagreeing with him. "When he smiled, half of his mouth went down," recalled his granddaughter Alice Reed Morrison. The senior class at Sidwell dubbed Harold "the old lamplighter" for his habit of switching on lights at the parties hosted by his daughters. Waterman in his memoirs described Emily's father as "a tyrant given to violence when annoyed." Before long, it was apparent that much of Waterman's attraction to Emily was based on his opposition to Dr. Morrison and the romantic aggrandizement of himself as her knight errant.

From the start, their fairy tale was marked by skewed judgment and patent bids for attention. One Saturday afternoon in May 1949, two weeks before Emily, who was planning to go to Cornell in the fall, was due to graduate, and just a few days before Guy's sister Anne was to be married in a big ceremony before the extended family, Emily and Guy went to the movies. When the picture let out, they lingered downtown for hours, rashly "necking" (as Waterman put it) on the steps of an all-night radio station. Knowing what ire would be aroused in the old lamplighter were Emily to return home so late, the couple headed for a classmate's house on the far side of Washington. They arrived after sunup. Guy called his parents, who had already heard from Emily's parents. All four adults were "quite upset." Mrs. Waterman told Guy to take Emily to the Morrisons' house and wait there for her and Hawee to join them. Emily told Guy she was tempted to run away. Well, why not? In for a dime, in for a dollar. They went to the bus station and bought tickets for points south with the idea of alighting eventually in York, South Carolina, near the Georgia border. The previous summer, Guy had attended a work camp at a church-run orphanage there. He'd been radicalized by his exposure to poverty, segregation, and bigotry; he'd been introduced to grown-up appetites: cigarettes, black coffee, beer at rural taverns. He'd had some fumbling first encounters with the opposite sex. He'd been intensely happy at the camp, sharing the fellowship of people from backgrounds unlike his, a happiness that crested when his fellow campers voted him "friendliest" at the end of the summer. Now he and Emily were headed back toward York. When they reached Virginia, they began hitchhiking, and by two A.M. the next day they had arrived in Raleigh, North Carolina. They lay down for the night in a weedy lot and momentously cast off the burden of their virginities. By Monday afternoon, they were back in Guy's old haunts and he was asking about jobs at the joint where he'd first tasted beer. No openings, as of yet, for a Yankee shaver scarcely a few weeks past seventeen. That night, they found a hay-strewn barn on the grounds of the orphanage and reconfirmed their passion, but were scared off from a whole night's rest by what sounded like a bull stirring nearby. Back on the road again, hitchhiking. They were finally stopped by a cop, who flushed out their real names, called their parents, and put an end to their frolic by clapping them in separate cells for the night.

Hawee and Guy's brother Neil made the long day's drive to fetch the runaways back to Washington. Anne was not happy about the distraction Guy had caused. Emily was allowed to graduate but was barred from the ceremony. Both families worked to keep the couple apart for the rest of the summer. Guy was sent up to Buffalo with his brother Neil, while Mary Waterman, conceding the reality of the relationship but hoping to cool it down, took Emily to visit various Mallon and Waterman relatives. As they were getting back to Washington, Hawee shunted Guy, who had returned from Buffalo, off to Maine for their final father-son canoe trip. But the harder the parents plotted to keep the kids apart, or at least moderate their fervor, the more determined Guy and Emily were to embrace their romantic destiny. They were yoked in an unspoken pact to vex the forces of respectability.

At this time, "Guy thought he had discovered African American culture," recalled his sister Anne. "When my parents expressed concern about the drinking and drugs in the jazz clubs, he banged on the dinner table, and said, 'Just because their income bracket is lower than yours doesn't mean they aren't good people.'"

There was a reprieve in the rebellion that fall when Emily went off to Cornell and Guy began his senior year at Friends. Guy was pleased to discover that the news of his escapade with Emily had given him an air of notoriety among his classmates. But his parents, concerned about his state of mind, were requiring him to see a psychoanalyst once a week. "I was defiant, and [the psychoanalyst] took the posture of being completely unsympathetic and caustically critical of my conduct," Waterman recalled. Not surprisingly, the appointments, in his inexperienced eyes, were "totally unproductive."

Perhaps here was one of the sources of Waterman's aversion to pigeonholes, for his impression of shrinks was soon to grow still poorer. Parental warnings and admonishments notwithstanding, Waterman kept drinking at the parties thrown almost every weekend by his classmates. More constructively, he continued to apprentice himself to the New Orleans style, auditing recordings in the collection of the Library of Congress, then trundling home to pick the tunes out on the piano. But his sense of guilt about his entitlements and his isolation from "ordinary folk" took the savor out of things that most high school teenagers enjoy without pangs of conscience. To his delight, for instance, Waterman made the football team as a small but speedy guard. And he was even more thrilled when he acquitted himself well in the first game and sat with the team's star halfback on the bus ride home. But then he abruptly left the team to take a sixty-five-cents-an-hour job jerking soda at a People's drugstore on the corner of Wisconsin Avenue and Albermarle Street, in northwest Washington. There, on weekdays from five to ten P.M., and sometimes on weekends, he could fancy himself a superior sort of "working stiff," rubbing shoulders with real people.

After just one semester, Emily left Cornell and returned to Washington. She and Guy began dating again. At parties, they would slip off to a bedroom. Guy had made what in the Waterman household was the rather heretical statement that he wouldn't go to college; he would play music for a living. In December, he got the call from Country Thomas for his first professional gig. Not long after that, he attended a jam session in Baltimore, where he sampled what then seemed the scandalously illicit, ticket-to-madness drug, marijuana. His parents' apprehensions were mounting. If he had been trying to get their attention, he finally succeeded.

He told the story this way:

One Sunday evening, my parents told me we were going down for a meeting with the psychoanalyst, to be attended also by Emily and her parents. At this session, the doc announced that I was a deeply disturbed young man, and he recommended prolonged psychoanalysis, either at the Mayo Clinic, in Rochester, Minnesota, or elsewhere, away from Washington. I protested, but still thought this was something that would take place in a week or so. Then I found that I was not to return home that night, but was taken instead to the psycho ward in George Washington Hospital, and incarcerated there on a floor where the stairway doors and elevators were locked. I was kept there for several days of tests and questions—including one session where they administered some kind of truth serum to me and questioned me about my musical friends, who had marijuana, etc. It felt very much like jail to me. I was very unhappy. . . . This confinement in the psycho ward had only the effect of hardening my hostility toward the adult world and the realm of respectability. I deeply resented the loss of freedom—though, as I'm well aware today, I had flagrantly abused the privileges of freedom hitherto.

Waterman's parents passed on a course of prolonged psychoanalysis in favor of removing the wayward boy to Ohio and the supervision of his big sister Bobbie and her husband, Joe Carney. The change of scene did the trick, at least for the time being. While Waterman's class at Sidwell went on without him, he entered West Carrolton High School, where he was "overjoyed" to be "sitting next to a black student," and making friends with "the common folk at last." Twice a week he saw a psychoanalyst in nearby Dayton. Where the first therapist had tried to confront Waterman, the second one just sat in silence, dogmatically waiting for his patient to start talking. Waterman found the new sessions no more helpful than the old ones, and perhaps these experiences instilled in him a bias against therapy in general. No thanks to the shrink (at least as far as he was concerned), Waterman felt himself changing all the same. When not studying, he spent most of his time reading and practicing the piano. "When I was cooking dinner he'd be playing the piano," recalled his sister Bobbie. "He would wink at me and play 'Ain't Misbehavin'.'" He slowly began to gain some perspective under the beneficent influence of his sister and especially of her husband, Joe, who worked in the local paper mill. "He communicated to me by example, not lectures," Waterman recalled. Joe told the young man that "we are all responsible for our own behavior, all accountable for our private morality. Alone of all the adults I was at war with, Joe let me know that he expected me to be responsible for myself, to accept the consequences of my actions."

While his life seemed to be stabilizing, a final campaign was yet to come. In retrospect, Waterman's behavior seems curiously linked to his father's success, as if he was determined to offset the heights of Hawee's professional achievements with the depths of his delinquency. That winter of 1950, Alan Waterman reached the apogee of his career when he was named by President Truman to be the first director of the newly created National Science Foundation. He edged out ten other candidates and survived a last-minute objection by administration screeners who wondered whether he ought to be disqualified because his wife had twice been to teas at the Russian embassy. Remarkably, in McCarthy-era Washington, sanity prevailed and Waterman was appointed to the job of organizing a new federal institution from the ground up. The NSF mission: to fund basic scientific research. The director's duties entailed everything from overseeing the first federal grants for university researchers to finding office space, hiring a staff, and writing the phone company to make sure the NSF was listed under "N" as well as in the government pages. Waterman became a frequent visitor to the White House and was reappointed to a second term when Dwight D. Eisenhower succeeded Truman to the presidency.

It would be the unusual teenager who could grasp the nature of his rivalry with his father or see what looms in retrospect as the conspicuous link between his aggression and his conception of his father's rectitude. The idea that Hawee was Ariel Incarnate dogged Guy Waterman when he was older and began, overtly and self-consciously, to measure himself against that mythical figure. When he was older, he seemed to find the lesson of his father's example in the idea of taking responsibility for yourself. But it's one thing to take responsibility for your actions and another to understand what motivates them. One has to wonder, in hindsight, if the control Waterman was eventually able to exert over himself came at the price of a more inclusive idea of the self. He seems to have accepted too readily that he was fated to pitch between the bewildering extremes of his mind's nature and to have given up on the possibility that the shadow within him could be reconciled with the light. Maybe in learning to cope on his own with the dynamics of his psyche he found it easier to repress his feelings than to understand them. Tilt the prism and another color breaks. Maybe he understood himself so well that he had no desire to contend further with what he was.

One of the more provocative assertions of modern therapy is that suicide is a form of "mistaken identity." Of course, many contrary cases can be cited, where suicide seems less a way of mistaking one's identity than of realizing it, even of liberating or redeeming it—acts of altruistic self-sacrifice, for example, those noble if irrational instances when a soldier throws himself on a hand grenade to save his buddies. And there seems to be no identity error in people who choose suicide to foreclose the agony of terminal illness. The premises of therapy in some sense have secularized the morality of the Christian taboo against self-murder. They recast the sin against God as an offense against the healthy self. But this notion has more to do with faith than science, and the implication that people don't kill themselves because they know who they truly are is absurd in light of

the postmodern view of the self as embedded in cultural biases and onto-
logical mysteries it cannot hope to transcend (a self that by definition is
largely unknowable, and thus is impossible *not* to mistake).

But then the prism tilts another way. If there isn't one "right" story
per person perhaps there are several "less wrong" ones. Maybe the script
that carried Guy Waterman onto Mt. Lafayette could have been changed.
Maybe with the help of a therapist or medication or some freshly awak-
ened sense of broader responsibilities, he could have seen the error and the
harm in his thinking. The uncertainty here takes us back to the general
problem of attempting to fix the infinite malleability of a man's life in a
conclusive interpretation. How many times do we go over the same
ground, seeing something different at each pass, before coming to realize
in the end that the ground is never the same, the phenomena can never
be definitely captured; the qualities of a cabin, a garden, a woods, a man
are always in flux? Narrative demands a clear-cut answer. Did Waterman fatally mistake himself, or in fact is his death best understood in the
tradition of those exceptions in which suicide is the ultimate act of self-
fulfillment? How can a storyteller say where exactly the narrative Waterman told himself went awry? Isn't there something more truthful in an
irresolvable contradiction than in any categorical judgment? Something
more truthful in the miserable equivocation of saying the answer is yes
and no? Yes, he mistook himself. No, he did not.

In May of 1950, Guy and Emily concocted a plan to elope. Only Emily's
twin sister, Harriet, knew the pair were secretly intending to rendezvous at
the airport in Charlotte, North Carolina—Guy coming from Ohio, where
he was waiting to graduate from high school, and Emily from Washington, where she was living with Harriet and some roommates and working as a clerk in a downtown bank. From North Carolina, the pair crossed
the state line to York, South Carolina, where they had lain in the hay the
year before. York was a sentimental destination, to be sure, but more important, it was in a state where eighteen-year-olds could get married with-

out parental consent. Waterman had turned eighteen three weeks earlier. Now in a civil ceremony held in the office of the county clerk, he and Emily entered into matrimony. They notified Harriet of the deed by telegram: "Whom God and the laws of South Carolina have joined together, let no man put asunder."

"Defiance to the end," Waterman recalled in his autobiography. "Clearly this long-planned and now-achieved marriage was not a product of love but of a joint rebellion against the adult world. The resulting relationship was predictable, once there was no adult opposition to join forces against."

"He wanted my husband, Joe, to call our parents and tell them that he got married," Bobbie Waterman Carney recalled. "When they came out to Guy's graduation in Ohio, he didn't tell them. And they told me, 'Don't let him get any mail from Emily.'"

The horse was out of the barn, of course. The newlyweds kept their marriage secret for nearly a month, and finally, in June, when Guy returned to Washington by bus from Ohio, he revealed the secret to his father. Hawee took it "quietly," Waterman remembered. He asked the couple to come to the family house so he could call Mary, who was away visiting relatives, and so he could notify Emily's parents, whom he promptly invited over. "There was an awkward session in which Emily's father carefully studied the marriage certificate." But both sets of parents were done fighting. The couple had made their bed, and now they could lie in it. Emily had found an apartment for them to move into, and Guy got a dollar-an-hour job laying sod in Washington's new subdivisions. Three months later, his first son was conceived, and the callow eighteen-year-old who had yet to find his way out of the maze of his old family was already deep into the maze of a new one. Rather than follow the well-worn family path to Princeton or Yale, he had planned in characteristically headstrong fashion to educate himself. He mapped out a course of readings in history, poetry, philosophy, and such, but after plowing through Plato's dialogues and realizing he lacked a context for the work and any sense of where the author stood in relation to other Western thinkers, the limitations of the autodidact seemed severe. Moreover, after a few weeks hauling rolls of sod, a job that entailed the use of the mind suddenly had a lot to recommend it.

Backed by his parents, his uncle Neil Mallon, and the money he had begun to earn playing piano around Washington, Waterman enrolled at George Washington University at the start of 1951. In April of that year, his first son, William Antonio Waterman, was born, and that summer Waterman got a regular gig playing jazz. Suddenly, he had structure up to his ears: family, school, a job, and an apartment on Newton Street, on the dynamic edge of segregation, where the black neighborhoods east of Fourteenth Street met the white ones to the west. Waterman was nineteen years old. At GWU, he studied in his car until he discovered a hall where students could read. He didn't socialize, or go to sock hops, or swallow gold-fish. He didn't make any friends. What he did was soak up the syllabus, earn a skein of A's, and carry a course load sufficient to compress four years  of college into two and half. Thinking of job prospects—a big change— he switched from history to economics. He got a letter from a university dean saying, in essence, we don't know what you look like or who you are, but keep up the good work. He graduated at the top of his class and, to the delight of his parents, was elected Phi Beta Kappa. In September 1952, his second son, John Mallon Waterman, was born.

All the while, Waterman was playing jazz three nights a week with a group led by a veteran trumpeter named Scotty Lawrence. The Riverboat Trio, they were called. Lawrence, a bespectacled showman with a savvy stage presence, had been blowing professionally since the 1920s. The trio became weekend regulars at the Charles Hotel, in the black part of segregated Washington, where they took the stage in the small ground-floor lounge; the crowd was usually more white than black—segregation barred blacks from white joints but not whites from black ones. They also had a gig on Tuesday nights at the Bayou, a large club located under the elevated K Street freeway in Georgetown. Waterman loved performing.

> I loved the sense of walking into those bars, moving slowly up to the bandstand, standing there a moment to light a cigarette, survey[ing] the crowd calmly, then sit[ting] down at the piano bench, play[ing] a couple of chords, giv[ing] Scotty his A, then wait[ing] until Scotty gave the signal to launch into the last eight bars (as an intro) of "I Can't Give You Anything but Love, Baby," which was the song we invariably opened each evening with. . . . On my better nights I could stand the audience on its ear with a powerful rollicking barrelhouse style, or tormented gutbucket blues.

Lawrence had had a drinking problem two decades back but had been attending Alcoholics Anonymous meetings since the forties and now wet his lips with nothing harder than coffee. He set an example Waterman was happy to emulate—for a couple of years, at least. But in 1953, Waterman began to hit the sauce again. Old classmates from Sidwell Friends sometimes dropped in to hear him in the lounge of the Charles Hotel. "Guy would be playing with a cigarette dangling out of his mouth and a glass of whiskey on the piano," recalled Oscar "Mike" Gottscho. "We had some great nights there." "Sometimes," recalled Marianna Taylor, a Sidwell alumna, "there'd be an entire bottle of whiskey on the piano."

Meanwhile, Emily was home with the kids on Newton Street. Guy looked on his course work as a kind of day job, with the advantage that he got home earlier than other working fathers. According to the custom of the era, child care was largely the province of women; fathers who worked all day didn't stray too far from the easy chair in the evening. The feminist critique of the peripheral male and the division of labor in the average American marriage did touch a nerve later, when Waterman was writing his recollections, but the fuzziness of his memory suggests a deeper and more personal sort of guilt: "I recall feeling that I spent more time than most fathers with my young family," he writes.

> I remember those years as enjoyable ones as far as my two young sons were concerned—though stormy ones in the relationship between my wife and me. I think I recall many afternoons when I would take the kids off my wife's hands and go to the zoo with the them, or play in a park, or visit relatives in the area.... I mention this with some nervous hesitation. In today's terms, I'm quite sure I actually left a huge share of the child-rearing to Emily, being gone most of the weekdays at college and three nights a week playing music. I am sure she felt that I was an absentee parent, and how much of that was justified and how much the result of the bad feeling growing between us, I cannot now judge.

I think I recall many afternoons ... Would that be something you would be vague about, the many afternoons you spent at the zoo with your young sons? Well, possibly; nothing is more treacherous than memory. Likely, if you were wanting to plump up the evidence that you took your share of the load and made an effort to be a good father, those afternoons might appear more numerous in memory than they actually were. During much of her pregnancy in 1952 Emily had a difficult time, and Waterman acknowledged that she did not find him to be particularly helpful or sympathetic to her plight. Things didn't get any easier when John was finally born that fall (on the eve, Waterman recalled, of a big political science exam). Johnny was an Rh-positive baby and received a complete blood transfusion in the hospital—an experience his mother was convinced had much to do with the odd behavior he exhibited later on. She said in a letter to Guy's sister Anne that she thought Johnny had suffered all his short life from the effects of post-traumatic stress syndrome.

There are no briefs as sad and bitter and reliably self-serving as the ones unhappily married couples level against each other. Whoever didn't contribute enough, whoever was too quick to criticize or apportion blame, the point is the bliss of that mad adventure was leaking away quickly, and with it the gaiety of being young, and sharing family life with two young boys seventeen months apart in age. Within a year of their getting married, Waterman thought later, the marriage had reached a stalemate; the golden notes of "I Can't Give You Anything but Love" were lost forever in the dissonance of recrimination. Plenty of men have left their wives (and wives their husbands) for less than the troubles waylaying Guy and Emily in the summer of 1953. They had long, soul-fraying conversations, circling the same ground over and over like zoo cats. Guy stalked out one evening, caroused all night, slept at a friend's apartment, and boldly declared he wanted a divorce, only to be shocked when Emily replied, "Okay, which one of the two children do you want to take?" "It had never occurred to me that she would require me to take equal responsibility for the kids. So more talks ensued." More talks against the backdrop of his lapsed sobriety. As the marriage teetered, the Riverboat Trio broke up, and Waterman's career as a jazz man and habitué of nightclubs fell by the way. He reflected later that his drinking had a lot to do with the demise of his life as a professional musician, the return of his alcoholism being but a manifestation of "that self-destructive streak in me which throughout my life has tended to surface and destroy whatever good things come my way."

Waterman's view that his drinking was an aspect of his character and not a disease placed his behavior under the purview of his will and may have helped him finally beat the bottle as he achieved his sobriety by dint of will alone, without the aid of AA meetings or the invocation of "a higher power." But the fact was that something he genuinely loved—playing music in the trio—was gone. The adulation of the audience was gone, the deep satisfaction of working in concert with other musicians was gone. The tensions in his stalemate marriage were temporarily reduced when his parents helped the couple buy a small house in a better neighborhood off River Road. But for the most part, all the gladder aspects and spiritual sustenance of the union were done and gone. He was twenty-one years old, awfully young to be faced with losing what he'd scarcely had. Perilously young, in fact, if what he was learning from the taste of loss was the dark, hard-hearted art of shutting down and moving on.

It was just a dress rehearsal, though. The bottom came ten years later, in 1963, when Waterman was thirty-one. After graduating from George Washington, he took a year to find a good job, but when he finally caught on as a research economist in the U.S. Chamber of Commerce, he developed a reputation as a quick study and hard worker. In a number of bosses he found men who slipped into the role of surrogate father. Chief among them was Emerson P. Schmidt, the Chamber's director of economic research, who gave him his break, first assigning him to update the Chamber's economic pamphlets and then letting him draft testimony on legislation pending before Congress. Emerson sharpened Waterman's writing and taught him the ways of Washington. Never make an appointment for ten or eleven, he said; always make it for 10:20 or 11:40, the better to project the aura of a busy man for whom every minute is precious. Emerson took Waterman to lunch with top economic advisors in the Eisenhower administration. He gave his young protégé a plum assignment as secretary to an important Chamber policy committee headed by Lemuel R. Boulware, a vice-president of General Electric whose corporate paternalism and anti-union views eventually became known as Boulwarism and were much despised in union circles. It was for Boulware that Waterman wrote the speech about "what makes man *man*," expressing the philosophy at the heart of his own views: "We are each inevitably and terribly and forever personally responsible for everything we do. . . . This is a tough philosophy. But it is the *only* one—as proved through the ages—by which man can turn his personal hopes into reality." Indeed it *was* a tough philosophy, and an unforgiving one as well. It may have intensified Waterman's contempt for himself in later years, when he discovered he was unable to live up to it, unable to evade its remorseless implications about the sort of father he was.

With Boulware, as with Schmidt, Waterman discovered that he "had an instinctive liking for the role of . . . assistant-to-the-man-in-charge."

He tucked himself into the good-son service of these worldly players and was duly rewarded for his productive work and near filial devotion. Schmidt often invited Waterman and his family to visit his farm in West Virginia. He let Guy's young boys, Bill and John, ride around the fields with him on his tractor. Sometimes Emily joined them on the trips. The marriage that had nearly ruptured in the summer of 1953 had settled into an uneasy coexistence for the sake of the children. Waterman confided in his recollections that he felt much closer to one of his secretaries than he did to his wife, but the fact that he was around the house more, not running off three nights a week to play jazz into the small hours of the morning, relieved some of the pressure on Emily. In 1955, a third son, James Reed Waterman, was born. (Guy later told a colleague at General Electric, "I have one son for each form of birth control.")

After four years with the Chamber, and a short stop in the fall of 1958 at what is now known as the American Enterprise Institute, Waterman found his way onto Capitol Hill for what proved to be the pinnacle of his career, what he called his "blockbuster eighteen months." In January 1959 he joined the staff of the Senate Minority Policy Committee, a standing Senate committee that seldom met and served mainly as a means of keeping a staff on hand to support Republican initiatives. Waterman became one of those archetypal young hotshot aides who are always plucking at the sleeves and whispering into the ears of the city's distinguished so-and-so's. He got to observe up close the face cards of the Republican party in the waning years of the Eisenhower administration—the minority leader, Senator Everett Dirksen of Illinois; Senator Prescott Bush of Connecticut; and his boss, the minority policy committee chairman Senator Styles Bridges of New Hampshire. He huddled in cloakrooms with his leaders, produced on-the-spot analysis of amendments, and drafted speeches to be used in floor debate. Many evenings he spent at Bridges' side in the senator's lavish hideaway office behind door P-49 in the Capitol building.

And so he found himself vaulted up into the heady heights of his father's world. What a thrill it was once to sign out at a White House gate after a long Sunday drafting an important Republican report on a deadline and to see that Hawee had also been logged into the White House that day—and then, when he next saw Hawee, to exchange a covert look acknowledging their common whereabouts that Sunday but never mentioning their business, observing the hush-hush tradition of discretion that was expected in the capital. After all, how important could your appointment at the White House have been if you felt free to blab about it? And yet even as he grew conversant with his father's world, Waterman seemed to be either reflexively or perversely determined to spite his own success and repudiate those sunlit values he associated with his father. His conservative Republicanism itself was already something of a rebuke to his parents' liberalism. (When he went to work for the Republican party, his mother said, "Guy, is there anything else you haven't told us? Are you a Methodist?") The habits of rebellion were hard to shake.

In a shockingly short time, Waterman managed to undo everything he had achieved: the catalysts of his downfall, in his opinion, were alcohol and his own hubris. One of the mainstays of Hill culture in the late 1950s was the after-five cocktail with coworkers, usually a shot of something stiff from a bottle a senator or senior aide kept in a bottom desk drawer. Whenever he started drinking, Waterman had little inclination to stop, and the collegial afternoon cocktails quickly undid the good habits he had acquired under the influence of his band leader Scotty Lawrence. Before long, he was boozing every night. It's hard to say whether liquor impaired his judgment or success swelled his head, or whether he simply began to tire of always being the short man in the grip-and-grin photographs he was saving for his scrapbook, the physically slight second banana, obliged to dance attendance on a clutch of stentorian egotists. But all the praise heaped on Waterman began to give him a big idea about himself, and before long he paid for it. When the staff director of the policy committee began to treat him as capriciously as he had less-favored employees, Waterman went into an imprudent snit. He considered the man "a crafty, small-minded, unscrupulous tyrant" who would remove someone from an assignment he was doing well and give it to someone who had no expertise in the area just to prove he had the power to do as he pleased. Rather than demonstrate the political judgment he'd proudly acquired when it came to tailoring reports and speeches, Waterman began to sulk conspicuously. Finally he decided to go over the director's head to Senator Bridges. Prompted by the staff director, the senator sacked Waterman.

My uprising against the staff director was regarded around the Senate as inexplicable [he wrote in his autobiography]. Everyone knew he was an SOB, a madman abusing authority. But exactly what I was trying to accomplish by resigning seemed vague. So a lot of the Senate insiders (staff) may have been thinking: yes, Waterman's brilliant, but surely unpredictable, unreliable. . . . So I had blown it. I had a job at the core of power, in the World's Greatest Deliberative Body . . . and I just walked away from it.

The drinking increased, exacerbating tensions in Waterman's marriage, although it's hard to see how the bands of that relationship could have been strained any further. Marianna Taylor remembered a large party Guy and Emily threw in 1958, attended mostly by people from Sidwell Friends: "They weren't talking to each other, it was real obvious they weren't getting along. Emily was a very private person, and the party was making her very nervous and very upset. I came away with a feeling of doom about their marriage." The fact that the couple continued to hang on together for nineteen years when their relationship had gone sour after one seems to have been less a tribute to their determination to make the marriage work than a testament to what they were willing to endure for the sake of their sons, and to their mutual inertia, fear of change, and the stigma of divorce among their prewar generation.

Among his guests at that party Waterman found an old friend named Warren Groome, who had been the archetypal most-likely-to-succeed guy at Sidwell: a tall, handsome track star, scholar, and president of the student body who had won nearly every honor available, and had gone on to Princeton. Waterman had always been grateful for Groome's friendship; now he was surprised to see that the tables had turned and Warren was unhappy and lost. A year later, Waterman was dumbfounded to learn that his once and former icon of confidence and grace had died of a self-inflicted gunshot wound to the head. The story haunted him all his life.

Around the time of Groome's suicide Waterman began to entertain the same temptation, describing himself in his autobiography as "borderline suicidal." One day he went so far as to drive down to the Calvert Street Bridge, a high span across the ravine of Rock Creek Park that, until a fence was erected decades later, was the favorite platform in Washington for people seeking to leap to their deaths. He walked out onto the bridge, contemplating this most drastic solution, but found he didn't have it in him. It would not be the last time he would find himself on the threshold of the abyss, filled with suicidal intent but paralyzed to act.

The election year of 1960 proved to be a reprieve of sorts from the downward spiral of self-destruction. Waterman found a temporary assignment working for the equivalent of the policy committee on the House side of the Capitol: a three-month gig writing and compiling back-

ground papers on defense and foreign policy and drafting an important report. When the campaign began to heat up, Waterman joined the Republican National Committee as an associate director of research. Lemuel Boulware had recommended him to the campaign as "the best self-contained economist, programmer, political pamphleteer, and speechwriter I know of on the conservative side." At the time, the move seemed to Waterman an economically necessary but less-than-respectable transition from academic economist to partisan researcher. Still, it was exciting to be on the front lines of what in other elections would be known as the "war room." The Republicans had set up an "answer desk" for their candidate and presumptive nominee, Vice

President Richard Nixon. Senator Charles Percy, the Illinois Republican who was chairman of the Republican platform committee, took Waterman and a couple of other staffers in to have a look at the Oval Office after a meeting at the White House. A month into the job, everyone in the office moved to Chicago for the convention. Waterman stayed up all night drafting planks for the platform and toasting the television when phrases he'd written actually came out of the mouths of the politicians making the speeches. Back in D.C., after one of the Nixon-Kennedy debates, he got a call from the White House and stayed up all night to write a white paper Nixon had promised to release to the public in the morning. On election day he passed out campaign leaflets and then went to watch the returns at the Wardman-Park Hotel with a legion of hopeful Republicans. The early returns made what would be one of the tightest elections in history look like a Kennedy landslide. Waterman began to drown his sorrows in bourbon. In the morning, he came face to face with the severity of his drinking problem.

> I awoke late the next morning to find myself in a jail cell: quite a shock. It unfolded that I had become quite obnoxious at the hotel, and apparently at some point was threatening to jump out of an upper window . . . and when a policeman intervened, resisted him. Well, I really know nothing about what happened, except that they did indeed stick me in jail to sleep it off. I was released the next morning—I recall sheepishly asking the officer on duty what had happened, and then asking: "I guess this means Kennedy won, huh?"

It's possible his "disgrace," as he called it, loomed much larger in his own eyes than in the eyes of friends and coworkers. There were more than a few Republicans who wanted to jump out of a window after Nixon's narrow defeat, and in those days drinking was much more accepted as a part of the culture. Waterman had a tendency to judge himself harshly. "I don't recall ever seeing him drunk, or even knowing that he had a problem," said one of his former colleagues, David Abshire, who went on to serve as the U.S. ambassador to NATO and to found the Center for the Study of the Presidency.

In any case, the episode at the hotel sealed a decision Waterman had been mulling. He had received an offer to move to New York City and write speeches for the executives running the General Electric company. "I felt that too many people I knew in Washington had been a bit shocked by my being thrown in jail for being so drunk. I was plain ashamed. Leaving town was a good way to put that behind me and start fresh."

Several times previously in his life—when he had left Taft in 1950, when he had moved from Newton Street to a house on River Road in 1953—turning a page had done Waterman good. But if the problems besetting him now had as much to do with his perception of himself as with his behavior, they would not be easily solved by a change of venue.

He accepted the job offer and went to New York that December, put up in a hotel, and commuted back to Washington on weekends. But the new job proved not to be the fresh inspiration he was hoping for. He missed the excitement of Congressional action. He began drinking more heavily than he had in high school or as a hotshot on the Hill. By March 1961, he'd moved Emily and the boys into a house in Stamford, Connecticut, down by Long Island Sound, in a nice neighborhood known as Shippan Point. Every night he would knock back three glasses of bourbon and water before the boys went to bed, then work deep into the bottle until he was too glassy-eyed to remember what he'd seen on the eleven o'clock news. After spinning a bunch of jazz records, he usually passed out on the couch or the living room floor. Then it was wake in the morning, badly hung over, and catch the late train to work. Thus the months went by, snowballing into years: 1961, 1962, 1963. He was thirty-one years old—a drunk doing just enough to get by in a job he didn't like.

For Emily those years were a nightmare. Aside from the spectacle of my getting drunk every night, she had to put up with the fact that it was all going on so secretly . . . so that she wasn't getting any sympathy from others for what she had to put up with. . . . I was destroying myself and I knew it. Of course, knowing what I was doing only intensified my self-pity and desire to get drunk. . . . My life was going down the drain fast. . . . I could see no way out of the trap I was in, had no vision of anything better than the miserable cycle of drunkenness and despair in which I was caught. Shame is the word for those years. I felt then a deep sense of shame over my conduct. And still today I recall that time with nothing but shame.

And then in 1963, the year he could go no lower—the year, coincidentally, that his father received the Presidential Medal of Freedom, made a trip to Antarctica, where he flew over the mountain that had been named for him in the Hughes Range, and retired from public service on a bed of laurels—Waterman had his epiphany. It happened in the summer, a few months after Hawee returned from the U.S. polar base at McMurdo Station. It took the form of a series of articles in *Sports Illustrated* about—of all things—the ascent of a mountain: in this case, a disastrous 1957 attempt on the North Face of the storied Swiss mountain the Eiger and the heroic efforts of the rescuers to save the stranded climbers. For many years, the Eiger's icy North Face had been considered one of the great "unclimbable" walls of the Alps, and the public's fascination with efforts to scale it had been intensified not only by the mountain's aura of danger and death but by the nationalistic rivalries of European states before World War II. The magazine articles, by Jack Olsen, were later shaped into a book with the Miltonesque title *The Climb Up to Hell.*

Any hell above had to be better than the one Waterman was foundering in below. Never did the symbolism of ascent seem so uplifting. Climbing means many things to many people, but to Waterman, mired in the pit of alcoholism, climbing was like the rope that appears before a man at the bottom of a crevasse. It was rescue and salvation. It was the one thing that had meaning and that he had to do. Certainly one could suggest it was also a new form of inebriation which was promising to supplant the old one without altering the compulsive pattern behind it. And to be sure, climbing in its way was no less melodramatic than drinking, no less an absurd and useless pursuit. But there was a glory in it that drinking could never have—the glory encapsulated in Shaw's epigram on how to tell the difference between heaven and hell: "Hell is where you just drift; Heaven is where you get to steer."

"I was swept off my feet," Waterman wrote in his autobiography. "Mountains and mountain climbing dawned on my drunken, shamed, lonely life like a beacon of hope. Here was a whole new world of aspiration and effort, contrasting with the nightmare my life had become. A flight of Ariel way up in the sunshine, distantly seen from the depths of Caliban's black hole. I turned toward it as a drowning man toward a distant beach. Was I too late, too far out to reach it?"

Everything followed from that moment of discovery—Waterman's own way out of the morass of his life, the work he would do, the books he would write, the little Eden he would piece together, the old marriage he would at last dissolve and the new one he would begin. Everything followed from that moment: even the kind of sons he would raise and send forth and lose, three boys who came of age in the crucible of mountains, close to the wildness that bewilders us all in the end.

5.

ROPING UP

✳

... I know
How a long life grows ghostly toward the close
As any man dissolves in Everyman
Of whom the story, as it always did, begins
In a far country, once upon a time,
There lived a certain man, and he had three sons ...

HOWARD NEMEROV,
The Western Approaches

Gentlemen: I would like to apply for membership in the Four Thousand Footer Club of the White Mountains on behalf of the following applicants, all of whom reached their forty-sixth peak together on Saturday, July 9, of this year: William A. Waterman; John M. Waterman; Guy Waterman; Ralph Waterman. The first two named are my sons, aged fifteen and thirteen respectively. The last named is our dog, who will be three next month, and is a collie-shepherd mixture.

GUY WATERMAN, *letter to the Appalachian Mountain Club, July 23, 1966*

L IKE HUNTING in its more noble forms and farming at its most contemplative, climbing urges on its adherents a kind of communion with the natural world. It is a way of seeing and feeling and weaving one's self into nature, but it is more intense than most disciplines because peril is part of its equation. To climb is to enter a labyrinth where the menace that awaits is nature's indifference to its own creation, an indifference you feel in those corrosive instants of self-estrangement that beset even the greatest alpinists: brink-of-oblivion moments when the proximity of the void draws a crushing tension between the nature within and the nature without. *What the hell am I doing here?* But in the payoff of its transcendent moments, in its therapeutic rapture, climbing can generate states of mind akin to the mystic's experience of unity, dissolving the distinctions of self and not-self so that the outer reality of wind and sky truly seems part of the terrain of one's inner life.

It's a game, to be sure, but one played for keeps and close to the edge, and one that rests on painstakingly calibrated physical statements rather than on intellectual propositions. To the degree they speak with their balance and nerve and gymnastic grace, most climbers cannot say what draws them up, or what they're after. Climbing famously has no point or moral rationale. Mallory's dismissive explanation for his pursuit of Everest—"Because it is there"—is memorable because it's marvelously succinct and eerily sufficient. The truth is, climbing is its own reward, and almost every climb begins where reason and good sense leave off. Which is not to say climbers are irresistibly impelled by tropisms like the force that draws the ivy up the trellis or moves sunflowers along the arc of the sun. There is art in what they do. There is consciousness. There is form, choice, and sometimes even a sense of composition, as if one were working out a series of variations upon a theme prefigured in the stone.

Anyone who climbs understands the relation of pleasure to risk and the great joy of escaping hardships you have brought upon yourself. And yet the risks can bring terror and all too often the tragic, senseless waste of life. In its extreme, state-of-the-art expressions, climbing often seems to approximate a kind of medieval asceticism, a form of suffering and mortification akin to what saints underwent to purify the spirit. Certainly their goals are profoundly different, but a special spiritual impetus seems to denominate saints and climbers, and on occasion, oddly, even suicides. William James identified this impetus in *The Varieties of Religious Experience:*

[M]ankind's common instinct for reality . . . has always held the world to be essentially a theater for heroism. In heroism, we feel, life's supreme mystery is hidden. We tolerate no one who has no capacity whatever for it in any direction. On the other hand, no matter what a man's frailties otherwise may be, if he be willing to risk death, and still more if he suffer it heroically, in the service he has chosen, the fact consecrates him forever. Inferior to ourselves in this or that way, if yet we cling to life, and he is able "to fling it away like a flower" as caring nothing for it, we account him in the deepest way our born superior. Each of us in his own person feels that a high-hearted indifference to life would expiate all his shortcomings. . . . [He] who feeds on death that feeds on men possesses life super-eminently and excellently, and meets best the demands of the universe.

This was the sport, subculture, and romantic order Guy Waterman embraced in 1963. In his last published book, *A Fine Kind of Madness,* he took the occasion of the discovery of Mallory's body on Everest, seventy-five years after the famous British mountaineer was lost, in 1924, to reflect on the idealizations climbers of Waterman's generation had been steeped in. "We were all brought up on the legend of 1924," he wrote. "[We] drank deep of the cup of romance of 'because it's there'; could not tear our imaginations' eye from the tiny figures disappearing up into the mists of the unattainable. This was just one of the many neological twists we learned to give the stark reality of death, that half-dreaded, half-invited angel ever brooding in the shadows of the climber's world."

In October 1963, having ransacked libraries in Connecticut and New York for books on climbing and its history, Waterman took his first steps toward the mists of the unattainable by enrolling in a rock-climbing course taught by the New York chapter of the Appalachian Mountain Club. Under the club's auspices, he was introduced to the cliffs of the Shawangunks, outside New Paltz, New York.

The Gunks, as they are known, are not particularly dramatic as climbing areas go. Routes are only two to three hundred feet high, but the hard, horizontally fractured escarpment of four-hundred-million-year-old conglomerate breaks like a crown out of the modest wooded hills overlooking the Wallkill River valley and the Hudson River valley further east, and the four major formations are detailed with countless ledges, ceilings, and cracks. Climbers have threaded the cliffs with more than five hundred routes—many of them spectacularly exposed, skirting overhangs and airy drops, or shooting up jam cracks, chimneys, laybacks, and friction pitches.

The Gunks were discovered as a climbing area in the spring of 1935 by the famous German-born mountaineer Fritz Wiessner, who glimpsed a break of gleaming white rock from afar and decided to investigate. Wiessner and his various partners pioneered many of the first ascents. Even three decades later, when Waterman showed up at what he would soon begin to think of as the first of his two spiritual homes—the other being Franconia Ridge—climbing was a still a marginal preoccupation, far from the interests of the mainstream. It did not take long to get to know the crew of regulars who would meet along the old carriage road under the Überfall, one of the easy exit routes, and then head off with ropes and clanking racks of pitons slung over their shoulders for the various starting points at the base of the main cliff.

The sixties were some of the last unself-conscious years of climbing. There were no glossy national magazines like *Outside* to rhapsodize on the exploits of the hotshots; no Starbucks-sponsored Internet updates from Everest's Base Camp. This was before the Wilderness Act of 1964, or Earth Day and the passage of the landmark environmental laws at the decade's end. It was the era of drab woolens, not neon Gore-Tex. It was the era when unreliable equipment and a general level of caution combined to establish the principle that the leader who ventures above his belayer—the person to whom the rope is attached—must not dare risk a fall. Ropes were made of gold line, not perlon; you tied in with a bowline around your waist, no fancy harnesses. Climbers carried metal spikes called pitons to anchor themselves to the cliffs, not today's complement of aluminum nuts and spring-loaded anchoring devices called cams. The heralding cry of "On belay!" was mingled with the ring of rock hammers.

Into this community of "aspiration and effort," Waterman made his debut on the aptly named climb Beginner's Delight, which is as savory an introduction to the vertical world as exists among the many cliffs sought by climbers in the northeast. At thirty-one, he was old to be roping up for the first time—an odd position for a man who'd been so early to the altar and had a precociously successful career on Capitol Hill. But after polishing off his second climb of the day, Gelsa, he was ecstatic. He understood the lines by Frederic Harrison he'd transcribed from James Ramsey Ullman's book *Americans on Everest:* "We need sometimes that poetry should not be droned into our ears but flashed into our senses."

A month later, one Saturday in November, he drove more than five hours north by himself from Stamford, Connecticut, to New Hampshire, following a route that would take him as near as possible to what were vaguely indicated on his gas station map as the White Mountains. Waterman had not been in that country since high school, when his father took him up mounts Chocorua and Washington en route to the Maine woods. He found his way to a trailhead in Franconia Notch, where he pitched a canvas army tent. On November 15, 1963, in light rain and dense fog, he made his maiden ascent of Mt. Lafayette, the broad, windswept mile-high pile of rocks named for the French nobleman and revolutionary hero after his visit to America in 1825. (In the White Mountains, rivers are generally registered by their aboriginal names and mountains by designations ascribed by—and often in commemoration of—white men. The name of the Franconia Range, which reaches its crest in Lafayette, was an immigrant moniker inspired by the range's likeness to Germany's Franconian Alps.) In work boots and cotton clothes ill suited for the dismal weather, Waterman slogged up the Old Bridle Path, following the route Thoreau took when he climbed the mountain in July 1858. He ran into snow at 4,500 feet, traversed the high alpine ridge that crosses from Lafayette over to mounts Lincoln and Little Haystack, and then descended via the Falling Waters trail, a beautiful, tumbling path that wanders among rock ledges and waterfalls. Despite being soaked and unable to see much farther than his nose, he had a fantastic time. Monday, he crossed the highway that runs through the Notch and climbed up to Lonesome Lake. Tuesday, he headed home.

So exhilarated was Waterman by his first exposure to Lafayette that he repeated the climb ten months later, in August 1964, accompanied by his son Bill and his nephew Tim Carney. In a vest-pocket notebook he kept a trip log he called "White Mountains 1964—25 Impressions":

Sunday evening. Lafayette from [the] Greenleaf [Hut]. Unquestionably one of the most awe-inspiring scenes in the White Mountains. From the western shoulder of Lafayette 4,000 feet up, the entire wall—Lafayette's north peak, Lafayette itself, Lincoln,

Little Haystack—towers above the long flanks plunging 3,000 feet everywhere but on the narrow col connecting the western shoulder with Lafayette. The four summits connected by a wildly broken knife-edge ridge. Especially dramatic at sunset of a near cloudless evening, gaunt against a darkening sky, brooding in awesome power over a tiny inconsequential shack full of people sitting on its side. Monday morning. Lafayette's summit in storm. A storm of rain hit the whole Franconia region, so that the Hut [caretakers] cautioned against venturing up on the wild ridge of Lafayette. We decided to move, and crawled through the fog from one barely visible cairn to the next (above tree line at this point). On the summit, rain, wind, and cold drove us on quickly with little time to savor our first 5,000-footer and no view at all. On the knife-edge leading to Lafayette's north peak the storm reached its worst. But as we descended the eastern side we emerged from the storm and into sunshine eventually, though the top of Lafayette remained shrouded by a storm cloud all day as we looked back.

In July 1965, Waterman made yet another ascent of Lafayette in rotten weather. Finally, a day later, on his fourth trip, he was rewarded with a panoramic view from the summit. He went up before breakfast after a night at the Greenleaf Hut, accompanied by his son Johnny. Something about the rocky bleakness of the peak, and the ridge trail linking Lafayette and its satellites, resonated deeply with Waterman. *Gaunt against a darkening sky* . . . He kept returning as one returns to the refrain of a ballad, in rain, wind, fog, snow—at first light, at dusk, when the last ice was melting off the alpine tundra in spring, when the blooms of diapensia and mountain avens and sandwort were ripening in the heat of summer, when the tinges of fall were creeping into the leaves of the low-bush cranberry and Labrador tea, and even in winter, especially in winter, when gales raked the great dome of snowbound boulders and sleet streamed sideways like trace vapor in a wind tunnel. Of all the mountains he climbed in New England, he climbed none more times than he did

Lafayette. He began keeping a record after that inaugural foray in November 1963. For thirty-five years, he logged all his activity on cliffs and trails, typing up the entries and binding them in a black loose-leaf notebook whose first page was a compilation of quotes that included a line from Byron: "Where rose the mountains, there to him were friends." When Waterman quit with the counting and logging, he had racked up three hundred ascents of Lafayette. The actual final number was even higher. He made no record, for instance, of the reconnaissance trip in December 1999, when he went up the mountain to scout a place to die. And, of course, there was the final unrecorded ascent on the day of his death.

Lafayette had long passed from being just another summit to check off in pursuit of membership in the Four Thousand Footer Club. It had become sacred ground. The trail was like a rosary, and climbing it Waterman's way of praying, if a man who is not religious can be said to pray. Or perhaps traversing the same ground again and again, year after year, had an effect like a mantra one repeats in meditation to break beyond the confines of the self. Perhaps he found in the trail a way of tuning his spirit, a bliss-inducing regimen for legs and lungs and heart and mind. As the anthropologist and nature writer Richard Nelson once said, "Sometimes there's more to be learned by climbing the same mountain a hundred times than climbing a hundred mountains once."

Many of Waterman's ascents were made in service of the mountain and the Ridge Trail, which traverses its summit. Waterman was one of the primary custodians of the route through the fragile alpine zone, and the head of a group of devoted volunteer caretakers called the West End Trail Tenders—or WETT, in honor of the conditions they often worked in. Waterman spent countless hours seeking ways to keep the heavy traffic of hikers from wrecking the beauty of the place, clearing debris to make sure water drained off the trail, hauling brush with which to form a protective cover for denuded areas, building cairns and arranging stones to guide hikers through especially sensitive stretches.

And by the end of his association with Lafayette, Waterman knew every nook of the mountain. Along the Ridge Trail, there was hardly a rock he had not touched. In a larger sense, there was hardly a spot not linked to his life's revisions. Lafayette was the terrain in which he had pursued salvation in nature. It was the stage on which he had shared the best adventures with his sons. It was the ground of memory itself, haunted by ghosts, high times, laughter, and loss. Its desolate slopes were as familiar to him as the woodlots of his homestead. To comb the mountain's reaches was to leaf through the book of his life.

The full measure of this affinity would be revealed in years to come. For the moment, the tyro of 1963 saw the physical challenge of climbing and hiking as a powerful incentive to get in shape. Waterman began to lift weights and squeezed a hand spring to strengthen his fingers. After moving his family to suburban Connecticut, in 1961, Waterman walked the nearly two and a half miles from his house in Stamford to the railroad station, and then back again in the evening. Even in wintertime he began to ride between the cars of the New Haven line on his commute—to escape the cigarette smoke but also to accustom himself to the cold. At work he skipped the elevator for the stairs, loping up two steps at a time, even when his office at General Electric was on the twenty-first floor. Heading out for lunch and at the end of the day, he would run down, too, often outracing the elevator, honing what proved to be a remarkable ability to bound down mountain trails at high speed.

As nothing else had, the rigors of climbing and back country travel drove home to Waterman the necessity of getting sober. Breaking the grip of booze was the hardest job he'd ever tackled. "The calendar year 1964 was one long ordeal of trying not to take a drink each night," he wrote in his autobiography.

Though I kept no record, I'll bet if I had it would show just about a straight-line projection, from say, thirty nights drunk out of thirty-one in January 1964 to maybe five or six in December. That is, thirty nights drunk in January, twenty-six in February, twenty-four in March, twenty-two in April and so on. Each night was a battle with Caliban, each sober night a great victory and source of pride, each drunk night a setback and source of despair. This entire campaign was waged alone: I never joined AA . . .

never talked with anyone about the problem or my struggle to overcome it. Emily gave no support or encouragement, viewing my every action with disdain—which I can scarcely condemn after all she'd put up with. By 1965—and this I recall distinctly—I had essentially reached my goal. I had one slip in January 1965 and another in June 1965. Thereafter it was one more drunk in June 1968 and a last one (so far) in November 1970, and not one drop since.

In a chronology of his life he drew up in 1982, Waterman placed his hiking prime in the late 1960s and his climbing prime in the early 1970s. He got steadily better on rock and maintained a respectable standard. He was able to "on sight" a 5.9 at age fifty—on sight meaning do the route on the first try; and 5.9 being the designation for a degree of difficulty. (Once at the outer limits of free-climbing skill, 5.9 has long since been exceeded, with climbers today pushing past 5.10, 5.11, 5.12, and 5.13 to a subtly calibrated frontier that sounds more like a section of the federal tax code: 5.14d.) Waterman's friend John Dunn, one of the five men who carried his body off Lafayette, remembered that Waterman would always sing while he climbed, except at a crux that was at the edge of his ability. Like many climbers, he preferred to lead—that is, to put the rope up, climbing above the belayer. (If the leader slips off his stance, he falls twice the distance from his last piece of protection, and so the consequences are much graver than falling as the second, who always has the rope above him ready to catch a slip immediately.) Waterman's sense of himself was keyed to leading. "Guy subscribed to the principle that the leader must not fall," Dunn said. "He thought it was breach of style if the leader put in too much protection. It was a sign of weakness. Yet eventually he pushed those principles to the point where he couldn't climb anymore because it was too frightening. The principles became handicaps."

If roping up induced him to get sober and roused him from the slough of self-pity, its most haunting effect was to bind him to his sons in a vividly literal way that paradoxically underscored the family's emotional disconnections. It is difficult to understand how father and sons who were lashed together by a 150-foot rope could have lost each other so completely. Are the ties that bind us so fragile?

The question of exactly what sort of father Waterman was, and what sort of judgment can be fairly rendered, is as tricky as it is important. It was not just the journalists arriving after his death but many of Waterman's relatives and friends who were left to infer what kind of job he did as a dad, and more than a few of them reluctantly concluded it wasn't a good one—that he was still a boy himself, in over his head, too callow to appreciate the range of his responsibilities, too self-involved to meet some of the key ones. "I can imagine there were times when Emily must have thought she had four boys at home," said Brad Snyder, a climber and former professor of German at Mt. Holyoke College, who was one of Waterman's most insightful friends and his most valued writing critic.

It's not that Waterman couldn't be bothered with his boys, or that he didn't take them to the zoo or the beach or Mets and Yankees games, or sign them up for Boy Scouts and help show them how to lash tripods and start fires with flint and steel. When they were old enough to hit the trail with him, he took them to get their feet measured for pairs of handmade Limmer boots, one of the premier status symbols in White Mountain hiking circles. Waterman's willingness to soldier on in a bad marriage and not quit on the family can be read as a powerful testament to his concern for his sons' welfare. And what better measure could there be of how he valued his sons than the obvious torment he felt in losing them—a depth of pain that may have made the temptation of shortening his own life harder to resist. His sister Bobbie was characteristically generous in her estimate: "I think Guy was a good father," she said. Even Emily Waterman thought Guy had done a good job raising their sons, in their early years, and into their teen years. She told her niece that Guy had spent a lot of time with the boys and they in turn had "adored" him. The problems came later.

But the very intensity of Waterman's relations with surrogate sons implied a longing to atone for mistakes. What mistakes? He never made that clear. He was loath to discuss the subject. One of the sharpest appraisals of his patrimony came in a confidence his youngest son, Jim, once shared with a cousin: "Dad was a good father as long as you wanted to do what he wanted." Perhaps Waterman's anguish about his sons reflected his sense of complicity in their sad ends—his remorse about the guidance he was unable to provide when they were older, ostensibly mature and out on their own. In retrospect, the fledglings seem to have escaped—or to have been pushed—from the nest before their wings were ready. Waterman's own precocity as a star student and teenage father of two might have blinded him to their difficulties. Maybe he expected his kids to make the transition to adulthood as expeditiously as he had. But to others, it was apparent his elder two boys were groping for direction on the margins of society, caught up in forces that strained their tenuous family connections to the breaking point.

"Without pointing the finger of blame, those boys were victims of divorce," said Dane Waterman. "Guy didn't exactly cut off his sons in any hard way. It was by presumption. It was 'Okay, we're all grown-ups, we have our own lives now.' Some of it has to be attributed to the hard fact of divorce. The home was dissolved. There was nothing there anymore."

It hadn't always been so, of course. In more lighthearted days, Bobbie hauled her brood down from New Canaan, Connecticut, where she had moved from Ohio, to visit her baby brother in Washington, and her sister Anne Waterman Cooley, who also lived in Washington, and who had four kids: three Watermans, three Carneys, four Cooleys. Bobbie's oldest son, Tim Carney, born between Bill and John, often played with Guy's boys. The gang of cousins buried snow in the backyard, insulating the cache with leaves for the unseasonable thrill of digging it up in the summer. They took train trips to visit Civil War battlefields at Fredericksburg and Gettysburg. When the Waterman family moved to Stamford, in 1961, the Carneys saw more of their relatives.

"Guy was a strict parent," recalled Tim Carney. "Emily was the homemaker, and Guy was the disciplinarian. I remember him one time coming home from work when they lived in Stamford and giving Bill and Johnny a spanking, and when I asked Bill what he'd done, he said, 'Oh, that was just our daily spanking.' But when the kids were bored, they'd go to Guy. He always liked to be with us, knocking around outside, working in the yard. He'd come out sometimes and do handsprings and back flips—he could do a back flip."

"They lived a few blocks from the beach in Shippan Point," recalled Guy's niece Jean Cooley. "There was a big tree in the front yard. We'd play kick the can with Guy in the summers, and paint the shells of dead horseshoe crabs. Bill was my favorite cousin when I was a kid. He was warm and funny. Johnny was a little strange. His room was completely taken over with thousands of little plastic soldiers, and the furniture was arranged as forts."

Of the three boys, Bill—the oldest—was the most socially adept. As a youngster he loved hearing stories of people who'd gone off to sea. He played the drums in a rock band. He was a good student—a star debater, his father proudly recalled in his autobiography, someone who "had real charisma among his peers." He earned the ten merit badges required to achieve the second-highest rank of Life in the Boy Scouts, and his troop once voted him "Boy Scout of the Year." He had his father's puckish humor, and some of his drive, too. "When he put his mind to something he really pushed it," recalled Tim Carney. "When Bill started playing the drums he was really terrible, but he got it to the point where he could play acceptably. He'd be on the third floor of their house, banging away. He would have been better on a keyboard. Maybe he didn't want to compete with his father."

As Waterman observed in his autobiography:

One thing I always admired about Bill, [was that] even in high school, he was always able to realize when he had made a mistake, and had the uncommon gift of being able to admit a goof, gracefully apologize (a rare art, especially in teenagers), and move forward. In his senior year we had some friction, as he got into the rebellious mode and I found that hard to take. But on the whole, at least through high school, he was doing very well and I was very proud of him.

100

Johnny had a bumpier road. Where Bill was sociable, Johnny was a loner. From an early age he seemed prone to frustrations that did not bother his brother. Emily, in a letter to her sister-in-law Anne, recalled that Johnny would be "inconsolable" if his building blocks collapsed. When he was two and the family was living in Washington, he fell out of a second-story window. "He kind of floated down on the screen—thank goodness he was not really hurt," Alan Waterman Jr. recalled. Johnny was hospitalized as a result of the accident, and according to his mother he was so restless the nurses had to tie him to the crib. Later he survived a bout of scarlet fever. In a letter, Guy said that Johnny, unlike his little brother, Jim, "was never cute, had no soft edges, was tough and stringy and hard from the cradle on." He seemed to have been born to push limits. When he began to climb trees, Bobbie Waterman Carney remembered, "He was always climbing up to where the branches were too thin." In school, he wasn't especially happy—it took him a long time to learn to read. He did, however, have his father's ability to vanish into an imaginary world, spending hours commanding his legions of plastic soldiers in epic battles.

As his father wrote in his autobiography:

Until the age of thirteen, his chief outside interests were the very elaborate games put out by Avalon-Hill, which took days to play, plus a minor interest in collecting comic books and, later, Civil War material. The relationship between him and me was always especially close from earliest years. I roughhoused and kidded around with him incessantly. He had a serious cast a lot of the time but would explode with delight at our antics.

And then at thirteen Johnny discovered mountains and mountain climbing, and underwent a transformation that mirrored the one his father had undergone at thirty-one. In the fall of 1965, Guy took both Bill and Johnny out to the Gunks and roped them up on a short 5.4 climb called Squiggles. The following spring he led Johnny up a longer 5.2 climb called Southern Pillar. By the spring of 1967, Johnny was climbing at a higher standard than his father. "His natural aptitude for climbing moves was immediately apparent," Guy said. "He seemed to know instinctively how to shift his weight for the best use of holds." Like his father, he began to train diligently. Guy walked to the station; Johnny walked to school. In the afternoon, he walked home, touched the front door, returned to school and then walked home again. Every night he did four hundred push-ups. He began to excel in his studies, motivated by the desire to keep his weekends free for climbing instead of homework, and before long joined his brother on the honor roll. In a systematic fashion, he laid siege to a variety of routes at the Gunks, mastering problems and techniques of increasing difficulty. "When Johnny began climbing at the Gunks, he always had a desire to push the limit," recalled Colorado-based climber Henry Florschutz. "But he had a hard time finding partners he really clicked with."

One of Johnny's early partners and a role model was a young Gunks climber named Howie Davis. In a letter to the climbing author and friend who coincidentally was named Jonathan Waterman (Jon, not John), Guy Waterman described Davis as "moody, brilliant, star-crossed." Davis encouraged Johnny to look at climbing as part gymnastics, part ballet.

> They used to bounce down the carriage road at first light, [Guy wrote], heading for their first climb, with Howie doing some gymnastic trick like a front flip and then Johnny matching him along the way. Howie was the one who, among the hushed throng watching Johnny at the crux move of Retribution, still age fifteen, quietly said, "Go, John" in the silence—and Johnny proceeded to make the move. Shortly thereafter Howie became enmeshed in an unhappy love triangle with another climbing couple and hurled himself off the top of [the climb] Jackie, trying to shatter himself on the Pebbles boulder. It must have been the crowning frustration in that instant when he realized on the way down that he wasn't going to reach Pebbles, but only come ingloriously down through a tree—thoroughly dead on landing, but not as spectacularly as he had planned. *That* had an impact on Johnny.

In the same letter, Waterman described a 5.9 route called Bonnie's Roof, which he led while his son belayed from below.

It took a bit to commit myself to the desperate moves with Johnny calling up encouraging exhortations all the while. When I finally pulled myself over the last move of the sequence, it was to the accompaniment of a peal of excited squeaks and squeals: Johnny almost beside himself with pleasure that I had done it. Then when he came up and got his hands on the final holds, I suddenly saw his feet swinging way out from the cliff: in his sheer exuberance and high spirits he just kicked his feet off for the joy of it, before putting them back on the rock and completing the move.

Climbing brought Johnny into his own. The sixteen-year-old boy who had seemed immature for his age emerged as a prodigy, filled with confidence and what his father called "an explosive energy and ferocious ecstasy on rock or ice." At a pint-sized five feet three inches, with a squeaky piccolo voice, a phenomenal strength-to-weight ratio, and daring vertical nerve, he acquired the nickname "Super Squirrel." He was, Guy wrote to Jon Waterman "masterfully competent" and pursued ascents with an "electric, volcanic, creative vitality." "He was not grace, he was power," his father said. "He was not control, he was uncontrolled joy. . . . I have never met anyone to whom climbing . . . meant more."

In May 1969, on the eve of Johnny's first trip to Alaska to make an ascent of Mt. McKinley with a group of climbers, Guy typed up a letter of permission with some fond fatherly teasing at the end:

To Whom It May Concern: This is to advise that John M. Waterman, my son, has his parents' permission to participate in a climb of Mt. McKinley in June 1969, as long as he takes along:

—an extra pair of mittens,

—galoshes, in case it's muddy,

—a flashlight, in case they're not back by dark.

A few months shy of his seventeenth birthday, his pack equipped with mittens and flashlights, Johnny became the third-youngest person to reach the 20,301-foot summit of Denali, as the mountain is called by Alaskans. The climb was led by the noted Yosemite climber Tom Frost and included among its members Guy's friend Brad Snyder.

"I had driven out west with Johnny in the spring of 1968 on a trip to the Selkirks," Brad Snyder told me. "For Guy and Emily to let Johnny go to the Selkirks was a daring step. When the Denali trip came along, I guess it helped that I was a known quantity. I was twenty-seven at the time. Johnny was one of two sixteen-year-olds on the climb, and both had difficulty because of endurance aspects. Johnny and I tented to-gether—and got along fine. Our tent was the source of uproarious laugh-ter, and every morning the others wanted to know what we were laughing about. We went up the West Buttress. We had to ferry loads from the airstrip to camp one—four round-trips. It was real drudgery. Johnny had an episode of pulmonary edema at 17,000 feet but he went down and recovered, and Tom Frost and I went up a second time so he could get to the summit."

Back east, in May 1970, a senior in high school, Johnny and a climber named Al Rubin put up the first ascent of a classic 5.8 route called Conso-lation Prize at Cannon Mountain, across from Mt. Lafayette in Franconia Notch. Johnny had begun to give slide-show lectures of his expeditions and climbing trips to various civic groups. He had taught climbing to classes filled with beginners older than he was. In a letter to Brad Snyder written after he had graduated from high school, Johnny recalled the nights he spent in tenth and eleventh grade preparing for climbs: "I used to pore over my equipment, spending hours organizing things. [I] used to stay up really late, having completely torn apart the room and my posses-sions, and before going to sleep, drowsy as can be, cleaning it all up again. Usually I'd be playing Beethoven late into the night. My parents must have thought it was weird. Always gave me a satisfaction to be all packed."

Johnny was the son Guy identified with most. Their special kinship was something Waterman underscored in letters and even in print, despite the proverbial injunction against playing favorites among your children. The identification was further enhanced by their resemblance to each other, their similar builds. For twenty years, Guy wore a pair of wind pants that Johnny had worn on Denali. Johnny adopted Guy's showy habit of turning cartwheels, but characteristically took it a step further. Turning a cartwheel in the yard was a birthday ritual Guy observed until he was sixty; Johnny once turned one on a tiny ledge in the middle of an epic solo ascent of one of Alaska's most difficult mountains. That bit of audacity on Mt. Hunter in the Alaska Range was witnessed by a white-faced bush pilot who was flying by to see if his client John Waterman was still alive. The Hunter climb in 1978—Johnny referred to the mountain as his "nemesis"—precipitated an alarming change. The late-night sounds of gear being sorted over strains of Beethoven were the emanations of an innocent eccentricity that eventually devolved into madness. As his mother put it bluntly in a letter to her sister-in-law Anne: "It was not until after Mt. Hunter, that [Johnny] seemed, well, very strange."

Finally, there was Jim, the youngest son, known as Scooter for most of his boyhood. He lives today with his wife, Kathleen, in Colorado, where he works as an environmental engineer, and where, like his mother in the Blue Ridge mountains of Virginia, he politely declines requests for interviews. In his correspondence, Jim exhibits many of the hallmarks of the Waterman family—a pressing concern for privacy, self-effacement, scrupulousness, and a fear of being misinterpreted. Like his brothers, Jim became a skillful rock climber, good enough to get noticed in climbing magazines. (One fall day in 1971 he led the Gunks 5.10 showpiece Retribution, with Johnny belaying below.) Members of Jim's extended family believe he was affected more than his brothers by Guy and Emily's foundering marriage. He was younger, and witnessed more of the upheaval. In his autobiography, Waterman noted that Jim was in the same position he'd been in when his big brothers went off with Hawee to the Maine woods during the "golden years." "I tried to be aware of this and give time to Jim," Waterman wrote, "but it was never the same." And that was about all he had to say on the matter.

And yet it was Waterman's sense that throughout the turbulence of the 1960s he was focused mostly on his sons, and that they got on together well, all in all, considering his short-haired, gray-suit conservative Republican politics and their long-haired, drugs-and-rock-music culture. Waterman insisted that his obligations to his sons prevented him from embracing climbing and hiking with the zeal he might have had otherwise. He waited until his boys—the first two, at any rate—were old enough to tag along. Tim Carney remembers that first adventure with Uncle Guy and Cousin Bill. August 1964. Eight days in the White Mountains. Lafayette in fog. The woods alive with the sound of . . . John Milton's poetry. Having whipped his body into shape, Waterman had resolved to do something for his mind as well and was then in the midst of memorizing *Paradise Lost* in the "free time" he had walking to and from the train station and during his lunch hour. (In most places a man striding around briskly declaiming Milton between bites of a peanut-butter-and-jelly sandwich would be picked up by the police, but in the midday pageant of Central Park Waterman fit right in.)

"I went through a pair of sneakers on that trip," Tim Carney recalled. "Five days into the hike, Bill and I got giddy. We would laugh at anything. On the sixth day, Guy started getting giddy, too. He was always reciting poetry on the trail. The first ten minutes it was exciting, but after half an hour it was a little strange. He would recite for two hours. I couldn't figure out how he did it. If he'd already been on one of the trails we were hiking he would know what was around the next corner. He seemed extremely knowledgeable. He knew all the plants and the wildflowers and the bushes, and if you asked him any question, he would have the answer. He loved to have you ask him a question; he'd go off on long tangents."

The next year, Waterman took Johnny up to the Whites for an eight-day hike. In the summer of 1966, shod in a new pair of Limmer boots, Guy led Bill and Johnny and their dog, Ralph, on a sixteen-day, 214-mile orgy of peak bagging. They knocked off all forty-six White Mountain summits known to be 4,000 or more feet in altitude. (More-accurate surveys have since increased the number to forty-eight.) What a trip, gentlemen! Brilliant blue skies and gloomy overcasts, broiling heat and thunderstorms, clear nights of matchless stars and even the yellow magnetic wraith of the northern lights. Days in isolation, days in crowds. Dad's cooking and the relative luxury of food prepared in Appalachian Mountain Club hut kitchens. They swam at Thirteen Falls, in Franconia Brook. They gazed in awe at the great stone cairn at Thunderstorm Junction in the col between Mt. Adams and Mt. Sam Adams ("a beautiful, almost noble work of man," Waterman called it). They drank water from the sweet spring at Edmands Col, and one near the summit of Starr King and one on Mt. Osceola, halfway across the traverse from Breadtray Ridge. There were paths they would never forget, like the Blueberry Ledge and Franconia Ridge trails, and the two slides on Tripyramids. Bill had a small problem with a nail in his boot. Poor Ralph, the dog, ran into a porcupine on the traverse to Mt. Waumbek and got fifteen quills in the face. "A real crisis until with blood, sweat and tears we got them all out." Their last summit was one of the most beautiful peaks in the whole range, Mt. Carrigain. They could see forty-two of the forty-six mountains they'd climbed, and that night, when they were camped atop Carrigain, the light from the town of Bartlett below was like a little island raised in an otherwise wild and unbroken sea of darkness.

In due course, their Four Thousand Footer Club certificates and patches arrived from the gentlemen at the Appalachian Mountain Club. But there was not one for Ralph, who had suffered more for the triumph than any of his companions.

A year later, Waterman found the season closest to his soul. He made his first winter trip into the White Mountains, once again accompanied by Bill. They set out on a holiday weekend in February 1967, planning to cross the Franconia Range. The temperature when they bedded down for the night in the Greenleaf Hut was near forty below zero. Not surprisingly, they had the hut to themselves. The next morning they tacked up Lafayette in banshee winds. Waterman ripped his pants on one of his crampons and got a case of frostbite on one of his knees that did nothing to chill his enthusiasm for inhuman weather. He was back with Bill in early 1968 on a winter trip in the Kinsman Range, a sub-range of the White Mountains, while Johnny was off on winter climbing ventures of his own.

Guy and Johnny finally made a winter trip together at the end of 1968, an epic that nearly undid them both. They started the day after Christmas, planning to follow the string of boarded-up Appalachian Mountain Club huts along the entire length of the Presidential Range and then traverse the ranges west, something no one had ever done in winter. The account Waterman wrote up, "Winter Above Treeline," was the most widely read and reprinted piece among his many mountain writings. He was still fairly green navigating the backcountry in winter, and he made a point of summarizing the lessons he and Johnny had learned from their encounter with the famously merciless conditions around Mt. Washington—the usual stuff about keeping dry and being prepared and expecting the worst, stuff you usually have to learn the hard way no matter how many books you read. They set out on snowshoes with eighty-pound packs in twelve-below-zero temperatures. They ran into a storm. They got lost in a white-out on top of Mt. Jefferson. They had to stay awake most of the night holding the aluminum poles to keep their tent from exploding in the wind. Their clothes got soaked; their down sleeping bags lost their loft. They beat a desperate retreat, hiking out to the road and then to a town where they found a Laundromat and dried out their gear. Bowed but not broken, determined if not demented, they started back in, walking up Mt. Washington's automobile road. They got to 5,500 feet when another storm hit—temperatures as low as twenty-six below zero, winds in excess of one hundred miles per hour. They spent four days holed up in one of the metal bivouac sheds that used to provide emergency shelter for road crews: 6½ Mile Box it was called. To get water they had to get completely dressed—boots, crampons, overmitts, parkas, face masks—go forth into the storm, chop at some icy snow crest with an axe, hope the gales blew some of the chips into a stuff sack, then dive back inside the box and melt what they'd collected. They played poker for lunch snacks with a handmade deck of cards. To his chagrin, Waterman discovered that Dostoyevsky's *Notes from the Underground* was no help passing the time whereas Johnny's trashy detective novels were riveting. The lesson of what to read when riding out a winter storm was simple: "Can the culture."

What Waterman got from the trip was an abiding fascination with the wildness of winter: bracing wildness that could restore the feeling of solitude and mystery to even an over-familiar, road-ringed, trail-ridden New England hillock with a cairn-topped summit tainted by boot prints, salami rinds, and truck noise trickling up from the interstate in the valley below. To submit to the thrill of the mountains, he wrote in *Wilderness Ethics,* was to glimpse the "scale of nature, its intricacy . . . the genius of its interrelationships . . . its raw power . . . its subtlety." (Like many outdoor writers, Waterman preferred to use the terms *wildness, wilderness,* and *nature* as loose synonyms rather than irritate readers with pedantically exact definitions.) Broken open by joy after his brush with the wild extremes of a White Mountain winter, Waterman believed that wildness ought to be fostered, and wilderness preserved, for the social good—that an encounter with nature in such primordial conditions was an intrinsically moral and perhaps even sacred experience, as sacred as any experience can be for a man whose overt spiritual observances didn't go much beyond a moment of silence before supper. When he picked up the cause of the northeast wilderness in the 1970s and began scolding hiking organizations and land managers for heedless practices and overly accommodating policies, Waterman seized on Edward Abbey's famous description of wilderness areas as cathedrals.

"There are some things you just don't do in cathedrals," he wrote in *Wilderness Ethics.*

You don't drive a dirt bike there; you don't play a radio; you don't fly a helicopter up the nave to the chancel, even if that would be an efficient way to supply wine and wafers for each Sunday's "users"; you don't mark the aisles with plastic ribbon to find your pew or to note where the carpet needs repair; you don't bring a voluble party of twenty-five friends. Notice that none of these

outrageous acts would physically mar the cathedral. But they out-
rage the spirit of the place.

The question is: what was Waterman worshipping at the altar of
wildness? What was the spirit that could be outraged? In just what way
was the experience of wilderness moral and sacred? "Guy had a deep
sense of joy in wilderness," said Dane Waterman. "That sense of ecstasy
hinting at some deep joy. But he didn't want to get too specific about what
it was because then it would become uncomfortable. He didn't believe in
God. If you pressed him on the topic, he would bob and weave."

Waterman never really explained his feelings very well in print either. In a telling passage early on in *Wilderness Ethics* he writes: "What
various kinds of wilderness have in common . . . is a vivid sense of both
the overpowering strength and the delicate intricacy of nature, and its importance relative to the simplistic dullness, even insignificance, of us
people. Maybe that doesn't quite put it right. Let's try again . . ." Capital
idea, because it's hard to imagine overflow crowds and the problem of
trail erosion in a cathedral that invites visitors to contemplate their simplistic dullness. Mountains can certainly strip away hubris and expose the
insignificance of human life, but can they hold a candle to the complexity
of a mammal's eye? Even the most awesome tableaux of stern and beautiful wilderness can just as easily highlight the preciousness of humanity,
the strength of our compassion, our interdependence, our visions and
revelations.

Even at the end of *Wilderness Ethics,* Waterman still seems to be struggling to define the moral rationale for seeking out wild places. He writes
in conclusion:

The mountain world (or that of the desert, or the sea, or the
polar regions) is so much more impressive than the proudest
achievements of humanity, so much more powerful, more beautiful, more important. . . . And yet, viewed in right relation to this
natural world, we can find humanity's efforts ennobled and en-

nobling. If we try to cope with a winter storm above tree line, we soon know our place, to use the language of intimidation. But if we do cope with that storm without too much loss of control or dignity—if we marshal all our strength, composure, knowledge painfully extracted from many experiences in other storms, concentration, courage, unflapped persistence with details, all those qualities that the unforgiving pressures of that storm ruthlessly demand from us—if we come down off the mountain perhaps a bit bewildered, battered, bemused, and more than a bit cold and exhausted, we feel a sense of achievement, an exhilaration of self, that few other experiences in life afford.

Set aside the debatable premise that mountains are more powerful, beautiful, and important than art or music or, to the degree that children can be claimed as a human achievement, one's own sons. Here is the lowdown at last: wilderness is an amalgam of cathedral, gauntlet, and junglegym. The outdoorsman sallies into the mountains to match his will against the will of the wild, hoping he may come through with a modicum of dignity and "not too much loss of control." The nature that gives us the deepest sense of ourselves is the nature that threatens to kill us, the nature whose powers of annihilation we forestall with skill and fortitude and luck, not to mention well-anchored belays and sleeping bags that don't lose their loft when wet.

The paramount characteristic of this view of nature as an adversary is the desire to remain in control. The exhilaration of the self Waterman realized in the grip of a mountain winter had to do with passing tests, meeting "objectives," and staying on top of himself and his situation. The premium he placed on conquering peaks and contesting tempests constituted a kind of morally displaced Romanticism that is a far cry from Wordsworth, who held that one could find in nature the ultimate truths of human life, "love of nature leading to love of man," as he once put it in a letter. Or Coleridge, who famously wrote: "The pleasures which we receive from rural beauties are of little consequence compared with the moral effect of these pleasures: beholding constantly the best possible, we at last become ourselves the best possible." Nor does Waterman's "exhilaration of self" seem especially consonant with the homegrown Romanticism of Thoreau and the New England Transcendentalists, who believed, in Emerson's words, "in the woods we return to reason and faith."

Perhaps, as was suggested to me by Dane Waterman's wife, Bernadette Waterman Ward (she's a professor of English at the University of Dallas in Irving, Texas, and writes her name in matrilineal style), Guy's view of nature has its roots in the disappointed idealism of Byron, the high-born, worldly, second-generation Romantic. Byron came to believe only in meaning that could be generated by one's own will, and saw the wild heights of earth that had once exalted man as serving now only to expose his baseness: "Gather around these mountain summits, as to show / How Earth may pierce to Heaven, yet leave vain man below." This line, from Canto III of *Childe Harold's Pilgrimage,* Waterman had copied into his climbing journal.

In a way, it was Waterman's life, not his work—the way he lived, not what he was able to abstract from it—that encapsulated the Romantic spirit. He was a master of practice, not theory, "a doer, not a thinker" as he defined himself. Whatever virtues his wilderness adventures were meant to instill, the fundamental impetus behind them was allied to the thrust of Romantic art, which as defined by the *Oxford Dictionary of Philosophy,* is "essentially one of movement, figured in quests, journeys, and pilgrimages whose aim is to return to a lost home or haven."

And, ultimately, Waterman was better able to articulate the values on which his homestead was based than the moral rationale of his commitment to wilderness and backcountry adventure. Indeed, the idea of nature as an adversary seems totally paradoxical in light of his pastoral life at Barra. It doesn't square with his exceptional sensitivity to the domesticated land of his haven in the woods. Where is the antagonism toward nature in a man who would wander his property for hours, ruminating on the condition of trees he knew by name, sometimes even putting his arms around their trunks in the spirit of pagan friendship? And on Franconia Ridge, he was the paragon of backcountry stewardship both in his trail work and in the way he would gently lead people to the conclusion that better campsites than the middle of a delicate alpine meadow or a junction of trails could be found. For his out-spoken commitment to the integrity of wild places, his respect-the-cathedral opposition to the intrusion of helicopters, cell phones, and Day-Glo parkas, he earned a reputation as "the conscience of the White Mountains." It went without saying he cherished wilderness and believed vital social values were at stake in its preservation.

But unlike Wordsworth or Thoreau, Waterman did not turn to wild nature to clarify the truths of our common condition. He first went to the mountains to escape the truths of how he'd lived. He went to mountains that he might be free of the pigeonholes back in town. Wilderness offered Waterman respite from the contradictions he couldn't reconcile, the responsibilities he couldn't live up to. He went to the wilderness of the mountains to escape the wilderness of families and the emotional and psychological complexity of their "interior worlds." He once said in a letter to Dane Waterman: "The interior worlds of people are so hard to describe, so easily injured, so hard to bring other people in[to] and show them." Wilderness offered Waterman respite from himself and his hard-to-show, easily injured, difficult-to-describe interior. There was a wholeness he felt in deep snow, a spiritual joy. How much easier and gladsome it was to navigate spruce traps and alder thickets than human entanglements; how much more exhilarating to be scourged by winter gales than one's own conscience. Starry nights in the mountains high above the settled valleys of New Hampshire and Vermont gave him hope, not for mankind but for himself: hope to believe that, as he wrote, "even one puny human being can be vital and alive, wonderful and mysterious."

The trouble is, no winter storm can scour away a father's sorrow or expiate his guilt. And there is not a wilderness in the world than can rehabilitate a man whose secret belief is that he is puny, half dead, and carries hell within him. It ought not come as a surprise that when his life was overtaken by profound misfortune one of the passages that affected Waterman most was from *Paradise Lost*; Satan has paused uneasily on the threshold of Paradise:

> *. . . and from the bottom stir*
> *The hell within, and from within him hell*
> *He brings, and round about him, nor from hell*
> *One step no more than from himself can fly*
> *By change of place: now conscience wakes despair*
> *That slumbered, wakes the bitter memory*
> *Of what he was, what is, and what must be*
> *Worse; of worse deeds, worse sufferings must ensue.*

In his later years, Waterman began to go alone into the White Mountains on extended winter trips, steadfast in his conviction that wilderness might imbue him with some sort of perspective-based grace or self-knowledge that would be as valuable for others as he felt it had been for him. But what *had* it taught him? In retrospect, those long solo excursions look like the last journeys of a tormented wanderer rehearsing for his final climb: that is to say they were futile changes of place engineered in a desolate season by a man who longed to escape himself, a man who was falling further from a family and a community he could not bring himself to beg for forgiveness or even to embrace for the sustenance of his own spirit. The nature that tested his fortitude could not challenge his narcissism or his pride. The saddest and most wintry of ironies is that Waterman's best times in the wild were always with other people, never more so than with his boys. What "exhilaration of self" could ever come close to the feel of one of them tugging on the rope?

And how Waterman must have hoped for years of adventures like those first winter larks! How could he not have hoped for winter after winter above tree line with his sons? Soon his youngest would be old enough to tie in and try the high ridges in lethal weather. They could scramble up the icy peaks, piercing to Heaven, then retreat to the shelter of the tent while gunshot gales sang in the guy lines and ice clotted in the cook pots. And when their objectives had been reached—Guy was always contriving new ideas for trips, new "objectives" to give his experience of nature the competitive structure of a goal—they could come staggering out of the mountains, bewildered, battered, speechlessly happy. How could he not have hoped he and his sons would always have this fellowship in nature, this luxury of finding each other in the medium of the mountains, relieved of their misunderstandings, restored to the best of themselves by their common pursuit. Waterman spoke often of Franconia Ridge being his "spiritual home." His trips up there were homecomings, as filled with the feeling of home as the home to which he actually returned in the lowlands, where his real family was beginning to disintegrate and another kind of wilderness was yawning.

In the late 1960s, when he wasn't off to the White Mountains, Waterman fled to the Gunks almost every weekend he could in order to escape his deteriorating marriage. (His mountain journal notes only one trip on which Emily ever joined him, and that was a White Mountain hike up Carter Dome with Jim and Johnny in August 1965.) "Nineteen years is a long time to remain in a bad marriage," he wrote. "I enjoyed being with my sons and did not want to walk out on them. Beyond that was a kind of inertia." What clinched his decision was an incident in December 1967, in which Johnny developed appendicitis and required surgery. Emily, who in Waterman's view "could never deal calmly with big events [such as] buying a house or planning a vacation . . . or anything involving major expenses" was, again in Waterman's view, worse than unhelpful. "She refused to take part in any of the decisions needed, then ripped me up and down unceasingly for each decision I made. . . . As soon as I'd take a new step (trying to find something to please her) she would heap scorn and emotional accusations on me." The experience left Waterman resolved to leave the marriage sooner than later. Coincidentally, the month of Johnny's appendicitis was also the month Waterman's father died. The example he was always trying to live up to, the paragon of judicious action and public service—the long shadow of Mt. Waterman—was gone.

In a last-ditch effort to accommodate his unhappy wife, Waterman moved the family in the spring of 1968 to a tract house in a development in Newburgh, New York, not far from where Emily's twin sister, Harriet, lived with her husband, Jim. Bill had left for a summer out west, and Johnny was climbing in the Selkirk Mountains in British Columbia. Waterman began to find some consolation as a teacher of climbing. The Alaska mountaineer Pete Metcalf, who repeated Johnny's route on Hunter, was a fourteen-year-old beginner when Waterman, then thirty-seven, gave him lessons at the Gunks, belaying him up the climb called Squiggles and then a much tougher 5.7 route called Laurel.

"He was very inspiring for a lot of people at the time when I embraced climbing," Metcalf recalled. "Everything about him was inspiring, from the hat he wore to the fingerless Miller mitts. He was a Hard Man, he lived that romantic climbing life. Climbing was life, and life was about climbing. He embodied all the facets of it. It could be pouring rain out and he'd say, 'Isn't this great!'"

While Waterman was impressing youngsters, Bill and Johnny began reporting back about their adventures out west. Waterman gave some thought to his decision not to visit the Rockies and the Sierras and the continent's ultimate peaks in the glacier-bound ranges of northwest Canada and Alaska. "Because of my [family] situation and my age," he wrote in his autobiography, "I had decided that I had a poor prospect for much of a career in the big Western mountains, and might be better off if I never saw them, so as not to belittle my vision of the Eastern hills in which I would spend my climbing life. So I had resolved never to go west to climb." One wonders if Waterman's "vision" was a way of not seeing rather than seeing—a way of sustaining an identity based on fantasy and self-deception. He made no bones about the degree to which the wildness of backcountry in the crowded Northeast was an illusion. The thrust of his work as an advocate, he said in *Wilderness Ethics,* was to increase the chances that "the precious illusion of exploration and adventure can be preserved for all who seek it."

And given that he eventually did make two trips west (persuaded by friends, he said), Waterman's reasoning here looks more than a little disingenuous, like his later explanation that he quit winter climbing because he'd ground the points off his old crampons and didn't want the expense of investing in new ones. It seems consistent with a pattern of rationalization that would grow more pronounced over the years, culminating in the rationale he offered for his self-destruction.

One of his trips out west was to the Bugaboos, in British Columbia, in the summer of 1970. The other, a year later, was an expedition to 14,573-foot Mt. Hunter, the third-highest peak in the Alaska Range and the mountain that, interestingly, Johnny had attempted to climb while his father was in the Bugaboos. In the Bugaboos, Waterman climbed three spires, but was distressed by the poor style with which he managed relatively easy routes. Mt. Hunter was a bigger disappointment, and had to have caused him a bit of embarrassment as well. Before the attempt on the north face, Waterman had been interviewed by a reporter from the Anchorage *Daily News*. He was photographed in his hotel room in his tam. The article in the Sunday paper quoted him musing philosophically about climbing and the prospects of his party of three men and two women. The group got a few pitches above their base camp before they were defeated by blizzards, avalanches, and what Waterman conceded was their mediocre ability. "We felt our attempt had been rather inept," he noted. "As this was the last time we went into the big mountains, it left me with a feeling of having flunked out on my only two tests in that awesome testing-ground."

After the Alaska trip, he did compose a long letter to Johnny and Bill, detailing the misadventure. Perhaps Guy's experience added to Johnny's desire to conquer the mountain that had defeated his old man, the mountain he would later describe in the American Alpine Club journal as "my nemesis." Perhaps the shadows of Mt. Waterman loomed over Johnny as they had loomed over his father . . .

Over the years, Waterman was able to make a virtue of whatever necessity it was that confined his adventurous mountain spirit to the pip-squeak peaks of the Northeast. He became like a scholar who finds a wide and worldly range of themes within his narrow specialty. He put it best in the epilogue of his masterwork, *Forest and Crag:*

> Whatever else, these hills of the Northeast have been and will be unfailingly *interesting.* Certainly they are small—absurdly small to be called mountains in comparison with the world's great ranges. But that smallness gives them their intimate connection to people. . . . The very scale of the world's big ranges limits the possibilities of human activity in them. Only the few well-trained mountaineers can make them their playground or experience their varied moods. But the hills of the Northeast—capable of savage ferocity on occasions but friendly and welcoming on others—are available to all who respond to the natural world. . . . Considering the scope, diversity, and depth of their human rela-tionships, these little hills may well be the most interesting moun-tains on the face of this earth.

Let us pass over the ironies of mountains with intimate connections to people but people without intimate connections to one another, for all the Watermans were soon to face the ways their fates were interlaced. Soon to come was a series of hard, hard turns: the misfortune fell first on Bill, fresh out of high school in 1969. He was heading west, hopping freight trains on a great adventure. On the night of June 19, dodging railroad crews in a yard in Winnipeg, he scooted under a box car just as an engine gave it a nudge. A steel wheel rolled over his left leg above the ankle, crushing the bone. He crawled out to a road in agony, his foot hanging by little more than tendons and skin. Doctors surgically reduced the fracture and managed to save the foot. Bill was confined to the hospital in Win-nipeg for fifteen weeks and didn't return home until late September. It was several months before the doctors removed his full-length cast. "He had thought with high school over he'd be free to go off on his own and be footloose and adventurous for a while," Waterman wrote, perhaps thinking about things other than the unfortunate connotations of *footloose* in this context. "Instead he found himself homebound, severely limited in mobility and stuck in an awful development [tract] house."

"We saw him after the accident, in Durham [Connecticut]," Tim Carney recalled. "He tried to be happy and witty, but you could see he was just putting on a show. He realized his life had changed. It was harder for him to play the drums. It was tougher to go hiking."

The bone never healed properly and two years later, Bill decided to have his left foot and part of his leg amputated and a prosthesis attached. He was living in Alaska at the time, and his uncle Peter Morrison found a surgeon at the hospital in Fairbanks.

One of the things people remember about Bill was his streak of dark humor. He liked to drink beer in a sawdusted Fairbanks bar called the Howling Dog. Sometimes, if he was sitting among friends with a newcomer in their midst—a *cheechako*, they're called in Alaska—or even just a local who knew little about Bill Waterman's life, he'd take his big hunting knife out of its sheath, toy with it a while, and then suddenly fling it into the wooden leg under his green wool pants. You could hear the silence quiver around the blade, and then the first black laughs spreading like a ring of ripples from a bitter fate. Anyone who was in on the trick always had a hell of a laugh.

6.

THE GABRIEL
BIRCH

✳

Nature's first green is gold,
Her hardest hue to hold.
Her early leaf's a flower;
But only so an hour.
Then leaf subsides to leaf.
So Eden sank to grief,
So dawn goes down to day.
Nothing gold can stay.

ROBERT FROST,
Nothing Gold Can Stay

Thanks for the mailings, especially the obituary of Lindbergh. Oddly, it's the deaths of big names from the past that constitutes the only category of news which we miss seeing. All other outside events are better left unknown.

GUY WATERMAN, *letter to Brad Snyder, September 23, 1974*

I N JULY 2000, I drove up to visit Laura Waterman in East Corinth, Vermont. It had been six months since her husband's death, and just six weeks since she had gathered friends and family to help her scatter his ashes over the homestead that had sustained, defined, and circumscribed their marriage for twenty-seven years. The week after the memorial service she had begun to dismantle Barra—the sad, stop-and-sob work of sorting and boxing and packing and eventually, again with the help of friends, removing all the whatnot of their life together: the pictures of her mountain adventures with Guy, Guy's climbing journals, their manuscripts, their correspondence, their gardening tools, their large menagerie of stuffed animals, including the two cats Waterman had had with him at the end, Guy's father's outsized ice axe, which had been retrieved from Mt. Lafayette with his body, even Laura's now-antique collection of opera recordings, which had sat under the grand piano all the decades the couple had lived without electricity, happy to make their own music when they were not communing with the quiet of the woods. What she had to pack mostly were their books, thousands of books with smoke-tinged spines and pages redolent with the dank must of earth. Books on the shelves had helped keep the cabin warm in winter and cool in summer. Books had enlivened their nights year after year as they read aloud to each other by the soft yellow glow of the kerosene lamps. Laura had felt the soul of Barra beginning to ebb when she started pulling down the books.

All the stuff had been shuttled to a newly built house that sat near the village on six acres of land that sloped down to the Tabor Valley branch of the Waits River. Page Hollow, Laura was calling the place. Guy had come up with the name, and had supervised the design of the house. When it was being built, he'd portentously referred to it as "Laura's house." It was a handsome gabled structure made of giant barked-and-varnished pine logs. At night, it creaked like a wooden ship. It had the full complement of twentieth-century conveniences: running water, a shower, a toilet, a gas stove, and fixtures that at the flick of a switch flooded the rooms with bright, overbearing light. Laura was still dazed by the modernity of it all, especially the magic that could conjure light without matches and wicks. For years, when she and Guy had gone to shop for supplies, he had jok-ingly put lightbulbs in their cart. Now she was buying them in earnest.

I found her on the back porch on a sunstruck summer morning. She had been working in the new Page Hollow garden and was dressed in a heathery wool sweater and blue cotton work pants. She was sixty years old, her salt-and-pepper hair was chopped short, her hands were weath-ered, her knees were bad, but her eyes were clear and blue and she seemed much younger than her age. Partly it was her enthusiasm, which could make even a delivery of milk seem like a special occasion, and partly it was something genuinely childlike in her manner, an undefended open-hearted innocence that was reflected even in her letters, which were sprin-kled with words like *golly* and *yikes*. It was easy to see why friends were so protective, so willing to help her out, and so reluctant to disturb what seemed from afar to be her dreamy view of her husband's suicide and her role in it. She'd written an article that appeared two weeks after his death in a local newspaper, the *Valley News,* in Lebanon, New Hampshire. It offered a snapshot of her frame of mind at the time.

Guy Waterman, my husband, walked up into the mountains on Sunday, February 6, intending not to come back down. After this news was released, many people have found their way to my door, tramping the mile-long path through the woods. Some have come on snowshoes, some not. But all have brought to me an outpouring of their gifts of love, concern and tears. They want to know, first, am I all right? The answer to that is easily seen and quickly given. I am fine. The second, harder question—Why did their beloved friend Guy Waterman take his own life?—will probably never be fully understood. Nor should it be . . . Guy believed in the uniqueness of the individual. That we are all separate and unknowable in our deepest core, one from one another . . . He sought his death; it was his conscious choice to go with his boots on. He felt it was a rational decision. For me it is right that the mystery of our essential individual selves remains unrevealed. Seek not to rend the veil.

Laura wrote that people had been asking how she could have let Guy go, and that her answer was she could let him go "because I loved him." Love bound her to respect and honor what he wanted. She wrote that though she did not fully understand why he needed to get out of life, she could "talk around the question." And as for why her husband did not seek medical help, she found that hard to explain other than to say, "It was not Guy's way."

After Guy's death, Laura had given interviews to obituary writers and had sat for a lengthy interview with a feature writer from the Associated Press, an experience which had left her so drained she declined all further requests. My visit in July was the result of a correspondence we had struck up after I sent her an article I'd written about Waterman's life. In her reply, she touched on everything from factual mistakes to what she felt were my errors of judgment, big and small. Guy's handwriting was much too legible to be described as a "scribble" she said. His color-coded index cards would probably not be used for recording the name of a dog he'd met, much as he loved dogs and had a special bond with them. More broadly, she had misgivings about the emphasis I'd placed on his death.

It is very hard [she wrote] to read everything that has been ap-pearing about Guy in the media. I'm sure he would have been ap-palled to know that his death had shot him into this kind of limelight—that national reporters were going around and talk-ing to all his friends, even his family, trying to find out things. What was he like? Why did he choose to die like this? What did his wife think about it all? This attention is just so opposite to how we chose to live our lives. Barra was a private place for us.

Six months after Guy's suicide, however, Laura's views were chang-ing. Time, a new home, fresh prospects had given her some distance and perspective. She'd received a stereo as a housewarming gift, and was start-ing off each morning with a tonic draught of recorded music—arias from Leontyne Price or Maria Callas turned up loud enough to rattle the win-dows and roust the tribe of stuffed animals from their lairs in her bed-room quilt. She was planning to travel abroad; trips to Scotland and South Africa were on the horizon. She had generously offered to put me up for the night at Page Hollow, and when I arrived she greeted me warmly. One of the reasons she was anticipating my visit, she said, was that she was planning to write a book of her own about her days at Barra with Guy. She was excited to talk about some of the themes her husband's life had raised.

And for my part, I had a list of questions, many based on her article in the *Valley News*. What lay behind Guy's belief that we are all separate and unknowable? Did Laura share that view? If the intimacies of mar-riage ultimately prove only that we are strangers to one another, why marry? And what did she mean when she had written "Seek not to rend the veil"? Was that to say we shouldn't search for why a man might want to take his life? What was this "mystery" that apparently could be compromised by a sharp question? And on the matter of depression and medical help: where did one draw the line between character and pathology? It was a long list. I was hoping Laura might expound on the nature of the love she had alluded to, love that in some blunt and unflattering interpretations might be said to have enabled the destruction of its most cherished object. Had she freely made the choice to let her husband go to his death, or had she been influenced—or perhaps coerced—by the balance of power in their relationship?

These were difficult and even obnoxious questions, certainly not in keeping with the public impression of the Watermans' partnership. To many of their friends, Guy and Laura were the epitome of togetherness. The lived together, gardened together, hiked together, climbed together, camped together, wrote together. For a while, they had even entertained themselves together with pieces for four-handed piano. They cosigned most of their letters. In winter, their baths, which they took every Thursday night in a cattle trough by the cabin's wood stove, were an accomplished pas de deux of pouring, washing, rinsing, and toweling; Guy would always help Laura shampoo her hair. One of their young friends, Rebecca Oreskes, had described the intense intimacy and mutual consideration between them; she'd been particularly struck by how appreciative Guy was of Laura. In pictures of them together, he always seemed to be gazing at her. "You could see his love for her in the way he would look at her," Rebecca told me. "You could see it in the way he would listen to her when they were talking. You could hear it in the way he would speak about her. Once a bunch of us were standing around and I saw him scratch 'G♥L' in the dirt."

But as we began to talk, it was apparent that Laura's transition to a new order of life was not as complete as her flow of cheer implied. Despite her claim that she was fine, despite her excitement about writing a book about her history at Barra with Guy, despite the exhilarating draughts of opera she was taking with her morning coffee, and despite even the invitation she had extended to me and her ostensible willingness to delve into her husband's ideas and principles, the questions I broached stopped the conversation cold. She fumbled for words. She looked upset and pained.

It seemed she could discuss life at Barra only within the framework of Guy's point of view, in his sunny and ultimately self-serving terms. She was determined to view his death as the culmination of his ideas about freedom and personal autonomy. He died in the spirit in which he lived. She said at one point she thought Guy "was being responsible to his life in the way he ended his life," ending it before he was incapacitated by an accident or the infirmity of old age. And that sounded plausible to me at first, until I began to hear echoes of the Vietnam War double-think that argued villages had to be destroyed in order to be saved. Some weeks after our first meeting, I received a letter from Laura in which she mentioned a discussion she'd had with Rebecca Oreskes about whether the word *suicide* was the apt description for what Guy did, or whether his actions could be better characterized by a phrase such as "going out on the ice," a euphemism sometimes heard in northern parts. Reach a certain point in your life and you can "go out on the ice" with a minimum of moral hand-wringing from your survivors.

When I would ask what Laura had thought, what *she* had felt as opposed to what Guy's feelings had been, she often seemed perplexed, as if she were being asked to drive a car without a steering wheel. Whether out of habit, or love, or solidarity with a ghost, she would almost inevitably slip into the first person plural, gravitating to that seductive enchantment of "we" in which she'd been living and narrating her life for decades. But the fact could not be ignored: one half of the "we" had unilaterally severed itself from the other. *Seek not to rend the veil?* Wasn't that a warning to herself not to look too closely at the story she'd been telling herself? A way of saying, in effect: *Seek not to disturb the dream I have been living.*

In July I didn't know enough to press Laura on these notions. Indeed, I was hearing her point of view in person for the first time, and it was only natural to react with sympathy for what she'd gone through rather than with skepticism about what she had or hadn't done, or truly believed. And really, how could it ever be less than impertinent to question her point of view? Certainly, on that July morning, she sometimes seemed like a woman who had managed to get through a terrible event by pretending it wasn't terrible, but if she said what happened wasn't terrible, wasn't she entitled to the benefit of the doubt? She'd been there! Whose version of what had happened and what it meant could be more authoritative? Maybe what was terrible was having a stranger with a legal pad on your porch implying things weren't how you knew them to be—having to stomach all the stories and letters to the editor and Internet chitchat by commentators who didn't let sketchy thirdhand knowledge stop them from projecting their morality onto your husband's death . . .

Still, there was no getting around that the story Laura had been telling looked like a coauthored fairytale, even to people who would never say so out of concern for her welfare. It varnished her husband's suicide and obscured the extent to which she'd collaborated in it. Was it not the case, as one of her more probing friends would bluntly say to me later, that the heart of the matter was a stark bargain struck by a wife who had traded her silence and consent, her assistance and willingness to dissemble on her husband's behalf, for the quid pro quo of a house?

God knows, in July this was not an interpretation Laura was remotely prepared to examine, much less accept even if voiced more diplomatically. And yet, even that summer the conflict within her was patent. She seemed to be struggling to find words for impermissible emotions. Was it disloyal to feel relief now that the weight of Guy's depression had been lifted off her? Contradictions were pulling Laura apart. She was clinging to an official story as if holding on were a test of faith and repeating it might make it true. "I'm fine," she had said, and doubtless she was in some ways—secure in the memory of her husband's love, buoyed by the ways he had genuinely looked after her needs, the "small kindnesses" he had shown her. But in other ways, even an untutored eye could see she had blocked out an enormous trauma and was trying to cope with it by veiling it from herself. *Seek not to rend the veil.* Yes, of course. But the laws of the psyche as we presently envision them insist trauma doesn't really happen until the veils are rent and you recognize the ways you have prevented yourself from feeling.

To make matters worse, a large part of the trauma had to do not with Guy's suicide but with Laura's having been left to explain it. It had fallen to her to devise a palliative story that made sense of her husband's decision, a story with which she might persuade herself, friends, relatives, and even the strangers importuning her in the name of "the public interest," that his decision *had* made sense.

My visit that July was the first of four trips I made to Page Hollow. Laura and I also met to talk whenever she scraped together her carefully budgeted Social Security funds and made one of her trips to New York to see an opera. With each passing month, I thought I could see her knowledge of the ways she'd been compromised and had compromised herself deepening. The process really began to accelerate when she started her book in November, nine months after her husband's death. She was inspired, she said, by one of our two-day conversations, which had left her feeling particularly "raw" and stirred up. She began to dig into the ground of her life at Barra and to perceive some of the illusions she'd been mantled in. The process of exchanging the old version of events for some uncertain new formulation continued all that winter and into the spring and summer of the following year as she rolled sheets of recycled paper into the carriage of her manual typewriter and wrote draft after draft. It was often like climbing in deep snow, where you flounder forward two steps and slide back one, Laura said. She had so much invested in thinking that her life had been a certain way. She kept a towel on hand to blot up the tears. She often found herself revving up for the day's excavations with arias sung by Callas and Price, as if the numb, unfelt parts of her psyche could not be cracked open under anything less than the pressure of operatic emotion.

But even in July of 2000, at the outset of our conversations, when she had not yet started her project and was still wedded to the account she had given in the newspapers, there was a moment when she stepped outside the pale of life with her husband. We had been talking all morning on the back porch, sidling up to the radioactive topics only to skitter away. I had put my legal pad in my backpack and was resolved to go wherever Laura felt comfortable leading. All morning the sun had been flashing in and out of a royal armada of white cumulus clouds, and we had been donning our sweaters when the sun vanished and shucking them off when it returned.

Around noon we went inside, and Laura fixed a lunch of yogurt, sliced apples, bread, and tea. We sat at the dining room table. She brought over some photo albums, and then a loose-leaf binder of Guy's poems, and then some of his notebooks. The conversation drifted to the short stories she had written. She loved to write short stories, she told me. In the days after Guy had left, when what he had done was still her secret, she had worked in a fever of inspiration on a short story set in her girlhood years, when all the poisoned glamour of adult life, all its subterranean longing, drunken chaos, and corrupt design, could be concentrated in the forbidden fruit of a gin-soaked olive. Writing stories was often how Laura figured out her feelings, she said, as if what she couldn't talk about might be divined with a typewriter. Emotions were easier to apprehend on the page than in person. Unlike Guy, she revised doggedly. She sent her stories out to little magazines, and persisted through rejections. She had had more than a dozen stories published—Guy always knew the exact number; he was always touting her latest small-press triumph in letters to friends and family, boasting with a curious mix of pride and, perhaps, envy. He had not found the same success with his own attempts at fiction.

While she was going over some files, I found myself thinking again about that air of innocence Laura had—the disarming ingenuousness which made people want to lend her a hand. She gave the impression of being naïve in some ways, but there was something resolute and even canny in her simplicity, a self-possession that seemed linked to her life on the land. For years she had lived close to nature, persevering apart from the structures and practices that prop up city people. She didn't depend on the A&P for food, or Consolidated Edison for heat. She was at home in the wild, and drew strength from her sense of place and understanding of the elements. When I was leafing through one of her husband's notebooks, I came across a quote he'd copied down. The lines by a Chinese writer, written circa 2500 B.C., spoke to the iron in the life the Watermans had forged at Barra:

When the sun rises, I go to work.
When the sun goes down, I take my rest.
I dig the well from which I drink.
I farm the soil that yields my food.
I share creation. Kings can do no more.

It was late in the afternoon now. Flashing sun and shadow filled Page Hollow with checkered light. We had been talking for hours. "What did you mean," I ventured to ask, "when you wrote that you 'did not fully understand why Guy needed to get out of life'?" Without hesitation, Laura replied that in some ways she'd been as much in the dark about Guy's motivation as anyone. For nearly twenty years, he'd been unable to share his deepest feelings with her. It was not that he didn't love her. Far from it. She could always feel his love. He was always showering her with valentines, cards, homemade presents, inscriptions in the dirt. He told her he could not have survived without her. But there were times when Guy was lost for days in what they called his "black moods." Days when his "demons" were running riot and he was unreachable. Laura would whisper over and over that she loved him and rub his back as he sat by the window of the cabin staring out at an ash-land he alone could see. She asked him to tell her what he was feeling, she implored him to take her into his confidence, but he couldn't, he just couldn't, and eventually she stopped asking because she felt selfish seeing how her need made his anguish worse. It was heartbreaking to her, the suffering in his eyes. What was it the old speechwriter couldn't say? The man with a thousand quotes who hid his feelings behind masks of literary reference. Describing what he felt would betray what was in his heart, he said. It would only beget more misunderstanding and yet more pain. His silence was out of Nietzsche: "That which we can find words for is something already dead in our hearts." Some things could only be borne in silence, some things were meant to be passed over in silence. There was nothing to say, nothing to share, nothing to confide or confess or discuss or load off onto someone else, even Laura whom he professed to love so much—whom he truly loved—and who longed so to help.

Who on hearing this account wouldn't pity Laura? She had stifled her desire to be confided in. She had sided with her husband against herself, defining his inability to speak to her as a kind of organic disorder against which he'd struggled heroically, like a paralyzed man battling to rise from a wheelchair.

"Was it that he couldn't talk about his feelings or that he wouldn't?" I asked.

Laura's eyes flew to the window, then back to mine, tears welling. She pressed her lips together, struggling on the brink of what I realized later was a momentous confession, a heresy: the beginning of the end of something.

At last, in a halting voice: "At first I thought it was that he couldn't," she said. "But recently I've been thinking maybe it was . . . the other."

We sat in the charged silence of *the other.* She seemed exhausted by the immense distance she'd traveled from *could not* to *would not,* and also dismayed by the idea of her husband as unwilling—not unable—to breach the wall between himself and his wife.

"It hurts," she said at length.

We went to dinner that night at an Italian restaurant in the nearby town of Bradford, and talked nothing about death, suicide, or implacable silence. Laura was excited because for two decades she and Guy had lived on two hundred dollars a month and had hardly ever gone out to dinner. It was a treat! When we returned to the house, she showed me to the guest room—one of a pair of built-in bunks upstairs that were like sleeping berths on a ship. I had books about dogs at my head and books about opera at my feet, but I spent an hour in the magic aura of one of Laura's new electric lamps reading her husband's climbing journal, a meticulous record of all the peaks he'd scaled when he first felt the summons of high places, in the years before Laura had come into his life. It was a clear night; stars bristled in the window. In the morning when I woke, the voice of Leontyne Price singing "Vissi d'arte" from *Tosca* was soaring from the stereo downstairs. Laura had fixed the breakfast she had routinely made on the homestead: steel-cut oats, wheat germ, apple sauce, fresh bread, homemade jam, berries in season, and yogurt sweetened with maple syrup from the Waterman sugar bush.

"So do you want to go up and see Barra?" she said.

One gets the feeling with many couples that they have been clapped together by chance and the respective parties might have been as happily paired with someone else had someone else been sitting in the chair next to them when the music stopped. Not so with the Watermans. Only providence or some calculating fate could have arranged their meeting. G♥L: it was a one-in-a-gazillion match. Guy and Laura together were like the reunited halves of a torn picture, a perfect synchrony of ambitions, passions, and predispositions. As Guy at eight had declaimed into the rain, "Methinks it is a fair day, God wot!" Laura in her twenties once looked out the window of her New York apartment at a cats-and-dogs downpour and said with all sincerity, "What a wonderful day!"

They had happened upon each other at the Gunks on a climbing weekend in the fall of 1969. At the time, Laura was living in New York City. She was twenty-nine years old, the oldest child and only daughter born to Thomas H. Johnson, a legendary teacher and scholar at the renowned Lawrenceville prep school, in Lawrenceville, New Jersey. "Deeply Deeply" her father was nicknamed, though to his face his colleagues called him Tom. His writing was salted with rich phrases like "As spring widens and the buds move from intention to truth . . ." He was one of the editors of the *Literary History of the United States,* and the author of the *Oxford Companion to American History.* His reputation for brilliance rested primarily on his knowledge of the life and work of Emily Dickinson. He had edited Dickinson's collected poems and had published an "interpretative biography" of the poet, which was dedicated to Laura and her younger brother, Tommy. Time and again, he found himself profoundly moved by what he called Dickinson's "lines of almost insupportable tension." Deeply Deeply was a very fine writer himself. Here, for example, is his description of the famous letter (#868) Dickinson wrote to her sister-in-law Sue, after the death of Sue's eight-year-old son, Gilbert—Dickinson's beloved nephew, who died of typhoid in October 1883:

> The most moving letter that Emily Dickinson wrote in all her many years of correspondence she now addressed to Sue. That is to say, the form it takes is that of a letter, but in a truer sense it is a poem, an elegy of surpassing eloquence addressed to the memory of Gilbert. One never tires of reading it, and reading it again. Here there is no cry of anguish, no flinching, no panic in the face of chaos, no suggestion of laceration. She did not write the letter until she had mastered her nerve and glimpsed in vision the unfathomable harmonies which now became her memories of the little playmate. A sense of vibrancy, rapid motion, and light predominate, and the figures of speech tumble over each other: the boy is a passenger panting, prattling, whirling like a dervish, soaring; she sees him in the star, and meets his velocity in all flying things; he is light, and dawn, and meridian, and the swift-footed Ajax.

For all his remarkable ability and industriousness, Thomas H. Johnson was also a very heavy drinker. Laura grew up amidst the pretense and secrecy of an alcoholic household, trying to put the best face on bad situations, ever dreading the tinkle of ice cubes in her father's glass. Even when he was sober, Professor Johnson was a remote and abstracted presence, with a critical bent Laura's younger brother Tommy bore the brunt of. In time, Laura and Tommy's mother, Catherine, drank as well—little nips of vodka throughout the day. But Father was the figure around whom the house was organized, and there was always uncertainty in the house as to his condition. One could never be sure at a holiday dinner whether he would fall down the stairs, or burst out at the table with some clattering incongruity from a train of thought he alone had been following—"Henry James was an ass!" Poor devoted Laura was always trying to smooth things over.

Laura was a chubby kid with long, coltish legs. "I took her up Mt. Haystack when she was twelve and Tommy was eight," recalled Thomas Johnston, who'd been a younger colleague of her father's at Lawrenceville. "Tom avoided exercise like the plague. He'd hide behind a tree rather than take a walk. I used to call Laura 'Ladybug.' She was a little butterball. It's fascinating to me that that ash-blonde little butterball became one of the better women climbers in the country."

Haystack was her first mountain. Laura spent summers with her family in southern Vermont, and did some mountain hiking later as a camp counselor. She had attended Miss Fine's School, in Princeton, and gone on to Hollins College, in Virginia, where she majored in English. In the spring of 1960, during her sophomore year, she was drawn into Moral Rearmament, an idealistic movement widely considered to be a cult. It was led by an American evangelist named Frank Buchman, who in 1938 had a vision of himself as the leader of a God-inspired crusade against the moral and spiritual depravity of mankind. The roots of Moral Rearmament lay in the Bible studies program Buchman had organized in England in the 1920s, which eventually became known as the Oxford Group. The Oxford Group's principles of confession and sharing served as the foundation for Alcoholics Anonymous and the epidemic of twelve-step programs that swept the United States four decades later. Despite remarks like "I thank heaven for a man like Adolf Hitler, who [has] built a front line of defense again the anti-Christ of Communism," Buchman enjoyed considerable prestige and influence around the world. But by 1960, the year before he died, Moral Rearmament was a soon-to-be forgotten fringe group associated with rabid anti-Communism, heavy-handed moralizing, cult-like recruitment tactics, and the coercively wholesome road show "Up with People."

Young Laura Johnson knew nothing about Communism in 1960 but still found herself avid to join the crusade to stamp it out. On a school year abroad, she visited the Moral Rearmament headquarters, in Caux, Switzerland, and shortly thereafter informed her parents she was staying on with the group and would not be returning to college in the fall. "Laura was a considerable idealist and always a very biddable girl," Thomas Johnston recalled in an interview. "She was easily led and easily influenced." Catherine Johnson flew to Switzerland, and over the course of several days pried her daughter free of Moral Rearmament. Laura returned to college, and after graduating in 1962, moved to New York City, where she worked in book publishing. Five years later, she took off for Europe, knocked around the Mediterranean on a freighter, and toured the Bavarian Alps. Home again in New York, she worked for an outdoors store before eventually catching on as an associate editor in New York with the newly formed *Backpacker* magazine. She began signing up for hiking and climbing trips upstate with the Appalachian Mountain Club. It was on one of those outings at the Gunks, on September 10, 1969, that she met a handsome gray-eyed man with a tam-o'-shanter on his head and coils of gold line jauntily draped across his shoulders. By late in the following spring, when the Achilles tendon she'd ruptured in a skiing accident had healed, they had each other on a tight belay.

"I fell in love with Guy the first time I saw him," Laura told me.

Waterman had left his wife just that fall, after nineteen years of marriage. He had moved into a group apartment in New York City, near Columbia University, taking along his oldest son, Bill, who had been quarreling with his mother while recuperating from the accident that crushed his leg in June. Johnny, who still had a year of high school, had stayed on with Emily and brother Jim in Newburgh.

> My feeling was that I had not wanted to desert my sons [Waterman recalled in his memoirs] but that Bill was coming with me, Johnny had only one more year of high school and would be seeing me every weekend at the cliffs during the year, so the only one I was deserting was Jim. . . . It was anything but a happy time. I recall particularly one evening when . . . Johnny came into the city to have dinner with me. We ate in virtual silence the whole time, what conversation we had being limited to ineffective attempts to articulate how sad it was that the family had broken up. I think both of us found it impossible to express our gloom over being separated. But that was me and Johnny. I

had no second thoughts or reservations whatsoever about leaving Emily.

Came the new year, 1970, Bill headed west again. He enrolled for the spring semester at Western Washington State College before heading up to Alaska. After graduating from high school in the spring of 1970, Johnny went west also, and then north up the Alcan Highway to Alaska. Waterman quit his group sublet in the city and moved upstate to an apartment above a print shop in Marlboro, New York. He left himself with a horrendous two-and-a-half-hour commute each way to his job at General Electric, but the compensation was his proximity to the Gunks, where he wanted to spend all his free time. His guilt about deserting Jim was assuaged somewhat when Jim, who had not been getting along with his mother in Newburgh, came up to live with him. Waterman confessed that he had mixed feelings about Jim's arrival. After nineteen years of monogamy, he had been looking forward to becoming a "carefree bachelor," but, as he noted, "there was no way I was going to give Jim the least hint that he wasn't entirely welcome—the last thing he needed was to be rejected by *both* parents." Father and son lived together for three years, and "managed rather well," in Guy's view. Dad was seldom around, however; his long commute did not bring him home until after seven at night, and Jim was often on his own, unsupervised. As Waterman recalled,

> This was the era of rebellion and defiance of authority in all forms, and Jim fully partook in all that. Once an angelic little boy, he had developed a harder edge from the turmoil of a broken marriage, the process of the break-up having impacted him far more than the others. He was still a relatively happy teenager (as teenagers go), I think, but he was on his way to developing a melancholy, if not morose, side. As an adult, Jim smiles little and not heartily, and prefers to spend much time by himself.

Waterman was now thirty-eight years old, a suit-wearing, conservative Republican economist with a background in jazz, three sons, and a divorce pending: not the typical Gunks climber circa 1970. The fact that a man with his baggage could meet, much less land, a girlfriend in the predominantly male fraternity of climbers is, if not a miracle, at the very least a testament to the fellowship of roping up, and perhaps also an indication of Waterman's charm and charisma. He was working that spring as a climbing instructor for the Appalachian Mountain Club. In his memoirs, he claims that he considered Laura one of a half dozen prospects, but he also admitted he had virtually no experience courting women. It hardly mattered. It was quickly apparent to both of them that destiny was at work. Laura was recovering from her skiing accident, but she hobbled out to the cliffs on her crutches just to watch the climbers, Waterman in particular, and by late spring when she could stand on her own, she and Guy were on belay every weekend. They were known as the Dawn Patrol for their practice of rising before sunup to be first on popular routes and to rack up as many ascents per day as possible. Guy invited Laura to join him on what proved to be the disappointing climbing trip to the Bugaboos, in the Canadian Rockies. By the summertime, Laura had moved into the apartment in Marlboro, joining Jim and Ralph, the dog.

G♥L: They had so much in common, from academic families to overlapping interests. Laura's mother told a friend once that Guy and Laura were more suited to each other than any two people she'd ever known. Both were children of fathers they were unlikely to surpass professionally. Both had been affected by the scourge of alcoholism, albeit in different ways. Both shared a desire for adventure. Laura was champing at the bit to hike and climb with Guy as Emily had never been. During their first winter together they made long trips to the Adirondacks to snowshoe and chop and crampon their way up frozen waterfalls and snowy gullies. Laura loved books as much as Guy did. She shared his ardor for music. She was capable, supportive, adoring. She was a conciliator, not a critic. Knowing that Guy, like his father, hated perfume and makeup, she seldom wore any, once even returning a gift of some moisturizer she'd received. She abided by the rules, one of which was that there would be no recorded music played at Barra.

While Waterman speculated in a letter that his boys may have felt supplanted by Laura, they appeared to get along well together. By the fall of 1971, Guy and Laura were engaged. They tied the knot on August 26, 1972. The ceremony took place at the Mohonk Mountain House near one of the main Shawangunks crags. The wedding procession passed under an arcade of ice axes brandished by friends. Guy wore a dark suit, Laura a white dress with a double strand of pearls around her neck and flowers in her hair. Johnny and Jim attended—Bill was in still Alaska living in a cabin off Chena Pump Road in Fairbanks and confounding

*cheechako*s at the Howling Dog with his knife trick. "We were expecting him to show up—Guy was hoping for that, too—but he never did," Bobbie Waterman Carney recalled.

Guy and Laura spent their honeymoon night in a tent pitched on a belay ledge two-thirds of the way up a 5.8 Gunks climb called Oblique Twique. An implicit covenant of their marriage was that confrontation and discord would be kept to a minimum. The Watermans almost never fought, and were so reluctant to quarrel they concocted the name "malawi" to stand in for "tomato," thus sparing themselves the friction of disagreeing whether it was pronounced *to-may-to* or *to-mah-to*.

Perhaps the most important point of the Watermans' agreement was their mutual willingness to relinquish their city careers for the dream of a cabin in the woods. They had begun thinking about the possibility just a little more than a year after they met. It was Guy's idea, but Laura typically embraced it without reservation and was eager to help make it happen. Waterman had gone up to climb in Huntington Ravine on Mt.

Washington one weekend in February 1971. He was accompanied by his friend Brad Snyder, who had led Johnny Waterman on his first snow climb in the White Mountains, and then with Tom Frost had helped the teenager scale Denali in 1969. Snyder had grown tired of teaching college students and was restless. As Waterman recalled in his memoirs, when they weren't climbing they were "talking about what you could usefully do in life." Snyder had been reading a book by a well-known pair of homesteaders, Helen and Scott Nearing. It was called *Living the Good Life*. It had been first published in 1954, and would eventually go on to sell more than two hundred thousand copies and achieve fame in the 1970s as the "bible of the back-to-the-land movement."

"You ought to read this book," Snyder told Waterman.

When Waterman got back to Marlboro, he did. Scott Nearing, who died at age one hundred, in 1983, in what is considered an act of willful self-starvation, had been an economist at the University of Pennsylvania. He was fired in 1915, in part for his persistent study and sharp criticism of the inequitable distribution of income in the country. He bitterly opposed America's entry into World War I, ran for governor of New Jersey in 1928, and after three years in the Commmunist Party was expelled, in 1930, for "non-Marxian conceptions." Homesteading for the Nearings was a way of walking the talk of their theories about economics and social justice. "We were seeking an affirmation," they wrote in *Living the Good Life*, "a way of conducting ourselves, of looking at the world and taking part in its activities that would provide at least a minimum of those values we considered essential to the good life."

Waterman was impressed by the book—not just the high-flown rhetoric about social justice but also the practical aspects of how to live off the land, how to minimize the potential drudgery of it. The Nearings' key "discovery" was vegetarianism, which relieved them of the need to keep animals and left them comparatively free to come and go as they pleased, especially in winter, when the garden was lying fallow. They were able to allot half their time to leisure and reflection, and wrote numerous books together.

Like *The Climb Up to Hell, Living the Good Life* was a signpost that pointed Waterman toward his future. In the summer of 1971, he and Laura began looking for land in northern New England. They had decided on the region in part because it offered such a welcome contrast to the forbidding vastness of Alaska, which they had encountered on their disappointing expedition to Mt. Hunter in May of that year. There was something homey and not overly wild about the leafy mountains of Vermont, the lichen-blotched rock in the notches, the stony rills and rivers, the insular little villages with covered bridges, the self-contained dairy farms, the relatively long summers and glorious autumns, and that Yankee spirit shaped by geography, climate, Puritan heritage, and the Transcendentalist tradition, which bid citizens to fling aside their Bibles and intuit spiritual truths directly from nature. Vermont was a northern stronghold of the church of the self-determined, and the Watermans were eager to join.

"We wanted to get away from the nine-to-five," Laura wrote in a letter to me:

> From bosses, from work routines that kept us tied to the city. But it felt like we were moving toward something rather than fleeing. It seemed like an interesting life to be responsible for growing your own food, working up your own heating with wood. [But] in many ways we just wanted to go live in the woods and play, like children. I think this was particularly strong for Guy . . . I think in a deep way Guy took to the woods as a way of keeping himself sane. We never really talked about this except in affirming how important living at Barra was, how impossible it would have been to return to the marketplace life.

In July, they bought for eleven thousand dollars a tract of thirty-nine acres in East Corinth, Vermont. (Twelve acres were later sold off.) In October, they spent their first night on the property, snug in one of Hawee's old canvas tents. "We elected to call our land Barra, after the island in the Outer Hebrides where my family came from," Waterman wrote in his memoir. They mapped out a two-year schedule: they would build a small shelter in the summer of 1972 and then by June of the following year—the year Jim would graduate from high school—make the big move, cutting the urban umbilical cord for good.

"Homesteading was so much in the air," Brad Snyder told me. "But I always felt one of Guy's motives for setting up Barra was that it was an environment that was alcohol free. He was creating for himself an environment that wouldn't tempt him to fall back into drinking. He had cured himself of alcoholism single-handedly, but he never had any delusions that he couldn't fall back."

Guy dived into the job of learning to live off the land as he had the intricacies of legislation during his tenure on Capitol Hill. First he drafted a set of principles. At Barra they would strive "to live simply, cheaply, unhurriedly, basically." They would stay out of debt, not use machines, and seek wherever possible to find multiple uses for their possessions. (Thus wooden spoons, when not stirring pots, might moonlight as props to hold windows open.) They would "create not simply the necessary but the beautiful." They would not hurry. They would keep no animals, except Ralph. Consonant with the forethought that went into Waterman's suicide, they would "plan all activities in detail and well in advance." It's telling that while Waterman insisted they would "maintain contacts with friends and climbing organizations" and would not "withdraw into isolation," he made no reference to keeping up with family. And, somewhat paradoxically for a man who had just itemized the nine principles that would guide the latter half of his life, he added a tenth: "Be dogmatic in nothing. If it's desirable to make an exception from any of these principles, do so."

With the ideology in place, Guy and Laura immersed themselves in the practical aspects of living on the land. Forgoing animals meant weaning themselves off meat. They eliminated bacon from their breakfasts in the winter of 1972; soon Laura was serving meatless suppers, and by early 1973, they were both card-carrying vegetarians. In Marlboro they began a garden, planting boxes of tomato, bean, and broccoli seedlings, which they kept track of by naming each plant after people in the local phone book. They built an outhouse of their own design. They read how-to manuals and pored over issues of *Mother Earth News* and *Organic Gardening and Farming*. Guy took thorough notes on all manner of subjects, from ways they might earn a little income (selling produce, working on fire crews, giving piano lessons, typing manuscripts) to ingenious tips to improve homestead life. To keep whetstones clean, put them into the fire until red hot. Use newspapers to scrub window glass. Pillows can be filled with milkweed. Including a bowl of buttermilk in Ralph's diet may help keep ticks off. Carpets can be inexpensively pieced together from sample swatches. For toothpaste, substitute powdered charcoal. Strawberries thrive when toads are present. Juice extracted from string bean leaves can help remove warts.

Waterman learned from the Maine *Times* that the Nearings had covered their blueberries with nets to thwart ravenous birds. He noted how long C batteries lasted in a portable clock. He reminded himself to recycle the sixty Christmas cards he and Laura had received over the holidays in 1972. He jotted down ideas for homestead entertainment: if perishing of boredom during the snowy months, they might try sliding down hills on shovels. Perhaps they might join the chorus in Wells River or visit the Weston Priory. He transcribed the number to call if they saw a rare bird, though making a report would entail a long trip to Bradford to find a pay phone. He made sketches for shelves, for furniture, for nut and flour bins. He wrote to a log home manufacturer. A friend advised him not to skimp on nail quality; for exposed areas, hot-dipped galvanized nails were essential.

In an article on bristle cone pines, Earth's oldest living things, Waterman underlined a sentence that contained an important idea: "Could what man has considered adversity actually contribute to a long life?" Barra might well tell. When the plans for the main cabin were complete, Waterman began ordering Sheetrock, storm sashes, cement blocks, interior birch doors, glazed windows, and hot-dipped galvanized nails. They had a road bulldozed into the property and brought in a backhoe to dig the cellar and the hole for the septic tank, which the law required even though Barra would have no toilet or running water. What the sketches specified was a sixteen-by-thirty-two-foot structure on a cement block foundation. Guy and Laura mused that life on a kerosene-lighted homestead might be like winter camping—but with a wood stove, an outhouse, and a truly storm-proof shelter: the lap of luxury when you thought about it. With only one bedroom, there would be no accommodation for family, other than tents and a storage shelter behind the woodshed. Nonetheless, the boys came up to lend a hand. Bill joined Guy and Laura on a Barra work trip on Memorial Day weekend in 1972—his first and only visit to Barra. Jim and Johnny helped out with the construction in 1973; Jim continued to help with the porch and the woodshed. (He also pitched in twenty years later to help with building the guest cabin, Twin Firs. And to bring things full circle, he drove east from Colorado to Barra four months after his father's death to pick up his brother's letters, his father's bagpipes, and other family mementos.)

By June 1973, Guy and Laura were ready to make the jump.

"We left the apartment we had to Jim," Waterman noted in his auto-biography.

> He was not planning to go to college right away, and would become financially on his own when we moved. . . . In fact, though I had put away a special account of money for his college education (and the completion of college for the other sons), I didn't even come close to allowing for the inflation in college costs. What it came down to is that I walked away from that responsibility, leaving my sons with a difficult time to finance their own college. My mind was on my own future, from which there was no turning back.

His last day at General Electric was June 8, 1973. When he left the office, he was a forty-one-year-old retired jazz pianist, retired economist, retired speechwriter, and—not unfairly—one could say retired father as well. His failure to consider the rapidly inflating costs of his sons' educations cannot be attributed to a lack of economic expertise. He planned to stake them to what he had and then wash his hands of further obligations.

Nine days before Waterman quit the city and headed out to the woods on the great adventure of his new life, he received a letter from his son Bill in Alaska, Bill who just a year before had helped his dad turn over the earth of Barra's new garden. It was dated May 30, 1973. In the letter, Bill told his father he was "going off on a trip." A trip not in Alaska. He said he would be in touch when he got back. And that was the gist and sum of it. Nothing in the letter alarmed Guy. Nothing Bill said seemed ominous in the least. Bill going off on a trip was in keeping with his character, as was the shortage of details. Bill, as Waterman knew, liked to be a bit sly and mysterious. Waterman didn't think much about it at the time. His mind, as he said, was on his own future and there was no turning back. He yanked off his tie and caught a train out from Grand Central. He was never to set foot in Manhattan again. Nor was he ever again to see or hear from his oldest son. He climbed into his packed Datsun station wagon the next morning and drove to Vermont with Laura to create what he hoped would be a piece of Eden in the woods, little knowing the doom that trailed him all the way north or the serpent already inside the garden-to-be, waiting for him to arrive.

We parked on the summer road and took the short way in, following an unobtrusive path that slipped through groves of hardwoods and white pine. Dry culverts were spanned by little bridges made of logs, each log sized and planed and scored by hand. Waterman had spent many hours building footbridges and grading trails to make the hill-and-dale terrain easier on Laura's knees. Had it been winter and the woods full of snow, we would have parked much farther away on the road into town and faced a trek of a mile or so through the homestead's woodlots and sugarbush. But after ten minutes, we came to the edge of a natural south-facing amphitheater. The clearing was backed by rocky ledges and oak trees clinging to a steep hill; it sloped down in a series of gentle terraces toward a palisade of spruce, fir, and hemlock: Barra.

To enter was like stepping from the dock to the deck of a boat. It was as if the path from the road did not connect the homestead to the village but had simply led down to the water's edge, where a vessel was waiting with an air of detachment, sufficient unto itself, governed by a code of its own. Nothing was particularly shipshape about the place; no mechanical ingenuity was evident, no special flair for engineering or architecture. But there was an easy natural relation between the modest set and the immemorial setting, as if the buildings had ingratiated themselves with the land.

The main cabin and the small barnlike shed to which it was joined by a covered porch were simple one-story structures painted drab olive with forest green roofs. At the bottom of the amphitheater was a large garden enclosed in a post-and-wire fence to keep out the deer. Two door-sized gates let you cross the planted ground to the woods below. Near where we had entered was Twin Firs, an open-air bunkhouse for guests intricately fashioned from burled and witchy-looking wood. West past pear and plum and apple orchards was the prominence of Pavilion Hill, and the Vermont countryside falling away toward the Waits River.

As we were approaching Barra, a black muddy-pawed poodle named Moozi came galloping down the trail. He belonged to Kate Botham, the young caretaker Laura had found to live at Barra for the summer. Kate was not far behind.

"No, Moozi! Down! Down Moozi!"

Kate had short black hair, dark eyes, and the shoulders of a rower. She was dressed in overalls. She was from Wisconsin but had just graduated from Dartmouth and was spending the summer by herself at Barra, hauling water and wood, harvesting the vegetables that she and Laura had planted. Laura was still stopping by every few days to explain what needed to be done, but Kate had taken over most of the chores and the work of preparing the homestead for winter. Come winter, another young caretaker would move in.

We went inside. While Kate and Laura chatted, I looked around. It took a moment to adjust to the gloom. An index card tacked to the wall of the front entrance had written on it in Waterman's hand a line from a book by Norman Maclean: "To woodsmen, if you don't know the ground, you are probably wrong about nearly everything else." There was no sink in the kitchen, just two water jugs, and a stained counter by the window, some pans hanging on the wall, and a cookstove. The Ashley wood stove in the living room served as Barra's furnace. A trapdoor led down to the hunch-back root cellar where the Watermans kept the fruits they'd canned and the vegetables they carefully stored to last them until next year's harvest.

I was struck by how confining and dingy the cabin seemed: smaller no doubt (in the way apartments look smaller when the furniture is removed) because Barra's book shelves had been evacuated. But even on a sunny day, the eight modest windows did not exactly flood the place with light. The bedroom barely had space for the bed. The ceilings were claustrophobically low. The table doubling as a desk and eating place wasn't much larger than the portable typewriter perched on it. Half of the living room was occupied by the looming bulk of the black Steinway grand piano around which the cabin had been built. Cabinets and rafters and walls were begrimed with years of smoke and soot. One could only imagine how cramped and gloomy these quarters might seem on those bleak November days when pineal glands all over New England begin to shrivel with the onset of seasonal affective disorder. All over the north country there were cabins like Barra, most of them products of insuperable poverty, not determined efforts to fulfill a vision of the good life.

But of course my impressions of hardscrabble squalor and confinement were wrong. Barra had been scrubbed and dusted and cleaned according to a religiously observed schedule, and what the atmosphere of the cabin reflected was not a lack of care and maintenance but rather its organic relation to the land. The grime and soot were in fact the residue of the woods, the residue of an intimacy with the earth that could only confound a denatured urbanite accustomed to daily showers, roll-on deodorants, and shrink-wrapped carrots. Part of the point of going "back to the land" was to unhook oneself from the mindless consumerism and advertising-induced behavior of mass culture—to quit, for example, the vain and endless "war on germs" waged by phobic housekeepers armed with highly profitable cleansers and bleaches. It takes time to find the eyes that can see the difference between the honest dirt of a garden and the filth of a city, or can appreciate the more permeable and less neurotic boundaries that define categories of nature on a homestead. In short, if you're wrong about the soil, you're missing the forest for the trees.

Kate suggested we have a picnic lunch, and we trooped over to Twin Firs and a little sitting area with handmade chairs. Kate brought out a tray of iced tea, fresh bread, honey, peanut butter, and florets of broccoli she'd just picked from Barra's garden. The sun was winking in and out of the clouds. The wind was swirling in the trees. Like the rocks on Franconia Ridge, there was hardly a tree here Waterman had not touched, appraised for its health, or in some way contemplated. What you wouldn't notice immediately were the subtle insinuations of his sensibility, the touches of whimsy and enchantment that had outlived him: the covered firewood bays behind the main cabin named for baseball immortals, or the wooden phone in Twin Firs, or the glen set with tiny furniture for the "little people." You came upon them as you would upon those moments in a conversation that reveal the grain of a person's identity.

After lunch we carried black nylon nets down to the blueberry patch, where a dozen or so bushes were arrayed in a circle. We spread the nets over the berry-laden branches to keep the birds at bay. Mounted on a small boulder at the center of the patch was the plaque no bigger than a postcard: Guy Waterman 1932–2000. It was the most modest of markers, as unostentatious as the moment of silence that preceded the nightly suppers in the cabin, and it was the only place at Barra, apart from the spines of his own books, where you could find the creator's name. His fingerprint was on everything, but his name was not. As a friend of Laura's, a psychologist named Susan Staples, memorably put it in a conversation we had later: "I always thought of Barra as being like a painting, and Guy was the little signature in the corner."

Laura wanted to show Kate the procedure for cutting firewood, so the three of us shouldered axes and bow saws, and marched into the forest. We crossed the stream, where Guy had dug out a pool deep enough to sink three-gallon watering cans. Barra didn't have running water; the water walked—or rather, it was walked. Daily, Waterman hauled the cans up to the cabin in his hands; if Laura went for water, she used a yoke to spread the weight across her shoulders.

We wandered past the grave of Ralph, who died long enough before that not even Moozi's keen black nose could detect a trace of him now. Farther on, we came to the streamside bathhouse, where several white buckets of cold water were standing in anticipation of Kate's next tepid, solar-heated bath. Past the stream, the sugar maples grew more plentifully amid the stands of oak and hornbeam, and soon we reached the sugar shed. Here, every spring, the Watermans had collected and boiled off sap from a grove that comprised about 250 trees, each of which they knew by a name and by character, if character can be ascribed to a tree's pattern of sap production. Guy had tracked the flow of sap in his sugar bush over the years and had established on the shed wall a hall of fame, which listed the winners of the Tree of the Year Award, including the eight-time champion, "Mad Dog," Barra's maple version of Babe Ruth, the Sultan of Sap.

The ground climbed toward the south boundary of the homestead. We came finally to a patch of woods where Laura had spied a thicket of saplings four inches or less in diameter. We worked for several hours, unsentimentally axing the young trees, trimming their limbs, then dragging their skinny trunks to a rack. They would season for a year or two before being pieced into four-foot lengths and hand hauled up to the sawhorses in the wood shed, there to be sawed, split, and stacked prior to their final transformation in the belly of the Ashley stove. It was hard, hand-blistering work, but rewarding. The tang of chopped wood and crushed leaves was in the air, and when we were done, sauntering home, the water in the stream and the light dappling the mat of pine needles seemed sweeter for the labor of the afternoon. We stowed the tools in the shed; the wood bins were half full. Standard procedure at Barra called for four and a half cords to be cut and ready by November. All of it done by hand. Waterman cut by hand, sawed by hand, split by hand, stacked by hand. And on the endless push-pull of the saw, he counted every stroke.

The light was mellowing over the garden now. I sat for a while on the porch where Barra's absent master had often lingered to listen to the song of a hermit thrush or watch the leaves sift down in autumn. Here, six months before, on a winter Sunday morning, he had stood by this bench made from the log of an ash tree and gazed at his woods, and then he had taken his snowshoes off a nail in the wall and walked down the steps. Four steps. I found myself counting them, as he had counted each pass of the saw through the wood stacked in the shed at the end of the porch. Perhaps you too would have counted the steps had you been sitting on the porch, wondering about the man who was so conspicuously absent, whose signature had dissolved into his painting. Had he closed the sketchbook all at once, or had he shut it page by page, in increments of renunciation? Good-bye porch. Good-bye bench. Were there ten and twenty elegies in every moment, or had all the moments tumbled blankly past? Had he marked each step, or skipped numbly down the stairs, his mind elsewhere already? Here was a ghost descending, stopping again to put on the snowshoes, then heading down the hill past the garden, shuffling over the blankets of snow and into the forest, never to come back, never to look upon any of this ground again as he moved from intention to truth, shedding his life as lightly as a leaf . . .

Barra was Waterman's vision of an idealized life, a life naturalized by weather and shaped by seasons and ruled by ritual and repetition. It was his recollection of childhood happiness. It was the life he had before the Fall, his fort, his garden, his home, his living, his long conversation with the land. And yet one winter morning, nothing Barra could say to him had mattered anymore. The principles stopped mattering. The number of blueberries stopped mattering. The consolations of wilderness stopped mattering. The love he bore his wife stopped mattering. The quality he prized most at Barra was its "tranquility," but even the great calm of the place, the enfolding sense of order didn't matter anymore. None of it could matter if what a man willed into being to exert control over his life could not hold back the chaos at the gates, or the chaos in himself.

Sitting on the porch where Waterman had last laced up his boots, I remembered a story I had heard from Danuta Jacob, the New Hampshire singer who had struck up a musical partnership with Waterman in the eleventh hour of his life. The pair had practiced regularly for six months and then agreed to perform at a local cabaret benefit just three weeks before Waterman died. During one of their last Wednesday-afternoon rehearsals, Guy told Danuta he'd risen in the middle of the night to get some water and had fallen through the open trapdoor of his root cellar, barking his shins. He'd forgotten to close the root cellar door. "Ow, that must have hurt!" Danuta said sympathetically. But she was startled to see Guy peering at her with what looked like exasperation, as if she hadn't heard what he said, hadn't grasped the seriousness of it. She realized later she had misread the impact of the accident on him. He had not seen it as some trivial pratfall. Its significance transcended the injury to his shins. The misadventure had undermined his sense of dominion. It was as if Barra had turned on him, as if there were a trap built into his premises, and he'd sprung it on himself.

Guy Waterman once drew up an organization chart showing Barra's executive structure. There was little fat in the echelons of upper management. Laura wore multiple hats as Chief Executive Officer, Vice President of Cabin Services, Vice President of Food Supply; she headed up various other homestead divisions. The duties of Guy Waterman were self-effacingly listed as Director of Research and Chief Statistician. On the occasion of their tenth anniversary at Barra, the Chief Statistician worked up a detailed report. With his mania for "Barra stats," he was able to state authoritatively that he and Laura had canned 1,977 jars of various fruits and vegetables; they had eaten 421 kohlrabi, picked 1,356 spears of asparagus, and hand-cut 68.7 cords of firewood. They had read ninety-seven books aloud after dinner. (Reports in later years would include quarts of Ben and Jerry's ice cream consumed—157 in 1997—with a breakout by flavors revealing the household's strong preference for vanilla.) On trips away from Barra, they had bagged ninety-eight peaks in the White Mountains. They had withstood one hundred and five nights of homestead temperatures at ten below zero or lower, thirty-two nights of temperatures at twenty below or lower, and one night of temperatures at thirty below or lower. After ten years, their plum trees had finally yielded an inaugural harvest of seventy-nine plums. Their ground had been drenched by 322.16 inches of rain. Their maples had issued 15,758 quarts of sap, which they had transported with the help of friends to the sugar shed, a cumulative load of approximately sixteen tons. The ten-year yield of syrup: ninety-nine gallons, most of it consumed or given away to friends. They had picked 5,009 tomatoes. They had spent the entire decade below the poverty line, neither paying nor owing Federal income tax.

And for the first eight years, they had never been happier.

Every year they celebrated June ninth as "Barra Day." The day they went off the grid. That first summer they had lived in one of Hawee's old canvas tents and a three-sided shelter they'd built the year before. "Our world here seems so self-contained," Waterman had written in July 1973 to Brad Snyder. "We are conscious of so much detail—the endless parade of wildflowers, the morning and evening song from the birds, moss and fern on rocks near the stream, the shades of green at the edge of the woods as you look from the shelter."

They threw themselves into getting a garden established first, and then turned to the construction of a cabin. Plenty of friends and family members came up to help over the next five months. Fifty-eight people contributed 446 hours of volunteer labor, according to the Chief Statistician. The volunteers helped pour cement, string floor joists, nail decking, assemble stud frames, and make loft ladders. They helped muscle Guy's 1913 Steinway grand piano into the living room after bringing it through the woods in the back of a lurching pickup truck. The Watermans officially moved into the cabin on August 26, their first wedding anniversary. The fact that Laura got stung thirty-two times by hornets and couldn't keep any food down and was living in a house with no walls could hardly crimp her happiness. The walls went up by Labor Day. Two stoves were assembled, one for cooking and the other, the Ashley, for heating. The front door was hung in September. The homesteaders were racing against the clock now, trying to make the exterior weather-tight before the Vermont nights began to bite in earnest. The insulation was completed by early November, when the countryside received its first big snow. Guy and Laura turned with new zeal to the task of filling their wood bins.

Curious chipmunks and red squirrels rustled in the underbrush; the local chickadees flitted about unafraid, like emissaries ushering the Watermans into a new world. All summer, the astonishing particularity of nature had begun to reveal itself, some of its nuances made vivid by Guy's keen sense of pitch. In a letter he thanked a friend for confirming the aural signatures of the birds that had been entertaining them, reporting that he and Laura were now satisfied "that two notes coming down a major second is [a] chickadee, and three or more notes with the first a minor third lower than the others is a white-throated sparrow; however, we still need to know one more [bird]: a six- to ten-note sequence, the first three of which are roughly C-B-G (descending) and the remaining all in F#."

Johnny arrived after another big snow, in mid-December, and helped finish the kitchen. Jim spent much of the first two months of 1974 completing the interior. By the end of their inaugural year at Barra, the Watermans had gotten the hang of life on the land, growing more and more confident they could sustain their gambit. They bartered their labor for loads of manure; each year they planted more of the 150-by-70-foot clearing they'd laid out for the garden. The earth erupted with lettuce and kale and Swiss chard, with broccoli, carrots, kohlrabi, beets, rutabaga, potatoes, and buckwheat. What they couldn't grow—peanut butter, wheat flour, cereals, powdered milk, Tang, cans of pineapple juice with the labels that could be recycled as stationery—they bought in bulk at a local co-op, along with supplies like kerosene and candles. In winter, they hauled provisions back to the cabin on two Flexible Flyer sleds named Orestes and Electra. In the root cellar, they stored carrots and beets in sand; turnips and onions and potatoes were piled on shelves. They learned the hard way that winter squashes had to be kept upstairs, out of the damp air of the cellar. They dried beans on the stove. Laura canned the rose hips and blackberries growing wild at Barra. They planted strawberries and blueberries and raspberries. They planted fruit trees and patiently waited for the crops of apples and pears and plums. They worked endlessly in the woods gathering firewood: oak, hop hornbeam, ash, beech, yellow birch—nearly eight cords a year for more than a quarter of a century. They managed their forest carefully, and there were more trees on Barra at the end of their tenure than when they'd started.

Over the years they added a porch, a woodshed, the sugar shack, and the guest house. They cut trails through the woods that you would hardly notice, and built three bridges across the stream that drained their land. They came to view their car as an eyesore, and the road an intrusion, and they decided to block the latter off with a couple of trees. Nature could have it back. Over the years, Barra became a universe of its own, where life had more in common with the seventeenth century than the twentieth. Guy's sisters loved to bring their families up for visits in the summer; older nieces and nephews often came for sugaring weekends in late March and early April. There was always a good laugh to be had discovering the ways Guy had lost touch with popular culture. He looked especially puzzled by the convulsions of hilarity that would ensue when a guest incorporated into conversation one of the ubiquitous advertising slogans of the day, saying, for example, after a vegetarian meal: "Guy, where's the beef?" Or, having finished a bowl of kohlrabi: "Guy, I can't believe I ate the whole thing!"

Those first eight years were the best of times—"the happiest of my life," Waterman recalled in his memoirs. He played the piano constantly, often after dinner. Each summer, he gave a benefit concert of jazz and ragtime at the Mohonk Mountain House. Laura was playing the piano in those days, too—sometimes with Guy, romping through four-handed pieces. They were able to earn some money writing articles for *Backpacker* magazine, and then after several years landed a monthly gig writing a column on camping and hiking themes for a regional magazine called *New England Outdoors.*

But it was the work of homesteading that gave the Watermans' lives meaning and shape, the familiar cycles of planting and harvesting, the structure of regular chores, the endless and unexpectedly absorbing rewards of hard physical labor. Waterman never tired of cutting and splitting the firewood, nor did Laura. Their hands, toughened by climbing, were stained by garden dirt and callused by axe handles. They'd gotten acclimated to extremes of heat and cold. Laura could reach into a pot of scalding water, and to shake Guy's leathery paw was to look twice to make sure he wasn't wearing a glove. "When we used to play dice baseball, the dice would bounce off his palms whereas they would settle into my soft lawyer's hands," said his friend Tom Simon, a Burlington-based attorney with whom Waterman had collaborated on a history of baseball in Vermont.

To be sure, there were moments on the homestead that disturbed Barra's cherished air of tranquility and tested not only Waterman's abhorrence of violence but his solidarity with all things wild. One evening during their fourth summer, they were sitting on the porch, Guy reading aloud, Laura looking out at the garden, listening, with her chin in her hands.

"Guy! There's a woodchuck!" she said.

The woodchuck was over by the compost pile, inside their eight-foot-high floppy-topped wire fence, which they had set up to protect their food supply from hungry deer, rabbits, raccoons, and woodchucks. Spread before the intruder was an undefended smorgasbord of kohlrabi, asparagus spears, and every other tasty vegetable the Watermans were counting on to sustain them for the winter.

"We didn't know what to do," Laura recalled. "We couldn't let him escape. He'd found a way in, and if he'd gotten in once he could get in again. So we reasoned that we had to kill him. An axe was the only means."

Waterman grabbed an axe and edged reluctantly toward the woodchuck, who'd retreated to the fencepost in the northeast corner. One time when Waterman had been digging postholes for this very fence, he discovered a garter snake and a woodland jumping mouse in the bottom of a thirty-two-inch-deep hole. It was a real puzzle how to get them out safely. He was able to extract the little snake by first covering it with a bit of dirt and then gently clamping it with the posthole digger and lifting it out. The mouse had to be coaxed out on a post set in the hole at an angle. Both creatures looked a little dazed by their ordeal but soon recovered and made their way happily back to their liberty in the woods.

"I can't do this," Waterman said, creeping toward the woodchuck.
"Guy, you have to!"

"This is the hardest thing I've ever done."

Summoning the energy of some atavistic passion, he struck a lethal blow with the blunt edge of the axe. There was no blood, thank goodness.

"I felt like Lady Macbeth spurring her husband on," Laura recalled. "But we had to do something. That was our food he was eating!"

They dug a hole at the spot of the slaughter and buried the poor trespasser. A few years later, curious as to the condition of the corpse, they dug up the grave but found nothing, not a trace.

How the years dashed by, measured out in seasons and the rhythmic refrain of chores. The program of one year was much the program of the next. January and February were the quietest times on the homestead, the months when the Watermans could get away climbing. Their trips were usually restricted to four or five days; if the cabin went any longer without a fire, the provisions in the root cellar might freeze. By early spring, they had to stick close to home to begin tapping their sugar  maples; they hung buckets on eighty-eight of the trees. Guy had been appointed to the board of the Mohonk Trust, a nature preserve of the land around the Gunks, and in late spring they always made a trip to the crags to attend meetings and climb. Then it was back to Barra to get the garden in. Summer was filled with home improvements and maintenance—

mending fences, cleaning gutters, gathering wood, lugging stones up to the site where they would eventually be used as the foundation of the guest cabin, Twin Firs. There were often visitors to entertain in summer, and days away for climbing trips too. In fall came the harvest, the picking, the canning, the preserving. The first frosts always underscored the urgency of filling the wood bins. After Christmas, starting in 1973, they taught a week-long winter mountaineering course in New Hampshire sponsored jointly by the Appalachian and Adirondack mountain clubs. The fourteen-year gig provided a steady flow of contacts and friendships with young climbers from around the northeast. As January and February rolled up again, they would return to ice climbing and snowshoeing, or, as was the case during the 1980s, apply themselves more concertedly to writing.

Within the cycle of the year were smaller patterns. Daily, weekly, monthly: schedules at Barra were carefully mapped in accord with Principle No. 1, "Plan all activities well in advance." On his color-coded index cards, Waterman would jot down the day's chores and errands. He normally rose before dawn and posted on the wall the quote of the day, along with any interesting facts or events associated with the anniversary of the date. Then he would turn to the couple's mail, which was always heavy; with no phone in the cabin, family and friends could contact the Watermans only by letter. Just before seven, Guy would head out to take temperature readings at the three weather stations on the homestead. His rounds measured out the day. He took readings in the morning, again at one in the afternoon, and a third set at seven in the evening, adding the data to the burgeoning store of Barra stats.

Once a month, Waterman would also prepare a schedule laying out the chores of the upcoming three weeks. Specific times were allotted to wash the water jugs, rinse the houseplants' leaves, clean the stove, inspect the fire extinguishers, and aerate the bags of cashews, peanuts, almonds, walnuts, pecans, and Brazil nuts to keep mold from spoiling what was, along with peanut butter and beans, their main source of protein. The books were dusted according to a schedule. Poetry in December. Works

by Scott, Dickens, Kipling, and Shakespeare in January. February was reserved for the collection in the southwest corner of the cabin. Fiction and
biography were dusted in March, and history in April. Three times a year,
in April, August, and December, the Watermans shuffled the pictures in
the cabin, the shots of Guy with Vice President Nixon, the portraits of
Bill and Johnny, the climbing photos of Johnny on the Ruth Glacier and
the summit of Mt. Huntington, and Jim on a 5.9 climb in the Gunks
called Jacob's Ladder. They budgeted time for cleaning windows, and of
course worked out a system: Laura would wash on the inside while Guy
washed on the outside, one mirroring the other with only a pane of glass
between them.

In his memoirs, Waterman confessed that his account of the happiest
period of his life probably seemed a little "bloodless" and did not convey
the joy and pride he felt. Pride and joy at making a go of the gamble in
Vermont. What a risk it had been—like a bold climb at the limit of his
abilities. And how "humiliating and depressing," it would have been to
have been forced to "crawl back to the world of 'work' and ordinary living." And he was just as proud of the strides he'd made as a rock climber
in those years, and of his growing mastery of mountain terrain above the
tree line in winter. And, finally, he wished to redress any misimpression
he might have given about the depth of his feelings for Laura. Here is
how he put it in his memoirs:

I'm an odd mix of Yankee reserve . . . and an almost absurd
heart-on-the-sleeve emotionalism. That is, I used to cry in movies,
still do [at] books (especially dog stories!), love *Wuthering Heights*
and *Green Mansions,* and easily get too choked up to finish speaking anytime my emotions are primed. Yet I also dislike confessing
personal matters. Maybe I could just say that Laura proved both
the perfect homesteading mate—hardworking, perseverant, re-
sourceful, steady (much steadier than me, which helped)—and
the perfect companion for me—fun, compatible as to interests
and tastes and priorities, unceasingly sympathetic, warmly affec-

tionate, unbelievably patient through my bad moods. So great, after nineteen years of a bad marriage, to be embarked on this great
adventure together.

When the Watermans first came onto the land at the start of their great
adventure together, there was a tree not far from the cabin, an old yellow
birch that shaded a spot just up the path from the woods. Waterman
called it "the Gabriel birch" for the way it stood like a winged angel at the
entrance of their little Eden. But in the spring of 1981, it became just a tree
again with no angelic power to ward off the disorder of the world.

Imagine that year beginning as previous years had begun, with the
Watermans in the White Mountains, surrounded by a flock of admiring
students. Their weeklong winter mountaineering course always concluded with a square dance on New Year's Eve, which sent them home on
a festive, hopeful note. Home to the solitude of Barra in the tranquility
and stillness of winter. Home to the leafless trees, the gray trunks aglow
against the drifts of deer-tracked snow. To the lamplight throwing back
the early dusk. To the train of gelid nights and beloved Orion rising beyond the bedroom window in the east. That winter, Waterman was reading *Ivanhoe,* the novel his mother had read to him in the waning days of
his boyhood on the Farm.

Suddenly, here was April. The work in the sugar bush was nearly
done. The last snow in sight of the cabin was spied on the third. The next
day, it was balmy enough to spread the year's first picnic on the porch. By
the fifteenth, when much of the country was poring over tax forms, Waterman was noting the progress of the melt; now anyone who wished to
walk in to Barra via the summer path could park halfway up the road. It
would be May before the ground was free of the winter's last frost and one
needn't light a fire in the Ashley to ease the cold in the cabin at night. But
everywhere in the widening light and aching buds you could feel the intimations of spring.

And then, on the twenty-first of April, at 4:30 in the afternoon, Waterman heard ominous footsteps on the porch. Nearly every visitor to
Barra made arrangements by mail weeks or even months in advance.

Now two unexpected young people from the village were knocking on the door, and telling him when he opened it that they had been dispatched to fetch him to a phone—the postmaster in East Corinth had been called by a park ranger in Alaska who'd been a student at the first winter mountaineering course the Watermans had taught. The news Guy was shortly to learn was very grave: his son Johnny, twenty-eight years old and one of the most renowned climbers in the country, was missing on Alaska's highest mountain.

7.

POISED UPON
THE GALE

✳

When, to their airy hall, my fathers' voice,
Shall call my spirit, joyful in their choice;
When, pois'd upon the gale, my form shall ride,
Or, dark in mist, descend the mountain's side;
Oh! May my shade behold no sculptur'd urns
To mark the spot where earth to earth returns.

LORD BYRON, A Fragment

To guard against losing their way—which could have been disastrous—the son would go out from the last identified cairn as far as he could and still see it. Then the father would go out from there as far as he could without losing sight of the son, and stand there waiting for some brief lapse in the wind to try to squint forward into the fury of the storm in a forlorn effort to find another cairn.

GUY WATERMAN, *Wilderness Ethics*

L ET US SQUINT FORWARD into the storm, knowing there is a point where the cairns leave off and trails can go no further. The father had three sons; two lost their way. One vanished into the catacombs of a glacier in the shadow of Denali, the other into the uncompassable wilderness of the disappeared. Beyond the issue of what happened to their bodies, which were never recovered and thus make their deaths probable but unconfirmed, lies the more complex question of what happened to their lives.

In some ways, the first two sons of Guy Waterman were dramatic opposites. Bill was as obscure as John was famous. Bill was as determined to withdraw in a mantle of secrecy and silence as John was to advance in a mad excess of self-disclosure. One a man of too few words; the other, of too many—and neither of them men, really, more like wild wounded boys drawn to the cold flame of the north. In the end, they were different only in ways that underscored their likeness.

Bill and John were only seventeen months apart, but in a picture of them taken in Fairbanks in the summer of 1972 Bill looks much older. They are sitting in a metal skiff on the Tanana River with a big king salmon on the floor of the boat. Bill is pointing off to his left, his

face pale, his eyes ashen, his shoulder-length brown hair tangled and ratty. He's wearing a gray wool shirt; the left pant leg of his jeans is sliced at the seam to accommodate the prosthetic foot, which rests awkwardly on the floor of the boat by the beautiful fish. Johnny is wearing half-frame glasses, sneakers, brown pants, a brown shirt; his hair is neatly combed. He looks happy, smiling faintly as he glances over his shoulder at whatever Bill is indicating.

Another snapshot from the same summer shows Bill by himself leaning against his ramshackle cabin in the woods off Chena Pump Road. He has managed a rare smile for the camera, a smile all the more heartbreaking for the sense of despondency it masks and the onlooker's knowledge that in less than a year, a month past his twenty-second birthday, he will be a ghost, gone, leaving not even the tracks in the snow that Johnny will leave eight years later. There are circles under his eyes, good-bye eyes half-filled with shadows, and too many hours in the coils of LSD, and too many nights in the sawdust of the Howling Dog, pitching a knife into his dumb foot.

It is not hard to imagine how that catastrophe in the Winnipeg rail-yard in the summer of 1969 might have devastated Bill's spirit. Eleven days before the accident, he was in the Gunks showing what his friend and fellow climber Keith LaBudde thought was a newfound confidence on rock as he lead LaBudde up a 5.7 climb called Overhanging Layback. And then, as he was tasting his first real freedom, it was yanked away. It is not hard to imagine how both the patterns of his family and the Dionysian appetites of the era could have deepened his alienation. He drank, though not so secretly as his father had drunk during the first twelve years of Bill's life, when Guy was battling the bottle. He summoned the genie of acid without guidance or structure, an invitation Tom Wolfe once compared to "tying yourself to the tracks to see how big the train is."

After the accident he was laid up for most of the year, first in the hospital in Winnipeg, where he received a visit from his father, and then during his long recuperation at his parents' house in Newburgh, New York, where he limped around on metal crutches, his leg in a cast. The limp didn't get much better when the cast came off. When Guy and Emily split up, Bill went to live with his father in a group apartment near Columbia University, in New York City. They roomed with another climber and two Columbia students. They slept on mattresses on the floor and kept all their clothes and things in cardboard boxes. Guy would turn the light on in the kitchen to scatter the roaches before buttoning himself into a three-piece suit and heading off to write speeches for the big shots at General Electric. Guy camped in the apartment until the following April, but by January 1970, Bill was well and able enough to strike out on his own. He enrolled at Western Washington State College, in Bellingham, north of Seattle. Far from home. He'd been a National Merit Scholar finalist in high school, and had impressive test scores, but his semester at Western Washington State in the spring of 1970 was his only term of college. In the view of his uncle Peter Morrison, what happened was no mystery. "Bill was a casualty of the sixties," he said. "Drugs fried his brain."

Bill arrived in Alaska in 1971, and stayed with the Morrisons in Fairbanks until he could get settled on his own. Uncle Peter, Emily's older brother, lived with his wife, Katherine Macdonald Morrison, and their six children in a big house three miles north of Fairbanks, on the Steese Highway. The family had moved to Alaska in 1962, just three years after the territory gained statehood. Peter, with his doctorate in zoology from Harvard, eventually became the director of the Institute of Arctic Biology at the University of Alaska, in Fairbanks. Katherine had been a school-teacher, and in one of those novelistic twists, had had Guy Waterman in her class when she taught at the Shady Hill School in 1945. Both Morrisons were fond of Bill, and of Johnny, too, and were confounded by what appeared to be Guy's indifference to his sons' marginal situations. It was also perplexing to them that kids of such intelligence should have so little direction, or should keep themselves so poorly even in an era known for its bedraggled hippies. Katherine Morrison despaired of ever getting Bill to wear pajamas, and complained of having constantly to wash the sheets he slept in.

Even after Bill got settled he would come by for supper on Sunday—the one day of the week he was sure to have a decent meal. He didn't have a car, and had to hitchhike everywhere, or walk. He walked with a pronounced limp, and his leg was constantly giving him pain. "Some days he would go through a whole bottle of aspirin," recalled his cousin Alice Reed Morrison.

"Bill didn't take good care of himself," recalled Barbara Belmont, who had befriended the whole Waterman clan at the Gunks in the late 1960s, but considered herself closest to Bill. "He was straggly and dirty, and hippie-like. He did a lot of drugs, and there was alcohol, too. I would say he was really depressed after the accident. I'm sure the immediate cause of his suffering was the shock of his leg, but it also had to do with him not knowing what he was going to do with his life, where he belonged, who he was. The whole family seemed to have an aura of hard times around it. It just seemed there were a lot of emotional scars. And yet Guy also seemed the most wonderful dad in the world, and Billy and Johnny were very connected to him. Of the two, Billy seemed the more wounded. He didn't talk a lot about his past, but I remember him talking about feeling hopeless about his life, and me trying to convince him that there were reasons for being alive. Over the last year and a half before he disappeared, I went up to Fairbanks for ten or twelve visits. We wouldn't go out, we would sit and talk in his cabin. Drink beer and share a meal.

He was pretty destitute. He had no money. He had no car. He had to hitch everywhere he went. Lost is the only word I can use. Lost and disconnected."

In the spring of 1971, still encamped with his mother's relatives, Bill was excited to learn that his father was coming to Alaska in May. Guy was flying up with Laura to join a small party of climbers attempting the north face of Mt. Hunter. Johnny was away traveling and climbing in Europe, but for Bill in Fairbanks, the prospect of a visit from Guy in Alaska was big news. His father didn't like to fly and was already beginning to cultivate the defensive provincialism that would constrain him to what he called the "dinky" mountains of the Northeast for the rest of his outdoor career. He had had to be cajoled into joining the Hunter party. This would prove to be his only visit to Alaska. Surely if he could get to the airstrip in Talkeetna (from where he would fly into Hunter), he could get a few hours farther north by train to Fairbanks to see his oldest child, whose mobility was constrained by his lack of cash and the pain in his leg. As Peter Morrison recalled: "Bill was desperate to see his father. Guy was supposed to come up to Fairbanks, and then he called and said, 'No, we're not coming.' Bill was crushed."

Alice Reed Morrison had no doubt about the impact of the canceled visit: "I know it broke Bill's heart. Guy was coming to Alaska and he couldn't even be bothered to see him. I think that was the end of Bill emotionally because he idolized Guy."

When Guy returned east after the failed attempt on Hunter, he wrote an eighteen-page letter to Johnny and Bill, giving a "piton by piton" description of the abortive climb—a letter whose pitch descriptions and careful sketches of topographical features would surely have been of less interest to Bill than to Johnny, who had attempted the mountain the year before and would return again in 1973, and a third time, in 1978, for his mythmaking solo ascent. Guy noted toward the end of his letter that he and Laura had been flown off the Kahiltna Glacier on a Sunday in late May and had lingered two nights in Talkeetna, till Tuesday morning, "hoping Bill might possibly show up."

It was not the first time, nor would it be the last, that one of Waterman's sons would be injured by his father's failure to budget enough time for a visit or to improvise some leeway in his highly structured and carefully scheduled life. Some of the young climbers who came to feel like surrogate sons of Waterman complained of the same thing—with Guy, it was always the case of having to bring the mountain to Mohammed. What was this curiously passive and character-defining tendency to wait for people to come to him? Was he not capable of extending himself, of going the extra mile? He was famously considerate and sensitive to the needs of other people in some ways, and yet at other times he seems to have been paralyzed by pride or some existential confusion as to his own agency, feeling himself to be at the mercy of relationships that either "happened" or "didn't happen" as he would say in his memoirs. Laura explained Guy's reasoning to me in a letter:

We definitely wanted to see Bill when we were in Alaska in May 1971. When we got out from Mt. Hunter we looked into the train trip up there [to Fairbanks] and discovered that we would have exactly time enough to take the train up and immediately take the train back to Anchorage to make our flight home and NO time at all to see Bill. We decided it just wasn't sensible or feasible to make the trip. I know that Guy was very sorry about this, since seeing Bill was something he wanted to do.

This missed opportunity in the summer of 1971, coupled with seeing the extent to which Bill had been left on his own to cope with his soon-to-be-amputated foot, sealed Peter Morrison's poor opinion of Guy Waterman's paternal instincts. "I think he was a terrible father," Morrison said bluntly during a telephone conversation we had in the fall of 2001. "His boys were desperate for some fatherly attention. The story of his life is that he was completely self-centered."

Later that summer, after his father had come and gone, Bill worked as a cook in a mining camp for a couple of months. He dropped a note to Johnny saying he planned to visit him in the fall, when Johnny would be starting his first year of college at Western Washington State in Bellingham. After Johnny had graduated from high school in the spring of 1970, he had followed Bill's route out to Bellingham; his semester at Western Washington State in the fall of 1971 was the first of his two terms there.

Bill made good on his word and arrived on campus in October. Johnny described the visit in a letter to Brad Snyder:

The ol'brers showed up finally. Is up in Vancouver trying to get emigrated to Canada. Has a fair amount of loot in the bank at present. Was in good shape. Gets around on his leg OK, but going to the hospital to have something final done about it. If he gets into British Columbia he may have to wait awhile before the hospital has room so he may be down here for a while. If not, he'll go to Alaska and stay in Fairbanks while he's incapacitated. He likes the North Country pretty fine. His plans are very indefinite. Sounds like he learned some pretty decent skills up there in the northlands. . . . Intend to do some good drugs with my brer when he returns from Vancouver. We figure maybe some things can be learned from some kinds of drugs but then, we'd neither of us put our money on it.

One of Bill's favorite expressions, Johnny reported, was "Hell with that."

After spending part of the winter in Telegraph Creek, British Columbia, Bill was unable to get himself "emigrated," and returned to Fairbanks, where his uncle Peter and aunt Katherine found the surgeon to finish what the train wheel had started in 1969. Johnny confessed in a letter to Brad Snyder that things had not gone so well between him and Bill—Bill, who used to be the only person in the world he felt understood him. "Actually," he wrote, "I didn't (hmm, I guess) relate (is the best word) to Bill too well when he came down. I was feeling guilty about his leg being fucked up, last thing in the world he needs."

At his uncle's suggestion, Bill enrolled in a University of Alaska electronic-technician training program geared toward the handicapped. He started in early 1972, the spring term. In May, he went east. On a broiling Memorial Day weekend he drove up with Guy and Laura from Marlboro, New York, to the new property they had bought in Vermont the previous summer. They pitched a tent in the clearing. Bill helped Guy remove the sod from the ground that would become Barra's garden. They picked out a corner marker, a large rock that came to be called "the Barra stone" and served as a place in the garden where you might sit, or lay a trowel or a sweater, or keep a bottle of water cool in a bit of shade. Guy and Bill hiked up the steep hill behind the clearing where the cabin would rise the following summer and looked for large rocks with which to build a fireplace. They made a game of bowling the rocks down the hill through the ten-pin woods. "I sensed a bit of competition between father and son," Laura told me in a letter, "but mostly it was just high jinks, the two of them enjoying each other's company." On the way home, they all squeezed into the tan Volkswagen Bug Guy was driving then, Guy and Laura in the front, Bill, Ralph the dog, and all the gear in the back. It was hot; the windows were wide open. Bill took off his prosthetic leg and gave it to Laura to stow up front so he could have more room in the back with Ralph.

"We stopped at a gas station somewhere in Massachusetts or Connecticut," Laura recalled. "The attendant came out to pump the gas. Bill wanted to get out, so he said, 'Would you pass me my leg, Laura?' I handed it back to him. You should have seen the attendant's face as Bill's leg flashed by him in the window. It was immensely funny to us, and we howled over it as we drove down the highway. That was the last time Guy spent with Bill. I know it was a comfort to him that Bill had seen Barra. We talked now and then about the work we had done with him in the garden. Guy knew that Bill knew how to find his way back, since he had once been there."

Bill returned to Alaska for the rest of the summer and spent some time hanging out with Johnny. They went fishing with Barbara Belmont on the Tanana River. She took pictures of them sitting in a metal skiff. Let that boat drift and it would go down to the Yukon and then out the great artery of the subcontinent to the Bering Sea. Johnny was all vivid with the triumph of his prize first ascent on the east ridge of Mt. Huntington; Bill was staring at the abyss, the forlorn effort to find another cairn plainly visible in his eyes. *Hell with that.* Sometime that year he sent his father a knife with a carved whalebone handle. It was smaller than the one he liked to throw into his foot. He returned to the electronics training class and continued his course work through the fall and into the following spring. He received an Associate in Electronics Technology degree from the university on May 20, 1973. Ten days later, he mailed his father his final, cryptic note: "Going off on a trip. Not in Alaska. Will be in touch when I get back."

Friends were quoted speculating Bill had gone to Vietnam, or South Africa. Or maybe he'd emigrated to Canada after all. There were rumors he'd gone to live with Athapaskan Indians north of Fairbanks. Guy was quoted as saying he liked to think his son had gotten "engulfed" in the life of an Eskimo village. But to Barbara Belmont, remembering the picture of Bill and Johnny she took the summer before, during one of their last moments together, it was not so easy to sustain a fantasy about the mystery into which Bill had vanished at the age of twenty-two. As she told me over the telephone: "I remember a desperation on my part to convince Bill to keep on living. To make a connection with him that was meaningful enough to keep him from doing what he did. Given how depressed he was about the purposelessness of his life, and my experience of him, and how hard I was trying to convince him to stay alive, I would say there's a very good possibility he walked off alone into the bush to die— that he committed suicide."

His uncle Peter's wife had no doubt. "My mother said right away, 'Bill is dead,'" recalled Alice Reed Morrison. "'He walked away and committed suicide.'"

Johnny Waterman's reputation as the "crazy genius" of Alaska mountaineering was entrenched long before the spring of 1981, but it was his last rapture in the wilderness that year that secured his legend. His exploits were proclaimed in articles and chapters of books. A short story titled "Vreelund" about a climber based closely on Waterman was published by a Fairbanks fiction writer in 1987 in the *Alaska Quarterly Review.* A satire in *Rock and Ice* magazine had him faking his death and living incognito in Arizona, where he was illegally soloing sandstone towers on Navajo land. In a series of tributes published in *Alaska Mountain,* friend Don Logan quoted from Kerouac's *On the Road:* "John was one of the 'mad ones, the ones who are mad to live, mad to talk, mad to be saved, desirous of everything at the same time, the ones who never yawn or say a commonplace thing, but burn burn burn, like fabulous yellow roman candles exploding like spiders across the stars . . .'"

More than two decades later, Johnny Waterman's picture still hangs on the office wall of the Northland Wood Company in Fairbanks, where he worked on a sorting machine during the summers from 1973 to 1977. He used to amuse his bosses by holding his hard hat in one hand and turning a one-armed handspring with the other. For a number of years in the 1980s, the Alaskan Alpine Club held an annual John Waterman Memorial Auction in Fairbanks. A spirited crowd vied for various items of Waterman gear and paraphernalia, and the competition was always especially boisterous at the end, when one of Waterman's old socks was offered for sale, sometimes fetching prices upwards of $150. Sentiment surrounding Waterman's memory was strong but probably not strong enough to support $150 for an old sock: knowing bidders expected to find some choice contraband in the toe.

Johnny Waterman shared many of his father's traits, but they were often comically inverted or exaggerated to the point of parody. Johnny had Guy's love of music but not his talent. Guy with his gifts was always a little shy about performing, even as a pro; Johnny with marginal gifts needed no encouragement to give a concert. In summer, he sometimes sat naked on a car alongside a well-traveled road, strumming a cracked guitar he'd rescued from a dumpster and bandaged with tape. He took the stage of a bar in Cantwell, Alaska, to honk Christmas carols on the clarinet, undaunted by booing patrons or the bartender, who plugged in the jukebox. One time a friend was in the middle of an intimate dinner and Johnny, who happened to be working at the restaurant as a busboy, raced over and set up a large reel-to-reel tape deck in the middle of the table, then switched it on so one and all could hear his latest songs.

Where Guy was highly private and rarely if ever talked about his feelings, Johnny was almost compulsively confessional, broadcasting his inner turbulence and anxieties about his loneliness and lack of a girlfriend. During a famous slide show he gave of his triumphant solo ascent of Hunter, he brandished his right hand and joked about the love they'd shared. Guy was fenced off with boundaries even old friends dared not test; Johnny had no boundaries at all. "He'd ask to borrow your toothbrush," said Dane Waterman. Father and son shared a thirst for attention, but Johnny lacked Guy's offsetting, almost Victorian, self-restraint. Where Guy was carefully agnostic, Johnny took up as a born-again Christian for a while. Guy's signature tam—the very symbol of his discreet showmanship—became in Johnny a full-blown costume: he swept around Fairbanks in a black cape and oversized Elton John glasses with a big silver star glued on the bridge. He had his father's mania for recording the minutiae of daily life, but again the contrast was startling. Guy jotted notes on color-coded index cards, which he kept stacked neatly in his left shirt pocket: red for expenditures, orange for short-term projects, yellow for the day's chores, green for seasonal tasks, and blue for the shopping lists of needed supplies. Guy also prepared a daily calendar on which he noted visitors due to arrive, intriguing homestead events like the appearance of a new bird, and significant anniversaries such as the death of John Milton, the birth of Thoreau, or the end of Lou Gehrig's hitting streak. In lieu of index cards, Johnny had small spiral-bound notebooks and a Harpo Marx–like entanglement of clipboards. His mania for indiscriminate documentation bordered on madness as he tried to record the second-by-second flux of daily life.

"You'd run into him outside the post office in Fairbanks at twenty-five below zero and he'd log the time of your encounter on one of his clip-boards—ran into so-and-so at 3:04 P.M.," recalled an old climbing friend, James Brady, today a fisheries biologist with the Alaska Department of Fish and Game.

An even stranger similarity was that both men had political hanker-ings. When Guy left Washington, D.C., in 1960, one of his ambitions was to get involved in Republican politics in Connecticut—a dream eventu-ally dashed by his realization that he was temperamentally unsuited to the glad-handing and genial salesmanship of political organizing. Johnny actually mounted a quixotic campaign for a seat on the Fairbanks North Star Borough school board, running on a platform of free sex and drugs for students. He got 1,598 votes out of some 8,700 cast. Undeterred—or perhaps the word is emboldened—he aimed higher and announced a bid for President of the United States.

It's hard to know how seriously Johnny took any of these antics. Was there a method in what would seem to be a prolonged chapter of sopho-moric acting-out? Some bit of calculation in turning his life into Dada theater or a piece of drug-addled anti-Establishment performance art? Was he expressing hostility toward his father in the grotesque caricatures of Guy's traits and interests? Or was it all innocent, son-father modeling run amok—a case, perhaps, of "Johnny picking up Guy's football and running it right through the end zone," as Brad Snyder put it. In the last period of his life, people viewed Johnny's behavior as certifiable madness.

Guy had seized his own independence as quickly as both Bill and Johnny had seized theirs, but his initiative gave him the responsibility of a family, not freedom—it saddled him with obligations neither he nor his parents could ignore. The result was that Hawee and Mary helped him set up house and find money for his education, and got him on his feet. Where Guy had sons, his sons had only freedom, and nothing but freedom. Johnny, as his cousin Alice Reed Morrison suggests, was too smart to be written off as a weirdo goofball, despite his efforts to seem like one. It's hard not to see his antics as an extreme response to loneliness and the stress of the risks he was taking, and to wonder if there wasn't some pathology at work in his relation to nature. No one took the challenge of mountains more seriously than Guy Waterman's son. Climbing was his lifeline out of loneliness and adolescent confusion. It gave him focus, purpose, and prestige. In time it became the preoccupation that set him apart. And when many of his teachers and partners were killed in the mountains, climbing taught him existential lessons most people don't grapple with until late in middle age. In *Breaking Point,* the climber and journalist Glenn Randall listed the mentors, friends, and partners who, as Johnny would say with the hallmark bravado of the subculture, had gotten "the chop":

> Dave Seidman, the first person to tie him into a rope, had died in an avalanche on Dhaulagiri. Boyd Everett, who had introduced him to ice climbing on New Hampshire's Mt. Washington, had died in the same avalanche. Chuck Loucks, his partner on many early climbs in the Shawangunks, the Alps and the Canadian Rockies, had died falling off an easy climb in the Tetons. Neils Anderson, a partner on the first ascent of Huntington's east ridge, had died on the tourist route on the Matterhorn. Rocky Keeler, another Huntington partner, had died in Scotland. Warren Blesser, who had climbed with Waterman in the Canadian Rockies, had gone down with Neils. Ed Nester, who had climbed McKinley with Waterman when Waterman was sixteen, had died when his rappel anchor failed in the Selkirks. Lief Patterson, another Canadian Rockies partner, had died in an avalanche.

In the end, for Johnny Waterman climbing was the cause of as much loneliness and suffering as it cured, and the death toll of his pals and partners betrayed the wintry inhumanity in Byron's line: "Where rose mountains, there to him were friends." Johnny took that Romantic sentiment literally, to the point where the most unfriendly and unforgiving landscapes of nature seemed if not benevolent at least sympathetically alive, animate presences with whom he might commune. Climbing had become his way of being—of dreaming, grieving, and redeeming. But this was in the final chapter of his life, when his mountain genius was unraveling in destructive obsessions and he was lost with no rope to belay him back or cairn to guide him on. Perhaps we can see further into the storm if we go back to when he was still a kid—when the world was all before him.

May 1970. Johnny Waterman is seventeen years old. Emancipated from high school and headed for his first meeting with the mountain he would come to call his "nemesis." Fresh off Denali the year before, he'd bumped into a Harvard medical student, Dean Rau, whom he knew from the Gunks. Seven years his senior, Rau had just been rebuffed by Mt. Hunter, the 14,573-foot peak south of Denali. Hunter's massive summit plateau is a mile lower than Denali, the roof of the continent, but Hunter's steep flanks present many difficult climbs. The mountain, known to the Athapaskan Indians as Begguya, Denali's Child, has been called the hardest 14,000-foot peak in North America. Waterman had caught a ride with Rau down the Alaska–Canada Highway, and by the time they were back to the East Coast, he had shared his obsession with Hunter and was eager to join the second attempt Dean was planning for the next summer.

The team tackling the mountain in 1970 also included Paul Harrison and Duane Soper. Soper gave Johnny a ride up to Alaska in his Peugeot. On the way west, they stopped in Minneapolis at Soper's parents' house and made snow pickets and the snow anchors known as "dead men." They wangled some freeze-dried food from the Outward Bound program. They arrived in Alaska in June. After waiting nine days in Talkeetna for the weather to clear, the Alaska bush pilot Don Sheldon flew them into the Tokositna Glacier, near the south face of Hunter. The route called for them to work their way up through two ice falls to a col on the mountain's south ridge where the hard climbing would begin. It took a week to get their supplies to the col. They dug a large snow cave, only to see a thundering avalanche stop just short of it. The weather went to hell. They camped for fifteen days at the ice cave with only three or four days of good climbing. Rau later estimated they received twenty-three feet of snow. When they could climb, Johnny did the bulk of the leading. They got about 1,500 feet up the ridge, but turned back in the face of storms, equipment shortages, and the daunting prospects of the Happy Cowboy Pinnacle. Glenn Randall, who climbed it with two friends ten years later, described the pinnacle as a "nightmarish" ice tower that looked "like something conceived by Salvador Dalí" with its "razor sharp edges capped by snow as unstable as a house of cards."

As Waterman and the other three climbers retreated to the col, another blizzard hit. The snow fell so heavily they had to shovel in shifts all night to keep from being buried alive.

"We got rat-fucked," Johnny said later of the climb. But Hunter had set its hook in him, and he found himself brooding about the peak, eager to return. He moved to Camden, New Jersey, that winter and worked at a salvage company, saving money for the summer of 1971, when he took off to travel and climb in Europe. It was Guy Waterman, "dear-ol-Dad," who headed for Hunter that summer, on his maiden encounter with Alaska and the staggering wilderness of the Alaska Range. From abroad, Johnny confided his concerns for his father in a tender letter to Brad Snyder. Beneath the flashes of jocular competition lay the fear Guy might end up like Johnny's mentor, Boyd Everett, obliterated in an avalanche on Dhaulagiri. Eighteen now, Johnny had enough perspective to marvel at the swelled head he would have had had he succeeded on Hunter the year before:

I don't take [failing on] Hunter as a bad thing. God! Think if we had made it, a seventeen-year-old pioneering a major route in Alaska, God, then I'd really be fucked up. As it is it is hard enough to be humble, though I try to keep it in sight. It would be quite something if Dad did get up ol' Hunter. But God, look at his insane winter antics in the [Franconias]. Can there be any doubt which of the two of us is more of a tiger? Dad's really OK. I don't think I want his life but I have the utmost love and respect for him. And then I'll be busy enough having my life. . . . It isn't the technical problems that will get [their party]. Never is. The route will either be too flagrantly, blatantly impossible or it will probably be within their grasp. Still, technical things seem to be more difficult and freak people out in that environment (not so much for me). But that part is psychological. Then of course there is avalanche danger and personal conflicts . . . I hope dear-ol-Dad is wary. I'm not sure how much Eddy [trip leader Ed Nester] or anybody can judge this. The wall did not appear to show any feasible routes to me when we were there. But then I wasn't looking. I just hope they note the [avalanche] activity before getting into it, but with their limited time they will probably want to rush into it. The time is the biggest thing against them. I just hope they will be sensible. I should imagine they'll do something of worth whatever and Dad will fall in love with the place. I hope the [north] face [of Hunter] isn't too much of a shock. You have to build up to those things. I know every year my ability increases with experience. Make sure Dad knows about the danger. I wouldn't dig a Dhaulagiri scene for someone I love. Boyd hurts enough.

Dad came through unscathed. Concerned as he was for Guy, Johnny had worries of his own. It was burning at him that he'd never kissed a girl, much less found someone with whom he could shed his virginity. At the start of the year, he had confided to Brad Snyder that "there might be something wrong with me mentally" and said that he was going to see a psychiatrist. "Lately it's become much more notable to me how uptight I am and how much trouble I have just relating to other people on even the simplest of levels. I find myself thinking twice and worrying about everything I do." He wished he didn't care so much what other people thought of him. He wished he didn't have so many anxieties about climbing.

I'm afraid if I continue to climb at such a high degree of intensity I won't live a year more. I'll either fall somewhere or "flip out," either of which will result in the removal of myself from this earth (death). I think things out very carefully and am not likely to do anything very hastily, but once I make up my mind I'm sure to follow it through. As things stand now I'm still only living for climbing, and if it continues at its same level of intensity, I'll soon realize how little I'm living for. I'm not disillusioned with climbing, just climbing only. Lately I've been thinking of myself as a climbing machine with a very small and suppressed human element in my brain. It craves expression but the rest of me shuts it out as if I should know better than to try to be human. I've been thinking about it too much for my mental health.

There was his father's fingerprint: *I think things out very carefully and am not likely to do anything very hastily, but once I make up my mind I'm sure to follow it through* . . . Later in the month, Johnny dashed off another letter to Snyder:

I get so depressed these days that I really wonder. There's always hope unless you give up hope. Sometimes I think I'm not so far from giving up hope. On the other hand, what if I have a climbing accident and perish, I imagine all my worries will be ended, but man what a waste. . . . Mostly I think my suicidal thoughts are really attention-getting devices. Sometimes I wonder, at any rate. I've started seeing a psychiatrist. I've been once (one hour, thirty-five dollars). I'll go a few times (four at most) and then have to decide if there's any point in it because then I will have to figure out where the money is coming from.

Dad said he'd be more than happy to help but is also appalled by the cost. I don't see how it could do anything constructive. I've got to want to change and I don't really want to. I just want a girl-friend.

In Scotland that summer, Johnny traveled up to the Hebrides to see Barra, where his paternal grandmother's family had come from. He was very moved by the beauty of the place and the harmony of "man blending in so well with nature." It was a great lark of a summer for him. He got all the way to Turkey, then came back through the Dauphiné Alps, in southern France; he camped in the Bois de Boulogne, in Paris, went up to London, and finally returned to the States in late August. He and Guy climbed in the Gunks together, doing all sorts of "nice routes." Then with his brother Jim he did "some hard routes." Sorry, Dad. He visited with his mother, and then went up to Cannon, where he soloed a White Mountain test piece, V.M.C. Direct, and climbed the classic Whitney-Gilman Ridge with Guy's new girlfriend, Laura.

Laura is a very fine climber [Johnny reported]. "I've noticed with women that they are very trusting. To use a case in point, I don't think I could talk you [Brad] into trying a move you didn't think you could do already (at least not without a lot of hysterics), whereas it seems Laura would just follow instructions through a hard move. Yeah, I think Laura's pretty nice, I could dig having a girlfriend like her. Hope Dad appreciates her.

Before heading out to Washington State to start his first semester of college, Johnny visited the Gunks again with his brother Jim. Jim led Retribution, but Johnny kept falling off it even though he'd led the route himself a few years earlier. He felt he was out of shape despite his months of climbing abroad. A crowd of spectators gathered on the carriage road at the base of the climb to watch the two brothers. Too ashamed to be lowered off, Johnny let his baby brother haul him over the crux. While he was happy for Jim—Guy reported in a letter that Johnny was "delighted" by his brother's success—Johnny told Brad Snyder that it "hurt me very badly to do the climb so poorly." And yet, he went on in the same letter:

> I've gotten pretty disgusted with the whole climbing scene. It seems like one big exercise in decadence that people should devote great amounts of time and money to such useless endeavors. It's pretty obvious to me that a major reason I dug climbing was that it boosted my ego greatly. And yet I despise the publicity, or need or desire for publicity, that I've shown in the past. Maybe it's my rather subdued masculinity that's trying to assert itself. Yeah, maybe I feel that climbing is a real he-man sport and that excelling in it makes up for the lack I feel elsewhere. Yes, elsewhere, when it comes to action, I'm pretty submissive and weak. It seems a pretty good joke on me that this great effort I go to to sublimate my great drive brings me no closer to females. Just leaves me pacified for a time.

That was the great thing about college: when Johnny finally got to Western Washington State University in the fall of 1971, it brought him closer to females. He signed up for classes in German, English, history, and art. And folk dancing. With a fizzy show of wit, he said of folk dancing: "In case all other means of communication break down, that will be my last hope." And then finally, in October, he conquered the sexual summit that had been tormenting him. The letter he wrote to Brad Snyder gives a wonderfully comic and uninhibited account that stands in frank contrast to the Victorian restraint with which his father narrated his own deflowering in a weedy lot in North Carolina in 1950.

"Well, it finally happened," Johnny said. "I'm sort of in love and no longer a virgin."

He had met the girl at the student center. She was on the heavy side but had a really pretty face. Unlike most of the girls he'd met, she was unpretentious, and she seemed sort of interested in him too. It was amazing how much they had in common. He liked geology; she liked geology.

He wanted to study archeology; she wanted to study anthropology. She was so easy to talk to. He mentioned Europe; she'd been there twice already, in high school. She played the clarinet. He came from a musical family! Crazy! Where did the time go? She had band practice. Okay. Well, wow! Okay. Bye! Then: damn! He forgot to get her name! He went to where the band practiced; she wasn't there. He asked around about the girl clarinetist. Nothing. He went to a boating class because she had mentioned something about boating. Nothing. He'd blown it. He wasn't interested in anyone else. Oh man, it was world's oldest plot, obstacles to love. He saw a girl who looked like her, but she didn't remember them having any conversation before. He stopped by the band room again on Monday. Crazy, she was there! They exchanged names. Cathy, John; John, Cathy. Nice to meet you, etc. She lived off campus. She gave him her phone number. Okay, great. He called all week. They talked. He saw her on campus. They decided to go out, to a coffeehouse in town. Toad Hall, a basement dive, famous for fresh bread and yogurt. Always a bunch of long-hairs playing bluegrass and folk stuff. They hang for a while. There's a dance back on campus. Maybe they'll go. They stop by Cathy's house to pick up a joint. She really likes classical music, she says, so they bag the dance.

"I can't believe what's happening," Johnny wrote to Brad Snyder.

Really sort of moved. Finally we start kissing and that's really unbelievable . . . Kissing's really fun. I could do it forever, and holding and being held. Unbelievable the notion that she didn't mind my hands going anywhere on her body. Anyway I certainly didn't believe she would actually want to sleep together. Wasn't exactly prepared for it psychologically. It's fun to think how much I used to masturbate and yet I wasn't exactly overwhelmed by the passion. (Understatement.) I had no trouble having a hard-on the whole evening, but I didn't feel any sense of Urgency. So I suggest to her in the rather unromantic words, "Would you care to ball?" and she would. She's a virgin, she says, and I say, "Crazy, so am I!" which didn't bother her too much. For a second I wonder if I'm going to have a problem having an ejaculation but then decide "Millions of men before me have done it, why should I, John Waterman, formerly known as Super Squirrel and able to lead the 5.9, have difficulty?" Anyway she puts on Beethoven's Ninth Symphony, which is sort of neat and we got to it . . . I hope I didn't disappoint her. Maybe you'd better send me some more books on it or maybe we'll just figure it out better. Can't believe how I could jerk off so much when I was younger but only be able to "come" one time. . . . So maybe I was a little disappointed with myself. But let me tell you, I wasn't disappointed with lying there with her afterwards. I can tell you I felt a lot calmer than I can remember feeling in a long time. Her only stipulation she says is that she be able to keep up her studies, but as far as I'm concerned she calls the shots. . . . I've pretty much convinced myself I'm in love with her so I'm satisfied just being with her anytime. I can't believe I would find another person who I would enjoy talking to so much. . . . She hasn't mentioned being in love with me though, and I don't think there's any danger of her becoming as attached to me as I am to her.

Attached for a while, at least. No route on a mountain, even for Super Squirrel, who could lead the 5.9, could be as tricky as the paths of the human heart. By the term's end, Super Squirrel and Cathy were on the outs. Bill's visit in the fall had left Johnny feeling guilty not only about his brother's leg but about his own financial dependence on their father, who at that time was still receiving a salary from General Electric. Guy sent Johnny some articles suggesting anybody with a Vietnam war draft lottery number over 140 might be in the clear; Johnny's was 178. Johnny was doing fingertip pull-ups on the walls of buildings around campus, trying to get in shape for a climbing trip in the Canadian Rockies over the Christmas holidays with the famous American mountaineer John Roskelly. He wrote to Brad Snyder, wondering if Brad had any old down parkas and mittens lying around. He was, he said, getting psyched for climbing again:

> I may be able to evolve a philosophy towards climbing based on not dying which would be very healthy (of course then poetic justice would be to have me die). Funny, always in the past I [felt] sorry for myself (on the theme of love usually) and in climbing had a reserved, hidden idea that perhaps I would get the chop and be relieved of the burden of working things out. But I don't think that was ever true. I enjoy living, eating, all aspects of life too much. In a gluttonous way my mind would never reconcile itself to death. And I was playing games with people because I think I at times gave people the impression that "things couldn't get any worse," which is full of shit as I think I was only after pity. Now that is something basic from my childhood, desire for pity, always feeling sorry for myself. I thought the only way I'd get a girl was if she felt sorry for me.

The impulse to pity himself, then disgust for the weakness of it: another dynamic he had in common with his father.

"Hell with that," he said, echoing Bill.

Roskelly canceled the winter climb on Mt. Edith Cavell, leaving Johnny to stew about the time he'd wasted and the hundred dollars it had cost him to meet his would-be partner in Spokane, Washington. But in the late spring, Johnny went out to climb in Yosemite and then continued up to Alaska, where he and four other climbers claimed a highly sought-after mountaineering prize: the east ridge of Mt. Huntington. Though only 12,240 feet, the fanglike horn of Huntington makes the mountain one of the most beautiful in North America, and the east ridge had long been considered a deadly route. (The well-known climber and writer David Roberts had described its hanging glaciers as "sprawling obscenely down the ridge" in his climbing classic *The Mountain of My Fear.*) Glenn Randall summarized the 1972 Huntington east ridge expedition in his profile of Waterman published in 1983 in *Climbing*:

After landing on the Ruth Glacier, the five-man team began packing loads toward the saddle between Huntington and the Rooster's Comb. Over the next several days, they pushed a route up to a high camp, 1,800 feet below the summit. John led the crux, a vertical wall of deep, unstable snow that led to an overhanging cornice. Hanging precariously by one arm, he chopped a hole through the cornice and crawled . . . onto easier terrain beyond. From their high camp, a fourteen-hour push took all five members to the summit.

It was the fifth of July. While Johnny's partners celebrated, Waterman stared off at Mt. Hunter, five miles to the west, where he had been defeated the year before.

Johnny made other significant ascents that same summer, climbing the north face of Mt. Robson, in the Canadian Rockies. He was making a name for himself in mountaineering circles, but as he wrote to his father from college: "As far as John-the-climber goes, I've already defined my lines. It's John-the-rest-of-the-time that needs to be found now."

He returned east for his father's wedding to Laura. Bill did not make the trip.

Despite Johnny's resolve to broaden his interests, his time was increasingly monopolized by planning alpine campaigns. In the summer of 1973, he returned to Hunter, again with Dean Rau but now joined by two much stronger climbers, Dave Carman and Don Black. Again they went up through the two ice falls on an arm of the Tokositna Glacier and set up base camp in the col. Rau was struck by the changes in Waterman since they'd climbed on Hunter three years before. "On the first trip he was still a little kid," Rau told me. "Now he'd muscled out and matured. He was very quick and very good. He was climbing as well as anyone in the country at the time, especially in alpine terrain. But he seemed to be getting increasingly—I wouldn't say sloppy or desperate—it was more that he seemed to be disregarding the dangers."

The boy who'd been inconsolable when his blocks toppled had begun to show signs of a volatile temperament that unnerved his partners. Pete

Metcalf, who'd done some of his first roped climbs with Guy and had been one of Johnny's students too, had seen Johnny explode in a stream of blood-curdling curses. "John was waving his arms, screaming—I thought something horrendous had happened. After a one-minute outburst he said, very calmly, 'Oh, I just put a little rip in my wind pants.'" As author Jon Waterman noted in the chapter devoted to Johnny in *In the Shadow of Denali*:

> While waiting to fly into the mountain, Waterman's companions watched him slam the hardware rack on the floor as hard as he could, or rage at some passing frustration, swearing and scream- ing like Ahab. On the mountain, Johnny often sang strange dit- ties to himself. Although he became the driving force behind the climb, he was also fast to a fault. At one point Johnny did a sloppy job of hammering in a snow picket. When he started rappelling, the picket pulled out, and unbeknownst to him, Carman held the rope until Johnny reached the ledge.

Rau had been startled when Waterman told him in Talkeetna before the climb, "The only thing that matters is getting to the top." Rau had just finished medical school and had a nine-thousand-dollars-a-year intern- ship awaiting him in the fall in Minnesota; he found he wasn't nearly as ambitious as he'd been in 1970. Waterman, Carman, and Black pressed ahead without him. After three weeks of climbing, the three men reached, in a howling storm, what they believed was the south summit of the moun- tain. An apparent triumph, but when they returned to Talkeetna and con- sulted aerial photographs, Johnny was horrified to discover they had only topped out on a subsidiary summit. Hunter's true summit was another point farther along the ridge and two hundred feet higher. They had sur- mounted all the serious difficulties, and only the prissiest nitpicker would deny them credit for the new route, but Waterman burst into tears, the whole ascent suddenly a failure in his view. "He was very upset," Rau re- called. "But Don Black said they couldn't have gone any farther. Johnny said, 'You can *always* keep going.'" Rau could see the fixation taking hold as Waterman stood by the Susitna River back in Talkeetna. "I think when he realized he had not reached the summit is when he decided to climb Hunter's central buttress alone."

Salt in the wound was Johnny's discovery that he didn't have enough money to cover his share of bush pilot Don Sheldon's unexpectedly large bill. And then, a letter he was counting on to bring with it a check arrived instead with a bill for some furniture he'd damaged renting a friend's cabin.

Johnny moved to Fairbanks in 1974 and enrolled for the spring term at the University of Alaska. He had a work-study job at the university. Home was a thirty-foot trailer near the campus. He kept the place neat and well organized, and papered the walls with climbing photos. He was settling in, but some of his new friends were struck by the air of neediness about him, his propensity for compulsive disclosure and his almost spastic lack of social grace. "His soul was so bare, he'd confide in anyone he was talking to," recalled his friend and fellow climber Carl Tobin. "If he had an inner thought, he'd tell me. At James Brady's place once, he met my girlfriend, and he licked her shoulder. He'd do stuff like that a lot—why, I don't know."

Perhaps one clue to the gauche overtures and raw confessions was Johnny's dimming hope of being reunited with his brother Bill. It was now well more than six months since Johnny or anyone else had heard from Bill. "His brother's disappearance bothered him," Tobin recalled. "He brought it up initially when I met him. He related it in the context of all the climbing partners he had that had died. They all weighed on him—he had a long list of dead acquaintances and friends. He also had a problem with his dad. You could tell from the way he referred to his dad in passing—the tone and coldness in his voice. I thought it had to do with climbing, but he didn't talk about it."

It's possible Johnny was bridling at the pressure implicit in Guy's attachment to his son's prestige as a climbing prodigy. It's also possible the frost Tobin detected in Johnny's voice had to do with Guy's seeming lack of concern as to the whereabouts of Bill, an apparent indifference that could well have skewered Johnny with some sharp truths about the limits of his father's kinship and thus deepened the isolation he was already feeling so keenly.

In June of that year Johnny went back east to Washington, D.C., for his mother's marriage to her second husband, Richard Stimson. "He called us from the airport to come pick him up," recalled his cousin Jean Cooley. "I went with my brother Brian. Johnny had his skis with him. He was talking a mile a minute. We passed two girls on Wisconsin Avenue and M Street, and he was furious with me because we wouldn't stop and give them a ride. He stayed two days. He'd done a semester at the University of Alaska, and it seemed as if he had discovered sex, drugs, and rock-and-roll all at once. He was obsessed with our grandfather Hawee. He was wearing one of Hawee's jackets. He kept asking, 'Do you want to hear a song I wrote?'"

"Johnny was in our wedding," Richard Stimson recalled. "We had the reception at the Cosmos Club. He walked through a glass door. Sometimes his mind wasn't with him—he was probably on drugs. I got him a job sweeping up and doing dishes in Washington at a little bar where I ate lunch on Connecticut Avenue." He also made a five-day trip up to Barra at the end of the month to join the party of twenty-six friends Guy and Laura had gathered to help them frame the cabin's porch and woodshed. The "bash," as they called it, was made up mostly of climbing friends from the Gunks.

By the fall Johnny had returned to Alaska and was focused on music and school. He completed his sophomore course work and with the new year of 1975 started his junior term. He'd gotten engrossed in the Sturm und Drang Romanticism of Schiller's Wallenstein plays and found himself "becoming quite fond of tragedy." He had a job at the university's audio-visual department, which he had turned into an unofficial climbing clubhouse where local mountaineers gathered to look at slides and dream about routes. Johnny showed some of them how to cut teeth into their ice axes and change the droop of the picks so the tools could be used for more daring ascents. As he wrote to Brad Snyder in February:

I seem to have come through the darker phases of my "identity crisis." I put it in quotes because it is a cliché, but it is actually quite a valid phrase and really hits upon a true state (to my life) or else a number of years of my suffering had been for nothing. Climbing (the mountains, *die Natur*) does survive as my strong point (and I think our future does lie in our strengths). I am now skiing eight miles a day fairly regularly in and out to school and living in a nice cabin with a room-and-board arrangement—it's almost like having a home.

But the joys of books and the blandishments of a homelike arrangement could not compete with mountains and the epic ascent taking shape in his mind. Johnny planned to do some climbing in the Lower Forty-eight in July and August and then thought he might head east to visit his family and hike some of the familiar peaks in the White Mountains. "God willing, maybe Bill would be there, too," he told Brad Snyder. It was now two years since anyone had heard from Bill. About a year after his last correspondence, Emily had filed a missing-persons report. Johnny had also been looking for Bill. "Nobody knew what had happened to him," Jean Cooley recalled. "There was a rumor of a blonde-haired kid living with some Athapaskan Indians and calling himself Billy Jack. But that was it."

Bill, of course, never turned up that summer. And Johnny never got back east. Halfway through his fall term at the university, he dropped out. "Dad's loaned me a large amount [of money] which I no longer need," he noted in a letter to Brad Snyder. He had found a job working as a laborer for Alyeska, the consortium of oil companies then in the midst of building the trans-Alaska pipeline from Prudhoe Bay to the port of Valdez. He was daydreaming about joining the Peace Corps and climbing in Nepal, and wondering how he might capitalize on his talents as a mountaineer. Write a book, perhaps? "Do you know anything about book writing?" he asked Brad Snyder. "I'd like to do one in the style of *Mountain of My Fear,* next summer maybe."

Idle fancies, for the most part. More and more, Johnny's energy was

organizing itself around the vision of his nemesis, Mt. Hunter, and particularly around the central buttress of the south face, or what has come to
be called Hunter's southeast spur. He had glimpsed its rock headwalls
and long arêtes of snow and ice on his two previous climbs. The 1970 and
1973 expeditions had gained elevation by ascending two icefalls on the
Tokositna Glacier, but the more dramatic and natural line up the south
face began below the second icefall, to the east, where the buttress rose.
The route eventually rejoined the upper portion of the south ridge at
around 12,700 feet, airy ground Waterman knew from his 1973 ascent. If
he got up the buttress, he planned to traverse from the south peak across
Hunter's massive summit plateau (two miles long by half a mile wide),
climb the middle and north peaks, and descend by way of Hunter's north
ridge, which fell back to the main body of the Tokositna Glacier (and entailed plenty of difficulties of its own). Suffice to say, the route was long,
audacious, and terrifyingly hard. Writing about it in *Climbing* magazine
five years later, Glenn Randall described some of the obstacles on the way
up: "Cornices as airy as meringue jutted over voids a mile deep. The vertical ice walls were as crumbly as a bucket of ice cubes half-thawed then
refrozen. They led to ridges so narrow and so steep on both sides that
straddling was the easiest solution." Not only had the central buttress
never been climbed, it had never been seriously attempted other than a
halfhearted try in July 1977 by a party whose members didn't get more
than a few pitches off the glacier. To make the stakes supremely exacting,
Waterman was proposing to do the whole thing alone, solo.

In a log he kept of his experience on Hunter, Waterman marked June
1975 as the start of preparations for a climb he did not actually begin until March 1978. Hewing to his father's principle of "plan[ning] all activities in detail and well in advance," he trained all through 1976 and 1977.
He would go on long runs wearing crampons on his mountaineering
boots. One of his techniques for acclimating himself to cold temperatures
was the flesh-mortifying practice of bathing in an ice-filled tub; he was
once evicted from a motel in Talkeetna when the owner caught him hauling endless buckets of ice to his room.

During his period of intense preparation for Hunter, Johnny made a trip east to visit Guy and Laura, in mid-June of 1976, the first trip since he'd stopped by in 1974. He stayed for two days. Laura remembered him doing a one-armed cartwheel holding his guitar in his free hand. While Guy and Johnny were to stay in touch through letters, Johnny's visit that year was the last time father and son ever saw each other. It proved to be a grim year for Johnny. In August, his friend and mentor Chuck Loucks died in a fall in the Tetons. In December, his friend Lief Patterson was killed with his twelve-year-old son in an avalanche. "Kind of 'hilarious,'" Johnny said ironically to Brad Snyder in a letter dated January 1977,

> as part of the cause of [my] falling out [with Lief] was my interpretation of climbing as rather a desperately tragic affair. Oh well. It doesn't feel good to win that argument. Maybe he agreed with me anyway. Maybe I, or you, or anyone for that matter, will join them soon. Chuck [Loucks] got very upset with me once for the same reason. I don't have a death wish, but I am trying to be realistic.

He enclosed a greeting card he hoped Brad would mail him when he was done with Hunter: "Glad your operation's over!" it said. He told Snyder he'd gotten fired from his job at Alyeska. "The union is reluctant to support me as I pose nude on the snow at twenty below and write Congressmen on company (idle) time." He had been buying and gathering gear and supplies, and through the courtesy of Roberta Sheldon, was storing them in the Talkeetna Air Service hangar. He had 14,000 feet of polypropylene rope. He had ten Optimus stoves. A dozen Kelty packs. A bathroom scale to monitor the weight of his loads. He estimated that he needed to find three months' work in order to raise the rest of the money for the expedition. The projected total cost was fifteen thousand dollars— three thousand of which had come from his father, money Guy apparently thought should be used for school, not climbing. "Dad and I have had a bit of a disturbance over his giving me what remaining college money he has for me," he told Snyder. "Okay by me once I have it. (And I'll be happy to go over that in detail at some later date—it seems the only kind of help I get there is reluctant.)"

The same letter also contained a sardonic aside that was fast becoming the leitmotif in Johnny's song of experience. "I am enjoying life all the more for the fact that I realize imminent death is an integral part of *all life*. Therefore I watch TV a lot and listen to my hundred tapes of music almost continuously. Really recommend TV to lonely people. Jolly good to see heroes like Kirk Douglas dangling on a dam that is about to explode."

"He was fascinated with what it would be like to die," his friend Lance Leslie told Glenn Randall. "He expected to die on one of his climbs."

Years later, Guy dug up a letter Johnny had written to him in 1976 after learning from his father that Chuck Loucks had been killed climbing. (Loucks had also been a friend of Guy Waterman's.) "What can I say?" Johnny wrote. "Your letter said it all. Last person in the world I expected to live longer than . . . The thing forever removes all legitimacy from climbing to me, but will bring us all closer together, I think. Yes, it would have been good to mourn together—I've never been so touched, except maybe by Bill."

By late March of 1978, John Waterman was ready to go.

"I won't be seeing you again," he told his bush pilot, Cliff Hudson.

"You'll be back," Hudson promised.

And so began an ascent of which the noted American mountaineer Jeff Lowe once wrote, "There is nothing else in the history of mountaineering with which to compare it." One of the paradoxes of John Waterman's solo climb and traverse of Mt. Hunter in 1978 is that he was noted for moving boldly and quickly in the mountains—for ascents in what are called "alpine style." On Hunter, however, he chose the tactics of the so-called "expedition style" perfected by European climbers in their assaults on the 8,000-meter Himalayan peaks. Expedition tactics entail moving tons of gear with armies of porters who ferry loads up to a series of successively higher camps in support of teammates in the vanguard who make the final push to the summit. Waterman was his own army. Bathroom scale and all, he hauled his huge eight-hundred-pound base camp with him in repeated sorties up pitches that first he soloed, and then fixed with anchors and ropes that he could rappel down and then re-ascend with clip-on metal ratchets called Jumars. In effect, he climbed the central buttress a dozen times or more. He had 3,600 feet of rope and seventy-four bags, each containing five thousand calories of food. As the days went by, he would eat his way through much of this enormous burden of food and it would not be necessary to make as many repeat trips higher on the mountain. He kept a journal in which he noted the weather, the amount of fixed roped he placed, and the number of loads he carried, and in which he provided terse summaries of the day's highlights.

March 24: Lost a contact lens and probably further damaged my frost-bitten fingers of a month ago.
April 12: Read and sang verses from the Bible.
April 24: Cried bitterly.

As the days went by, Waterman railed at the endless wind. He wrote poems. He dug out from under blizzards. He repaired a rip in his wind parka with dental floss. He taped his fingers to keep from biting his nails. When a snow picket pulled out during a rappel, he was lucky not to die. To thaw out his ice-clogged Jumars, he sometimes had to blow on them till he was light-headed, and when that didn't work, he flailed at the ascenders with his ice hammer, attacking the very gadget on which his life depended. In a letter he wrote after the climb, he told Brad Snyder that when he was hauling his bags up the steeper pitches on the ropes he'd fixed, "I would occasionally stop and scream for twenty minutes." He prayed. He wept. He scratched himself savagely, discovering an infestation of body lice. "It was some comfort to know I was not alone," he noted drolly in an article he later wrote for the *American Alpine Journal*. His only connection to other people was a small AM radio and his citizens band radio, which he used to contact his bush pilot, Cliff Hudson, or other CB users who might get a message to him. On Mother's Day, via a third-party radio phone link, he was able to talk to his mother, Emily, in Washington. Father's Day came and went, but Guy at Barra was even more inaccessible than Johnny with a radio pinned to vertical ice in the Alaska Range.

> April 28: Wrote a song "Arbeit Macht Frei" comparing my Mt. Hunter climb to a concentration camp where inevitable death ensues. It summed up my dire thoughts.
>
> May 7: Noted I had the venereal condition known as crabs. Gouged myself in the leg trying to remove one of them.
>
> May 28: Jumars froze up on ropes today. Took up one load of pre-camp move items. Wrote "death" poem.

The names Johnny chose for his camps and for the rock and snow forms confronting him on the buttress reflected the enchanted, almost animate presence of the mountain in his mind, and his sense of himself as the protagonist in a saga: Valhalla, the Three Judges, Courts of the Lord, Little Prince. On his sixty-third day, he reached the juncture of buttress and ridge. He spotted ropes he and his teammates had left in 1973. He was running out of food and would not be able to be resupplied by airdrop until he reached Hunter's summit plateau.

> June 3: Worst winds yet. Three inches of snow and drifts. Dug out camp. Cried and prayed.
>
> June 6: Bad, windy. Marcus (AM Anchorage DJ) cut off his boss's tie. Crabs still present. Proposition 13 passed in California.
>
> June 7: Led the Happy Cowboy pitch. Cornice broke resulting in forty-foot fall.

By mid-June, past the hideous barrier of the Happy Cowboy, the going eased a bit. The high-summer nights were not dark enough for stars.

On day eighty-one, Waterman reached the blindingly white world of Hunter's summit plateau, where he could walk without having to claw the earth with his hands. It was no paradise, however. On June 26, it snowed six inches, Waterman nearly fell into a crevasse in a white-out, and in his log he noted: "Crampons came off boot three times, packing troubles, cried a lot." But in clear weather, Cliff Hudson was able to drop onto the plateau a fresh supply of food, including ten pounds of potatoes and a gallon of ice cream. At 1:50 P.M. on July 2, his hundred-and-first day on Hunter, Waterman went to the south peak and stood atop a wrinkle of the Earth that had haunted him since 1973. Then, tracing and retracing his steps, lugging his chattel into the endless winds, he moved across the plateau. He climbed the middle summit, and then went up Hunter's highest point, the north peak, on July 25. His CB radio broadcast from the summit was recorded by Roy Davies in Montana Creek.

"I'm standing alone on the summit of Mt. Hunter after a one-hundred-twenty-four-day climb of the central buttress. I'm a mighty tired man."

And then Waterman turned his attention to the north ridge and his exit. At the beginning of the climb, he had wept for fear he might die. But now, he noted in his log, he "cried at the thought of living."

Waterman spent an incredible 145 days on the climb, traverse and descent of Hunter. When Glenn Randall, Pete Metcalf, and Peter Athens repeated the route alpine-style two years later, in May 1980, they got up and down in thirteen days. They were pushed to what Randall called "the breaking point," and were hospitalized afterward with bad frostbite on their hands and feet. (Randall lost the tips of three fingers on his right hand.) Waterman's four months on Hunter were partly a function of his being alone, of having to do all the leading, all the ropework, all the packing, all the hauling, all the cooking, all the cleaning. When he fell, he had to extricate himself. When he wanted a photograph of himself, he had to set up the shot. (He was pleased enough with one photo to send it out later in the year as his Christmas card.)

But the time also reflected Johnny's desire to be alone on the mountain, to live amid the intensity of the place as one would live amid the intensity of a terminal illness. When he began to go down, it dawned on him that he might not die, and a song made popular by George Benson called "This Masquerade" began to haunt his thoughts.

That song [he told Glenn Randall in a telephone interview in 1981] seemed to say it all to me—the dual nature of what I was experiencing, this intense desire to live, and then this song, which suddenly had the influence of making me realize how sad it would be if I lived through the climb. Something far more precious would be lost if I lived through it than if I died. Living through it would mean that nature wasn't as raw as everybody wanted to believe it was, that man was far superior to the Arctic, far more capable than he had otherwise thought. Living through it would mean that Hunter wasn't the mountain I thought it was. It was a lot less.

Where his father had found uplifting and even "ennobling" elements in what a puny human being could achieve on a mountain—puniness redeemed, as it were—Johnny found only abnegation, and more subtle and complicated ways of perceiving the meaninglessness of his life. Where Guy had been humbled and yet somehow enlivened by blasting winter winds, Johnny had come away from his ultimate wilderness test with the vitiating conceit that because he was still alive, nature, mountains, even the elemental lethality of the Arctic, were overrated. It was not man that was puny, it was the universe. Here was the Byronic idealism of his father writ large: prolonged contact with the most sublime mountain landscape had only deepened Johnny's disillusionment; nature at its most savage could not compare to the wilderness of his soul with its drunk-on-oblivion logic and self-canceling superiority: *the only mountain I can truly respect is the one that denies me the glory of its summit and punishes me for the hubris of my aspiration.*

No doubt some of the disappointment Johnny felt about leaving Hunter—"discouraged about flying out" he noted on his last day on the ice in mid-August—reflected a strain of survivor's guilt as well. As Glenn Randall shrewdly observed, it didn't seem right that Johnny had lived when "all of his close friends, those who had taught him to climb and accompanied him on his greatest adventures, had died, often in senseless accidents. . . . It seemed perverse that he should be allowed to survive a solo ascent of a climb with far more inherent danger." In a sense, Johnny found himself in the untenable position of having to apologize to a jury of dead friends for not dying. His reasonable response was to belittle his own triumph. "My success on Hunter," he wrote to Brad Snyder, "was based on its having a worse reputation than it deserved, and my exploding the inaccuracy of that."

After the climb, Johnny borrowed twenty dollars from Cliff Hudson and returned to Fairbanks to resume a life that was in some ways much harder for him to negotiate than Hunter's icy arêtes. He got a job busing tables and washing dishes at the Switzerland Restaurant on Airport Road. (He had wept on Hunter because he'd been unable to renew his membership in a Fairbanks laborers union by CB radio.) He gave a slide show that fall at the university attended by upwards of two hundred people and then the next spring at a local climbing hangout known as the Sandvik House—both brilliant, funny, manic, self-disclosing performances that seared the memories of everyone who witnessed them. "We were all amazed," said Carl Tobin. But the shows did nothing to relieve his poverty or the larger estrangement of Johnny's life. He quit his job and by the end of 1978 was living on food stamps and unemployment and the generosity of friends.

To many people, Johnny wasn't the same after Hunter. Something had happened on the mountain. His friend the fisheries biologist James Brady said, "Johnny didn't feel the trip was a success." Johnny's mother, Emily, said it wasn't until after Hunter that Johnny seemed "strange." Guy wrote that Johnny's last years were filled with "achievement" and "mystique" but also with "madness"—madness "in the sixteenth century's usage of that term" he said, referring to when the word connoted extravagant folly and ungovernable rage. Lance Leslie told Jonathan Waterman that Johnny "was odd but little different [from] other climbers with his scruffy beard and down feathers clinging to his matted hair. But after Hunter he seemed almost dangerously psychotic." Dean Rau, the physician who had climbed with him on Hunter, said, "After Hunter, Johnny's eccentricities became mental illness." Even Johnny himself, in his last interview with Glenn Randall, acknowledged the existence of what he termed his "Mt. Hunter psychosis." He tried to explain it: "I get very upset if I think I'm going to be cold during the night I'm facing, if I think I'm going to be hungry in the next few hours. Even if I've got a lot of food and . . . a stove, if the food isn't ready to heat up and I haven't got it figured out so I can get it into my stomach real fast, I get very distraught."

Rau has always thought it was a shame Johnny's triumph was tarnished by the doubts about his mental stability. "He didn't get the full credit because people thought he was crazy," Rau said. The last time Rau saw Johnny was in September 1979. Johnny was collecting tickets at a kiddie ride at the state fairgrounds in Palmer, Alaska. "I just talked to him briefly," Rau said. "I told him I thought his climb was one of the hardest things ever done."

John Waterman is presumed to have died sometime on or after April Fools' Day 1981 while attempting to make the second winter ascent of North America's highest mountain. But there is less doubt about the doubt-shadowed facts of his death than about his state of mind at the end. Can the danger of the route he chose and the manner in which he launched himself upon it—alone and ill equipped—be taken to indicate an ill psyche bent on suicide? Where does self-dramatization leave off and true derangement begin? How does one gauge madness in a person who speaks lucidly about crazy ideas or subjects himself to extremes of danger in pursuit of an epic vision? Our culture is not so enamored now as it was three decades ago of the idea that schizophrenic behavior might be a sane reaction to the coercions of an insane society. But a school of thought does endure among some Fairbanks climbers that John Waterman was such a mountain genius he could not have died on Denali and that his odd behavior was simulated in service of his desire to disappear. In other words, the canny man might have faked his own death, and might well be alive somewhere right now, dropping psychotropics on a beach in Brazil or roistering with the yeti in Nepal. One of the most outspoken proponents of this view is Doug Buchanan, a Fairbanks climber who knew Johnny fairly well and who was one of the principals of the now-defunct John Waterman Memorial Auction. At the time of Waterman's disappearance, Buchanan helped organize a ground search in the area of Denali National Park where his friend was last seen.

"John Waterman was perfectly rational at the end of his life," Buchanan said when I spoke to him on the telephone in the winter of 2001. "He had discussed with an Anchorage attorney the ramifications of staging one's own disappearance. He once asked me to helicopter an old Buick body onto the South Buttress of Denali in order to distract the Park Service from what he was going to do."

Farfetched ideas are part of the magical realism of life on the last frontier, but in Doug Buchanan's defense, an Alaska magistrate in consultation with the National Park Service did wait six months after Waterman disappeared to hold a presumptive death hearing and issue a death certificate. The administrative procedure is typically scheduled within four to six weeks of when a climber is lost and presumed dead in the mountains of Denali National Park. The delay is both a tribute to Waterman's reputation for beating the odds and a testament to the fact that, even during his last days, he did not seem to be conspicuously out of touch with reality. Glenn Randall interviewed him over the telephone in Talkeetna on March 8, 1981, just three weeks before he disappeared. "The interview was long and rambling," Randall told me. "I probably asked half a dozen questions in sixty minutes and just let John talk. I believe he was borrowing a phone at some acquaintance's house. He didn't come across as outright crazy, but he certainly had very libertarian political views and was frank in discussing his use of recreational drugs. He didn't specify which drugs. In other words, he spoke coherently, in reasonably complete sentences, and didn't make completely bizarre, obviously untrue statements. He did have some very farfetched plans, as you know."

Were they poses? Well, probably. Very probably they were part of the Sturm und Drang show of the capes, the death poems, the born-again Christianity, the volcanic outbursts of emotion that left him shrieking obscenities into the wind, the vociferous talk-radio arguments on behalf of positions he didn't really believe in, the whole masquerade of self-dramatization, which was exacerbated by drug abuse and which perhaps climaxed in his bids for public office. It may speak more to the truth behind the masks of Waterman's melodrama to know that in 1979 he enrolled in a ballroom dancing class at the Tanana Valley community college. According to the university registrar, he was also auditing a course in disco dancing. What had he said about folk dancing at Western Washington State eight years earlier? *In case all other means of communication break down, that will be my last hope.* How much comedy ought we to wring from that now, knowing what end was looming?

The newspapers had not paid much attention to Johnny's 1979 campaign for a seat on the North Star Borough school board. His platform was not the conventional stuff of teacher-student ratios and standardized test scores. Instead, he advocated lifting restrictions on drugs and sex for students. Undeterred by defeat, he formed the "Feed the Starving Party" and announced a bid for President of the United States, which was otherwise shaping up as a two-man contest between Jimmy Carter and Ronald Reagan. As Waterman told Glenn Randall in his last interview, "My essential campaign priority was to ensure that nobody starved to death on the earth. I thought feeding the starving people of the world would be the most dramatic and difficult thing I could do."

Like all politicians, Johnny was looking to generate unpaid media exposure and hit upon the idea of returning to Denali, the mountain he had climbed ten years earlier, when he was sixteen. As with Hunter, he would climb it solo, but this time he would try for the top in the killing cold of winter. (The first winter ascent, recounted in Art Davidson's classic book *Minus 148,* had been made in 1967 by three members of an eight-man party; early in the climb, one of the climbers had died in a crevasse fall.) Waterman told Glenn Randall he would make his attempt hewing to a diet of flour, sugar, margarine, and protein powder, thereby demonstrating the immoral extravagance of American eating habits. On the face of it, the whole plan was rigged for disaster. Having identified cold and hunger as the triggers of his Mt. Hunter psychosis, Johnny designed a climb guaranteed to precipitate it. He flew in to the Kahiltna Glacier with a load of supplies on December 20, 1979. The temperature was fifteen below zero. On New Year's Day, his bush pilot arrived with another load of supplies. Faced with the prospect of not seeing anyone for 135 days, Waterman capitulated. "Take me home," he said, "I don't want to die."

"I just plain cracked," he said two months later. "If I didn't make it to the top, or if I died, if I died three days, five days, or fifty days from the point my pilot flew out, nobody would know. It would be entirely a mystery. There is some kind of morbid pain involved with the fact that nobody will ever see you again."

He returned to Talkeetna in February, planning to attempt Denali again before the end of the winter. He was so low on money, according to Glenn Randall, he had only vegetable shortening and white bread for food. He was staying in a cabin with a friend, Bill Hale. Lance Leslie's former wife, Lori Leslie, recalled that the roommates were kicking around the idea of starting a radio talk show. They would be cohosts.

But Johnny was clearly preoccupied by his defeat on Denali, and by his own precarious state of mind. Just how rickety it was can be gauged from a remarkable interview he taped on February 20 with Joan Koponen, a Fairbanks homesteader who had known Johnny's father at the Shady Hill School. Johnny had once presented his Mt. Hunter slides to an awed gathering at the Koponen homestead. His hope now was that the interview would draw attention to the Denali bid and boost his presidential profile. While he comes across as focused and intense, Waterman's positions on legalized drug use and voting rights for fourteen-year-olds were, at best, marvelously impolitic.

Koponen nudged him onto the topic of his Denali climb.

"I have to do it now, because the winter is almost over," Johnny said. "If I could do it, and live through it, and be healthy, it would be the first time it had been done in what mountain climbers call good style . . . I'm very nervous about it. I never expect to come back from any of the climbs I go on, and I certainly don't expect to come back from this one, much as I would like to. It's kind of like a kamikaze mission."

Johnny confessed to Koponen he was upset because he had just spent a hundred dollars on a prostitute, and he had very little money. After ten expeditions, he was perplexed as to why mountain climbing, "the height of what a man can do," had never sparked the interest of women or resulted in him getting "laid in an erotic fashion."

"Do you think of [mountain climbing] in terms of a suicidal thing ever?" Koponen asked.

"I think frequently yes. I think maybe it's because I've always been suicidal, even as a young child. Or I had a bent toward suicide. Or maybe I just found growing up in our country a very unsatisfying, unhappy experience."

Waterman criticized his parents, but like so many other aspects of his character, his notions of personal responsibility seemed to be a parody of his father's views. Anyone tempted to dismiss Guy Waterman as a negligent father who failed to supervise his sons adequately might be more sympathetic hearing his son Johnny argue that the dictatorship of parental supervision should be overthrown and even very young children allowed to solve their problems on their own.

"My argument against the whole system," Waterman said, "is that if a person was encouraged to be responsible and to actually run his own life at a younger age, you would maybe eliminate a lot of problems. Like let's say, bedwetting—and I like to get personal—I had a problem bedwetting, and I don't think my parents arrived at any solution. I used to sit there and wet my bed and I used to feel happy about it, because it was a pleasant experience. And for my parents, it was a big disaster. . . . My parents couldn't find a good solution to that because they weren't the ones doing it. If I had been directed to be my own boss at that age, I might have found a solution years ahead of the one that my parents and I worked out."

"You feel that some of this feeling of antagonism against authority is because you resent your parents telling you what to do, or what not to do, when you were little?" asked Koponen.

"I even resent it now. My mother detests my mountain climbing. She thinks it's some kind of suicidal activity, and she never supports me on it. My father is the exact other hand. He is a mountain climber himself, he thinks it is all I should do. And yet due to the fact that he's not the authority, I'm the one who eventually turns into the authority, [and] it's really been a total mess-up to my mind. I'm encouraged to be a mountain climber, but I'm not encouraged in a way that can be productive for me. A lot of times my parents . . . have the best intentions, but because they are putting their system down on my system—because they are attempting to guide me and they don't see through my eyes or have my conscience, because they use their conscience on me—they don't really see what's happening."

Two days later, on the afternoon of February 22, fire engulfed Waterman's cabin in Talkeetna. No one was hurt. Waterman was over at the Three Rivers laundry, writing in his journal. But virtually everything he owned or cared about burned up. Sleeping bags, files, journals, "two and a half feet of poetry." A man who had compulsively documented the moment-to-moment particulars of his daily existence was suddenly severed from the record of his life. And as his roommate and prospective cohost blamed John for the fire, the friendship and the talk-show dream were in ashes, too.

"John went berserk," Glenn Randall wrote. "He stormed into [bush pilot Cliff] Hudson's house, seized the telephone, and called the state troopers to demand a ride to the Alaska Psychiatric Institute in Anchorage. They refused. Hudson recalled the policeman saying, 'You don't sound crazy.' Waterman shouted back, 'What do I have to do, kill a kid?'"

His reaction, he told Randall, was part of his "Hunter psychosis."

The next morning, pilot Jim Okonek flew Waterman from Talkeetna to Anchorage, and Johnny committed himself to the Alaska Psychiatric Institute.

"I went to visit him at API," Carl Tobin said. "He was sad that he was in there. It was a self-committal—he thought he was crazy—but it was really sad. He had a song he sang for me about his Denali climb when he was sixteen. From his room he could look at the window and see Denali."

At the time, Mike Young, one of the mountaineers who would bring Guy Waterman's body down from Lafayette twenty years later, was a fourth-year medical student serving an internship at a hospital in Sitka, Alaska. At Guy's request, he called one of the doctors who had evaluated Johnny at API.

"I probably spent ten or fifteen minutes on the phone with the treating physician," recalled Young, now a research physician at the University of Vermont. "He said that he thought Johnny was a fragile fellow who had significant psychological disease and was in an environment that would throw him even more out of balance. He said Johnny's case seemed like a classic presentation of manic depressive disorder mixed with schizophrenia. It was progressive, and the drugs and his environment made the problem worse. With schizo-affective disorders, people retreat from society, they lose their fluency."

Waterman told Glenn Randall that he left API after two weeks because he was convinced the doctors were conspiring to deny him his civil rights. He returned to Fairbanks and wrote his father, who passed on the news of Johnny's misfortune to Brad Snyder in a letter dated April 12, 1980:

Johnny finally wrote. After flying out from McKinley after two weeks, he was preparing to go in again for an alpine-style attempt when the cabin containing all his gear burned. He kind of hit bottom, committed himself to a psychiatric institute in Anchorage briefly, but is now back in Fairbanks, working for the Census temporarily and wondering what to do in the future.

He had less than a year to live.

"I remember seeing him in the summer of 1980 at a folk festival," recalled Kate Bull, who roomed for a time at the informal mountaineering hostel based at the Sandvik House and now is living in Australia and working on a doctorate in geology. "He would sing a song onstage with a guitar. It would be amusing for a while, but it would go on and on. He came in to my apartment once, and I remember being struck by how strange he was, how much he couldn't relate to women. He'd make all these lewd sexual innuendoes. He just seemed so conflicted. Lost. Desocialized. People who loved him were always supportive of him and accepted him as a character. He was very intelligent, but just disturbed. He knew dates. He knew names of who had climbed what. He retained huge amounts of information about songs and about climbing. Even when his subject matter was absurd, it was all very articulate and well argued. Nobody realized how far gone he was."

Toward the end, Guy described Johnny's correspondence home as "scarcely legible scrawls with a lot of anguish." In a letter to Jon Waterman, Guy said: "[Johnny] would send me long fictional fantasies, heavily laced with sex and obscenities, and often involving his death. One of the things he didn't send me, but which surfaced in his effects after his death, was a very controlled and *under*written (in contrast with the grotesquely *over*written fantasies he did send) short story describing tersely my receiving a telegram notifying me of his suicide."

Johnny reactivated plans to solo Denali the next winter. On December 11, 1980, he applied for a permit from the National Park Service, choosing "Lone Wolf" for his expedition name and listing his objective as climbing the mountain by the South Buttress. As if his original idea was not ambitious enough, he now intended to walk in to the mountain all the way from the tidewater of Cook Inlet. The sixty-mile approach up the valley of the Susitna River would itself be an epic adventure for many people. He began in February 1981, tottering under the burden of an enormous pack. Sometimes he plodded on the frozen concourse of the Susitna, sometimes on the road. After ten days he reached Talkeetna, and knocked on the door of the Talkeetna Motel. Lori Leslie, who cooked at the motel and knew Johnny pretty well, said he had broken through the river ice and was soaked to the bone. She gave him some coffee. In the kitchen he picked up a knife and asked how you would hold it if you wanted to murder someone. It was all part of Johnny's show, in Lori's view. When he was warm and done toying with the knife, he turned back to the wilderness. Up the valley of the Chulitna River, the Tokositna River, the Ruth River, and onto the ever-frozen ice of the Ruth Glacier, shuffling along on snowshoes. On the glacier, some park rangers thought later, his routes betrayed a suicidal disregard for the dangers of crevasses. Waterman reached 2,000 feet, and then turned around and retreated to Talkeetna because his one gas cookstove had malfunctioned.

All that preparation for nothing. Had he balked at some intention he was reluctant to carry out?

Johnny lingered in Talkeetna for a couple of weeks, trying to make arrangements for a possible trip to Mt. Everest. He mailed a difficult-to-read postcard to Robert Gerhard, the supervisor of mountaineering rangers at Denali National Park. The card contained the details of his projected itinerary on Denali and the provisions he had made: he would be hiking in with fourteen days of food and eighteen days of white gas on his back. He had a cache of food and gas waiting for him at 2,000 feet on the Ruth Glacier. He was planning an alpine-style attempt on Denali, hoping to reach the summit on March 20, whereupon he would descend either to the northwest, with seventy days' worth of food and fuel waiting for him at a cache on the Traleika Glacier, or to the southwest, where one hundred pounds of food awaited him at a depot on the Kahiltna Glacier.

And so, in the second week of March, Waterman left once more to meet the mountain. "I won't be seeing you again," he told Cliff Hudson when he said good-bye to the pilot in Talkeetna. The same melodramatic farewell he'd spoken three years earlier when he set off to solo Mt. Hunter.

"You'll be back," Hudson said again, but this time, as Glenn Randall noted, Hudson had doubts.

The Lone Wolf turned off the Anchorage–Fairbanks Highway at Mile 141 and shuffled toward the Ruth Glacier on snowshoes. He eventually made his way up into the amphitheater of the glacier, one of the most spectacular mountain settings in North America. But rather than following the itinerary he had outlined, he spent two weeks fussing over his equipment and socializing with various groups of climbers camped in the vicinity of the Sheldon Mountain House at about 6,000 feet. The Mountain House, an octagonal hut perched above the glacier along a stretch of ice where pilots can safely land ski planes, is a little human fingerprint on the alien immensity of towering stone and white-blue ice. It serves as a storage shed, shelter, and informal gathering spot for climbers and visitors making fly-in day trips to the Ruth.

Waterman contacted Hudson by radio and asked him to bring in some already packed boxes. When Hudson delivered the cartons to the Mountain House, Waterman returned a hand-sized citizens band radio he'd borrowed from his pilot.

"I won't be needing this anymore," he said.

In late March, fresh off an ascent of the north buttress of Rooster Comb, Jay Kerr and Keith Royster skied down the west fork of the Ruth to unwind for a few days near the Mountain House. They were camped with a couple of other climbers in their party. Around midday on March 31, they were sitting outside on chairs made of snow blocks and sleeping pads when they saw a skier coming up the glacier. He was wearing blue pants, a blue sixty-forty cotton-nylon jacket, and hauling a red plastic sled. More notably, he was traveling unroped and alone on a course that cut an alarmingly direct line through the huge crevasse fields close to the flanks of Mount Barrille, where the Ruth Gorge opens out into the vast Ruth amphitheater. The line was exposing the skier to hazards he could have easily circumvented by swinging wider around the mountain.

It was John Waterman. Royster knew him; Kerr had only heard of him.

"We had a long visit with him—about three hours," Kerr recalled. "He talked about how he'd hiked in from Anchorage, and then hiked out because his stove had malfunctioned. We asked him why he liked to go through crevasse fields, and he said every time he crossed a dangerous snow bridge and it didn't fall in, he felt reborn."

Kerr was struck by Waterman's odd kit. No tent. No sleeping bag. Waterman told Kerr the gear he was pulling on his sled included a bivouac sack, a heavy one-piece snowmobile suit, vapor barrier boots, snowshoes, and about twenty wands for marking trail. His provisions were more bizarre—fourteen days of sugar, powdered milk, honey, white flour, and a plastic bag of marijuana that was mixed with pet hair, wood chips, and lint. Waterman said he'd dropped the pot and had hastily swept it up and put it back in the plastic bag. He told Kerr he was heading for the East Buttress and a steep, ambitious route that began at 9,000 feet in the northwest fork of the Ruth Glacier and topped out at 15,000 feet at Thayer Basin. It was unclimbed at the time, and remains so to this day. "It's a suicide line, a lot of big avalanches come down it," Roger Robinson told me. "It would be like playing Russian roulette."

Waterman told Kerr and Royster that after he reached the summit of Denali he would descend via the well-trod Harper and Muldrow glaciers, exiting finally at Wonder Lake, on the north side of the Alaska Range. His reward for taking the hard way up would be a relatively straightforward way down, though, again, the risks of traveling on glaciers alone are always considerable.

The day before, Monday, March 30, Kate Bull had been flown onto the Ruth Glacier with a friend. They set up camp about twenty minutes by ski north of the Mountain House and just a little south of Kerr and Royster and their party. When Waterman saw Bull's plane land, he came down from his camp near the Mountain House to say hello. His face was heavily plastered with zinc oxide to keep his skin from cooking in the fierce radiance of the glacier. Bull knew Royster, and two days later, on Wednesday morning, April 1, she stopped by his camp for a visit. They brewed up a pot of tea and lolled on the snow-block chairs. It was another painfully brilliant day. Waterman came skiing up. He was squinting in the brightness, wearing neither sunglasses nor the zinc oxide he'd had on when Bull saw him Monday. He was dressed in his blue jacket and a funky wool hat. He carried an old orange frame pack, which looked oddly empty to Bull.

"What are you up to, John?" asked Kate, struck by the fact that Waterman wasn't wearing sunglasses or sunscreen.

"I'm going to climb the East Buttress," he said.

He sat down and had a cup of tea. He shared the joint that was being passed around.

"Jeeze, John you should really have some sunscreen on," Bull said.

"Really? Wow! Okay."

In the edition of *Alaskan Mountain* magazine devoted to John Waterman, Bull wrote, "When I asked him about [not wearing sunscreen or sunglasses] he questioned [me about] the symptoms of snow blindness as if he had never been exposed to the potential before."

Waterman lingered about half an hour, answering some of the questions the climbers put to him about his solo ascent of Hunter. At one point, he commented on the size of the group that morning.

"That's the way to do it, all right," he said. "It's fun to have a big camp with a bunch of people."

And then he got up, shouldered his half-filled pack, and headed up the glacier for the northwest fork of the Ruth.

Looking back on the scene, Kate Bull is at loss to recall why she didn't put two and two together. "I just wasn't clicking in on what John was saying," she recalled. "I wasn't thinking about what it would take to do the East Ridge. He hardly had any gear in his pack and he was going off to do this major climb? Hello! I can't explain why I was such a dingbat."

Later that day, Kerr and Royster headed back up the Ruth for the glacier's west fork. For a while they skied along in the tracks Waterman's skis had left in the snow. Twice they veered off the line for a safer course. And then after several miles, the tracks cut away to the right and angled up into the northwest fork toward an area notoriously riddled with crevasses. Kerr followed the line in the snow until there at the end, he could see a dot-sized figure making a beeline through white swells of ice: John Waterman in the thrall of being born anew.

He was never seen again.

On April 4, a party of climbing rangers who knew that Waterman was traveling solo tried to pick up his tracks in the northwest fork, but two days before it had snowed heavily and the winds had been strong. The rangers couldn't see any tracks. On April 7, a Colorado-based mountain guide named Mike Covington skied into the northwest fork with two clients intending to climb the Southeast Spur of Denali. "They noticed a single set of tracks that were either ski tracks or those left by someone pulling a sled," according to the National Park Service "incident report," which was published in the American Alpine Club's 1982 volume of *Accidents in North American Mountaineering*.

> Covington felt that the tracks only went up the glacier and did not come back down. They also seemed to be oriented more toward the East Buttress than toward the other routes on the Southeast Spur or up the northwest fork. Because the area was very windswept from a storm the previous week, it was very hard to distinguish the tracks and no campsite was seen. From interviews with other climbers in the area, it appears that Waterman was the only one to travel up the northwest fork prior to Covington's group.

Covington eventually gave up the climb he'd planned; in his judgment, the avalanche danger was too great.

On April 15, the National Park Service began a small-scale search for the Lone Wolf. U.S. Army Chinook helicopters from Fort Wainwright were practicing high-altitude landings on Denali; ranger Roger Robinson and another park service employee went along on the flights and searched the flanks of the mountain. When Jay Kerr returned to the Talkeetna ranger station with his report of his encounter with Waterman, a more extensive search was started.

On April 21, ranger Dave Buchanan, whose life had been changed by his week in the Watermans' winter mountaineering course, called the postmaster in East Corinth and requested a message be passed to Johnny's father to call the Denali National Park headquarters. Buchanan was there to take the call when Guy telephoned back. "Guy was very calm when I described the situation to him," Buchanan told me. "It almost felt like he had been expecting a call such as this. I'm sure when he got word of a phone message from a ranger in Alaska, he knew what it was probably about and had time to contemplate what was coming as he hiked into town from Barra. It was the hardest call I ever had to make as a ranger."

On April 22, ranger Roger Robinson and guide Mike Covington flew up the Ruth in a Bell helicopter. They spent three hours flying in the area of the East Buttress. The weather was good. In the northwest fork, they picked up the single set of tracks Covington had seen earlier.

"You could vaguely make them out," Robinson told me, "and if you projected the line, boom! There was the camp. It was right in the middle of a crevasse field. You could see the crevasses under the snow more clearly from the air than on the ground. We could see tracks going into the campsite, but none coming out."

The campsite was at 7,200 feet. The pilot landed the helicopter on the glacier near what seemed to be an old tent site in the middle of a heavily crevassed area. Robinson belayed Covington from the struts of the helicopter as the guide cautiously probed the ground. Within a rope length, Covington gingerly found three thinly bridged crevasses. Both men, roped together, moved carefully around the tent site and vicinity, peering into crevasses for a body or some sign of Waterman. The only evidence they turned up was some pale human feces. Robinson scooped a sample into a Ziploc bag. "We knew what Waterman's diet was and we thought if we might analyze it we would be able to say conclusively we'd found Waterman's last known camp," he recalled. But in the end, the proof seemed pointless, and for years the stool sample stayed in the freezer at the Talkeetna ranger station until finally somebody in government service got tired of looking at it.

The signal conclusion was that any lone wolf who happened to be padding through that treacherous honeycomb of snow-covered fissures would not likely have survived for long. A private party hoping to conduct a more conclusive search was gathered by the Alaskan Alpine Club. The famed aviator Lowell Thomas Jr. flew four mountaineers in for free. Nothing they found in four days of searching shed any more light on Waterman's fate. Around that time as well, Dean Rau flew into the area where his old climbing partner and Mt. Hunter compatriot was last seen. "It wasn't a search," Rau said to me, apologetically. "It was really just a gesture."

There were a lot of accidents on Denali the year John Mallon Waterman vanished, the majority of them attributable to the weather. The exceptionally fair conditions of April—mostly clear and dry—lasted through May, when climbers begin to pack the mountain in earnest, and then continued for most of June. But in July, the sky fell in. A party camped at 17,000 feet on the West Buttress reported six feet of snow in one day, all of it scoured off twenty-four hours later by one-hundred-mile-per-hour winds. A camp at 14,000 feet recorded nine feet of snow in two days. Three climbers from Japan were lost in a massive avalanche as they approached the American Direct route on Denali's South Face; a fourth Japanese climber died of pulmonary and cerebral edema.

But the two most haunting deaths happened earlier in the season, when the weather was good. In May, the famous American mountaineer Jim Wickwire and his young partner, Chris Kerrebrock, were hauling a sled up Peters Glacier, on the north side of Denali. Simultaneously, they broke through a snow bridge and plunged twenty-five feet into a crevasse. The sled tumbled in after them. Wickwire, then forty years old, fractured

his shoulder in the fall but with his one good arm was able to chip out pur-
chase for his crampon points in the granite-like ice and get himself out of
the crevasse. Kerrebrock, twenty-five, was wedged upside down, pinned
by his pack so tightly between the narrow walls he was unable to move.
He was conscious, however, and kept saying, "You've got to get me out,
Wick!" Wickwire vowed he would. Once he freed himself, Wickwire
anchored ropes to the surface of the glacier and Jumared back into the
fissure. He pulled and tugged and hauled on his partner. He tried to
cut Kerrebrock's pack open. He worked for hours. Nothing he did succeeded in even budging Kerrebrock from the vise-like grip of the ice.
In desperation, Wickwire tried to call for help, but the barrier of the
Alaska Range prevented him from raising anyone on the radio. Night
was coming on. The terrible truth was dawning that Kerrebrock would
probably freeze to death in front of him, a mere twenty-five feet below the
surface, in a narrow, unyielding coffin of ice, and neither man could do
anything to prevent it. Wickwire described the last moments in his 1998
book *Addicted to Danger*:

After asking me to relay messages to his family and closest
friends, Chris entreated me to help him die with dignity. However, I could think of no way to ease his suffering or speed his
death. I asked him whether he wanted his body left in the crevasse or brought out. He said his father could decide. At about
nine-thirty, six hours after we fell into the crevasse, Chris conceded, "There's nothing more you can do, Wick. You should go
up." I told him I loved him and said a tearful good-bye. As I began my ascent, Chris said simply, "Take care of yourself, Jim."
Back on the surface, physically spent, emotionally exhausted, and
racked with guilt, I pulled on a parka and collapsed into my half-
sleeping-bag and bivouac sack—an uninsulated nylon sack used
in emergencies for protection against the wind. Lying at the edge
of the crevasse, I listened to my friend grow delirious from the
searing cold. He talked to himself, moaned, and around eleven,

sang what sounded like a school song. At two A.M. I heard him
for the last time.

It is hard to imagine a more heart-wrenching death. And yet twenty-
five-year-old Chris Kerrebrock, who went to Denali with no intention of
dying, was not alone when his last hour approached. The month before,
to an imperfect but adequate degree of certainty, there had been a different sort of death—unmarked, unattended, unheard. One of the last letters
Guy Waterman had received from his son was a mimeographed appeal
for funds in which Johnny referred to himself as "the man who may truly
disappear into the wilderness, and come to be part of something greater
than himself." Was the fate of the Lone Wolf sealed, as his father was in-
clined to think, by avalanches pouring off the East Buttress? Was he en-
tombed somewhere in the ice near that perilous, scat-marked camp in the
northwest fork? It's pretty to think of him otherwise, as myth would have
it, at large in South America. Maybe he truly wanted to disappear, not as
some cliché expat in Buenos Aires but into that encrypted country beyond
the cairns where he would never have to wonder why he was alive, after
the risks he'd taken, while his friends with all their caution were dead.
Maybe he didn't want to die; maybe he just stopped caring whether he
lived. No one can say. No one was there to relay his last messages or to
hear what song he might have been singing at the end.

The boxes John Waterman cached at the Mountain House were flown
back to Talkeetna and inventoried by the Park Service on April 25. Among
the items: a first-aid kit, batteries, Blazo fuel, a snow saw, ropes, a camera
case, a sleeping bag, boots, climbing hardware, a roll of film that had been
exposed on March 30, and, strangely, as he wasn't carrying a gun, a bunch
of bullets—twelve for a .357 magnum and nine for a .38 special. Inventory
item number eight included a box on which Waterman had drawn a picture of a man on a mountain and scribbled the famous Alfred E. Neuman
quip from *Mad Magazine*: "What, me worry?"

There was another note, which has been mentioned by almost
everyone who has written about or brooded over John Waterman's life.

Indeed, something indelibly poetic about it suggests an epitaph and invites us to imagine that the mad rush of a man's life, the confounding passions John Waterman tried to capture in the science of his clipboards and the daring of his ascents—all the wind and the cold, all the wild lonely drama, the mock-genuine joy and torment of his few short years—might be summed up in one final flourish of graffiti on a cardboard box: "March 13, 1981, 1:42 P.M. My Last Kiss."

8.

KNOTS OF THE HEART

*

Thou'll break my heart, thou warbling bird,
That wantons thro' the flowering thorn!
Thou minds me o' departed joys
Departed never to return.

ROBERT BURNS,
The Banks o' Doon

As with a climb that didn't go, I keep revolving in my mind (and heart) where things took the direction they did, how things might have gone differently, what was going on inside, what kind of father I was, etc. The special quality to all this is the utter blank impossibility of calling it back and doing it again. That Jacobean ballad which I used to think was too plain to be moving, that goes "Will ye nae come back again?"—that now says so much. When I was first up on the Franconia Ridge this year and looked over the non-road side, at all those mountains and ridges with cloud shadows on them, I thought why was there not this to come back to? Was there nothing for him to come back to?

GUY WATERMAN, *letter to Dane Waterman, September 4, 1981*

I T IS NOT A QUESTION NOW of where a man's death begins but of the faith he keeps as he struggles against it or doesn't, and of how we, for our part, might arrange his woes to reflect the right proportion of pathology and soul. Plainly, something died in Guy Waterman when the breath went out of his sons, but with his religious list of principles, his garden walls, his willful creed and yearning to believe, he could dare hope otherwise—was helpless *not* to hope otherwise. "One of the secret things about Guy," said his older brother Alan, "is that for a long time he wouldn't believe either of his boys was dead."

Is this a trait or a symptom? If a trait, is it the virtue of faithful hope or the defect of self-delusion? Waterman's fate and his character inexorably converged in the nineteen years between Johnny's death and his own, but it is hard to say whether his fate was made in the crucible of his character or his character was swept away in the current of his fate. Here, the man steers through misfortune; there, misfortune bears him off like a doll in a flood. Sometimes when he sits on his mountain to let the snow make his shroud, he seems to be fulfilling his faith; other times, to be fleeing it.

It's not illogical to wonder if a man enamored of the "illusion of wilderness" might be more prone to cultivating illusions about his life than the next guy. While it's an axiom of our psychotherapeutic age that everyone lives in the thrall of illusion and that all perception is distorted in the fun-house mirror of subjectivity, it's also true that we recognize a realm of common experience far from the shrink's couch where reality does not appear so infernally hard to know. Precious epistemological headaches about the illusoriness of truth pale before the death of a child.

Even were he so disposed, what illusions could Guy Waterman cling to after April 1981? The double blow of the brutal news was the way Johnny's death must have compelled him to face the likelihood that Bill was dead as well. Any fantasies about happy endings and the inconsequence of dropped responsibilities must have collapsed under the weight of guilt and grief. Can a father ask a more heartrending question than what kind of father he has been? Or how things might have gone differently? Could any romanticism be more poignant than Waterman's faith in the power of a Franconia prospect to draw his sons home? Here, finally, precipitated by crisis, was what he must have really believed to be the value of wilderness—not that it might provide asphalt neurotics with a potentially ennobling set of physical tests but that it might shrive a father and make a shattered family whole. That it might wash away his sins and dispense the mercy of forgiveness. It is impossible to say whether the faith Waterman invested in that roadless country east of the peak he died upon stemmed from his thinking so much of the land or so little of himself. *Will ye nae come back again, if not for my love then for love of this cloud-shadowed earth we once roamed together?*

Cold comfort that country was now.

That summer, on a crowded sunny day, Guy took his son's old Limmer hiking boots up onto Franconia Ridge, and then dropped down off the main trail, heading for a dramatic bluff opposite the crescent of the Cannon cliffs and Johnny's route Consolation Prize. He could see the spot on his approach and was concerned that his activity there would attract attention. But out of the blue, a thick mist drifted over the ridge, and as he gathered rocks and began constructing a cairn, he worked in the perfect privacy of a cloud. It took him three hours to find the right stones and fit the cairn together. In the center, he placed Johnny's boots, pointing them toward Alaska as best he could gauge the direction. Atop the cairn he laid a bouquet of mountain flowers. He sang some songs and recited poems. And then he hiked out the way he'd come in. Strangely, when he'd regained the ridge and looked down at where he'd been, the mist withdrew. He could see Johnny's cairn in a ring of mountains.

Having one place to grieve did not mean grieving only in one place. Climbing at the Shawangunks in the wake of Johnny's death, Waterman found himself faltering on routes he'd done dozens of times. His nerve was failing. It wasn't the physical risk of leading but the emotional pain of standing on ledges where he'd belayed his sons. By the magic of his mind's eye they were boys again, and himself their boyish dad cinching the gold line around their spindly waists and watching proudly as they inched up Squiggles and Three Pines. At the piano, in the aftermath, he found he had no heart for music either, not even for the blues for which he was now profoundly qualified. He quit the occasional concerts he'd been giving, and stopped his practice of playing rags and old-time songs at Barra in the evenings as Laura fixed supper. He did not touch the Steinway for a year.

In his marriage, he lapsed into a more insidious kind of silence. Laura noticed it for the first time on a trip over the Labor Day weekend in 1981, a little more than four months after the news from Alaska. All summer she had seen Guy suffering. By summer's end he'd built three cairns at mountain spots pregnant with memories of his son. Johnny's upcoming birthday on September 17—he would have been twenty-nine—promised to be especially difficult. Would company do Guy good? They had always enjoyed the annual Labor Day trip to Lou Cornell's house near the Cannon cliffs. It was a chance to catch up with old climbing friends from the New York area, many of whom had known Johnny and hadn't seen Guy since his son's death.

So the Watermans went, staking their tent in Cornell's yard with an eye for the view of Franconia Ridge out the front flap. On Friday, September 4, Guy wrote an anguished, self-accusing letter to his nephew Dane in which he asked, "Was there nothing for him to come back to?" On Saturday, at Cannon, while Laura and a friend did Consolation Prize, Guy scrambled up Eagle Crag. He sat by a cairn he'd built in August in honor of a climb Johnny had pioneered on that outcropping of rock. When Guy returned that evening, Laura was struck by how upset he seemed and by the distance he kept from their friends. Later that night, in their tent, she woke up, frantic not to find Guy in the sleeping bag beside her. It turned out he had responded to a call to help a benighted group of climbers get down off the Cannon cliff. But when he returned, his answers to her questions were short, and he seemed a million miles away—unreachable, unsympathetic to her distress. She was confused and hurt—he had never shut her out so starkly before. She recalled something he had said at the outset of their partnership about how he always hurt the people he loved. And now, out of nowhere, a wall had come between them. And in all their remaining years together, it never went away.

The first three years after Johnny's death were the hardest. In time, Waterman's grief moderated, or seemed to. In time, Laura learned to work around his "black moods." She came to accept that a part of him—

the very core, it seemed to her—was off limits. She entreated him to confide in her, but if he could not, he could not. And *could not* is how it seemed at the time; the possibility he *would not* share his feelings was unthinkable then. What Laura came to know for certain over time was that she still loved him. So she loved him, living for the intimacies he could share, enduring the shadow of the ones he could not.

"Our marriage changed after Johnny died," she wrote in a letter to me. "I had to learn to live with that change. The thing that saved me was that I never stopped loving Guy. Why *was* that? I don't know. He was vulnerable and strong at the same time. I knew he needed me, though he never told me that. I needed him, too. We needed each other for entirely different reasons, I think."

At the end of 1981, during the week between Christmas and New Year's, the Watermans again assembled a group of instructors and students for the annual winter mountaineering course. Tents were pitched on the grounds of the White Mountain School, in Littleton, New Hampshire. Busy days of classes and instruction. Convivial nights with everyone eating supper in the cafeteria, all the wet gear spread out to dry on the hallway radiators. During the week, a couple of instructors received a visit from a friend: it was Kate Bull, one of the last to see John Waterman alive on the Ruth Glacier. She introduced herself to Guy in a stairwell. He took her aside. They sat together in a room for an hour as he questioned her closely about his son, and listened intently to her answers. At one point, he said: "You know I lost another son, too."

"Everything about both sons just flowed out of him," Bull recalled. "He wanted someone to share it with. You could see how much he was hurting, in his face and in his manner when we talked. Everything had been taken out of him. He felt at a total loss for what the reasoning was—why Johnny had done it, why Bill was gone."

During the square dance on New Year's Eve, with recorded music and a live caller, Laura could see Guy was just going through the motions, there in body, dancing, but preoccupied in mind by Kate's story. At midnight, when the room filled with the sweet strains of "Auld Lang Syne" and its lyric Scottish nostalgia for the "old long ago," Laura found Guy in a far corner of the room, sobbing into his hands. "He told me the emotion took him by surprise," she recalled. "It was like he was hit over the head by grief." Guy didn't want any of the students or other instructors to see him so discomposed, and he and Laura slipped quietly away to their tent.

Three weeks into the new year of 1982, Waterman drafted a letter to Kate Bull, addressing what the conversation had stirred up in him. It ran to five handwritten pages, and he waited nearly a week to mail it, perhaps deliberating whether to send it at all, as it was one of the most emotionally bare and moving things he ever wrote, fraught with loss and confusion, fraught with forlorn rationalizations and a father's need for forgiveness. He seemed at points to be defending what he himself would find indefensible were some pivotal conception of himself not at stake. Other than a handful of poems written late in his life, the letter to Kate Bull may be the only time Guy Waterman ever really tried to explain what kind of father he had been. It begins by addressing one of the questions Kate Bull had asked him—why had he never gone to look for Bill:

> I think the main reason I've never gone on that quest is because there has never been a specific point in time when I could say he's really gone. That is, his last letter—May 30, 1973—said he was going on a trip, it wasn't Alaska, and he'd be in touch when he got back. For two to three years, then, I assumed he was off on an adventure. I confidently expected that one night there'd be a knock on our cabin door, and there'd be Bill with a big grin. He always liked to be a little mysterious and to surprise people by showing up unexpectedly.
>
> There followed a few more years when I began to wonder where he might have gone to. One of the last people to see him in Alaska in 1973, Barbara Belmont, told me she guessed he had gone to live in an Indian village and had been swallowed up in their culture. Finally, in the past two years and especially since Johnny's death, I have . . . come to the conclusion that the chances are slim that Bill's still alive. Not hopeless, but not much hope.

So one reason I never took off to look for him was there was never a single point at which I could say, "Now I've got to go see."

Another reason has been the selfish one that our life here is very ordered, and geared to not spending money, and very inter-dependent as between Laura and me. So there is no chunk of time that I could easily take off and go to Alaska, or wherever the trail (if any) might lead; nor do we have the money to spare for a long travel; nor are our lives set up so Laura could live easily without me for a period of weeks (nor I without her). All these things seem selfish and perhaps unimportant compared with see-ing Bill again, but in combination with other constraints, they are a practical reality.

Mainly though, it comes down to this: either Bill is dead or he is living somewhere quite deliberately not making himself known to me (nor to anyone else of his earlier life, as far as I know). If the former, it's probably unlikely I could tie down the circumstances, much as I'd like to. If the latter, then he would not want me to find him. If I were to show up and he was not happy to see me, it would break my heart. If he is alive and happy some-where or at least content, he must prefer not to be in touch.

Does all this, especially the last point, make sense?

Waterman goes on to confide that he sometimes thinks he would like to make a trip to Alaska so he could fly into the Ruth Glacier and see where Johnny last was. And to this pilgrimage perhaps he could add the task of looking for Bill:

By the time I might do this—if ever—any trail leading to Bill would long be dead I suppose, but there might be a chance. Bill is important to me now. I sense that my youngest son Jim has no de-sire to be in touch with me, and he may have good reasons. I think you know how important Johnny was to me. Even if we had drifted apart in the past five or ten years, nothing can ever extinguish the many years before that. Never did a father or son mean more to each other, I'm convinced. So you know what it would mean if that knock on the cabin door ever did come and there was Bill. There were evenings last summer here at our cabin, the day's work done, when I would stand at dusk and strain my eyes up the wood road that leads to our place, hoping to see a slightly limping form come down through the twilight and the years—before all went completely dark.

And finally, he concludes, apologizing for speaking so personally:

Well, I appreciate your raising that question so I can think through on paper exactly what I think on the subject, and [I] would be interested in your reactions—though as I said this has been for my benefit as much as yours. . . . I hope you don't mind this airing of very personal thoughts. Believe me, I don't usually speak of such things to people. It is just that you are, for me, a unique tie to Johnny's last years. I just don't know any of [his other] Alaska friends. Thank you for indulging me the chance to talk (last month) and write (this letter) about things I need to get out.

Did it all make sense? Waterman asked. Did any of it make sense? Such a woebegone question. Sure, it made sense—in all the small ways and none of the large ones. He had friends who would have happily lent him the money to go Alaska, could he have conquered his pride. Some would have liked to point out the folly of upholding an "order" that made you its prisoner. Granted, the chances of finding Bill were slim—but wouldn't it have done Waterman good to make the effort all the same? Wouldn't a college try have absolved him of some of the guilt and self-alienation churning in phrases like *All these things seem selfish and maybe unimportant.* Two sons were gone; relations with the third were hanging in the balance. There is no doubt Waterman's expressions of concern for Laura and their interdependence were heartfelt. But it's hard to understand how the same strong sense of marital responsibilities that kept him from exercising his duties as a father would not also then stop him from abandoning his duties as a husband.

It was Bill and John's mother, Emily, portrayed by Waterman as a passive figure throughout their marriage, who hired a private detective in the early 1980s. But the effort to turn up clues to Bill's whereabouts was unavailing. Emily had earlier given Bill's Social Security Number to the Salvation Army in hopes he might be located. When Johnny died, Emily established a small memorial fund for needy climbers under the aegis of the Alaskan Alpine Club.

What Guy mostly did in the wake of Johnny's death was mourn. He chose April 1 as the anniversary he would commemorate, and in the years to come, on that day, he would climb to the cairn off Franconia Ridge where Johnny's boots were secreted. He would recite some poems—including Robert Service's "The Men That Don't Fit In"—and sing three songs: "Lament for the MacLean of Ardgour," which had been skirled on the bagpipes at Hawee's funeral, "Auld Lang Syne," and "Will Ye Nae Come Back Again?" a lament for Bonnie Prince Charlie, the "Young Pretender" to the English throne from the House of Stuart.

The cairn with the boots was one of five Guy built in the White Mountains for Johnny. He did not build any for Bill. What may seem yet another example of favoring the son with whom he had a special bond was more likely a matter of not wanting to bury a son he could not be sure was dead. Every passing year made it increasingly probable that Bill too was gone forever, but with no final word there was always hope. For years, Guy would snatch up letters that looked as if they'd been addressed in Bill's handwriting. He would glance down the wood road thinking maybe . . . Even after Johnny's death, his hope that Bill was alive and would come back was never entirely extinguished. The most tender tribute to its persistence was the Christmas presents Guy bought in anticipation of seeing Bill over the holidays in 1973; the wrapped boxes sat up in the loft at Barra gathering dust for twenty-seven years.

And yet, the stark fact is that hope is about all Guy Waterman was able to do. Practical realities allowed hope, cairns, and not much else.

"Stones in lieu of sons," as Byron wrote. Waterman's hand was stayed by the tight budgets, the pressing chores, the prior obligations, or so he said. There was always something in the structure impeding his freedom to act and respond as other fathers might have. But then constraints were what he sought in structure—the ex-alcoholic bridled his demonic moods and latent waywardness with rules and limitations. Perhaps the element of his grief he could not communicate even to his wife was his suspicion that the structure so vital to his happiness, so much a part of his identity and success, had perversely contributed to the misfortune of his sons. Perhaps this was the unconfessable anguish: the possibility that he had only saved himself from the bottle, that the life he'd built to keep the world at bay had driven off his sons and thus implicated him even more deeply in their destruction. What despair lurked in the possibility that harm had come of the order he'd established—that the meaning he'd wrested from the woods was therefore bankrupt and the whole business of Barra a charade, a toy universe no less illusory than his ever-dimming hope that Bill still lived. How paltry his doctrines of freedom and self-determination seemed against the backdrop of his absent boys. He careened from extravagant hope to unpardonable guilt to depths of suffering too profound for words. Who in all decency could find fault in a man already finding so much fault with himself?

Where in this judgmental mishmash is the other Guy Waterman? Not the negligent, wounded, pitiable, self-dramatizing, and sometimes overbearing man, but the funny, compassionate, considerate, sensitive, scrupulous, socially conscientious man who was genuinely attuned to others, who volunteered at the local library, who played piano in an old folks home, who carried dog biscuits in his pocket and joked that he would use only one side of the tea bag and once wrote a limerick in Morse code, who enthralled people with deftly told stories, who encouraged and advised and mentored dozens of young climbers and writers and wilderness advocates. Where is the figure so often depicted by friends like Bonnie Christie, who said of Waterman when I stopped by her house near Lake Champlain: "He always seemed to know what people needed. He was very kind." Or Tek Tomlinson, an Ethiopian diplomat transplanted to

Orford, New Hampshire, who told me the first time I went to see him: "Guy was an unusually beautiful person. He had a way of getting into your depths." Or New Jersey–based writer and teacher Anne Barry: "He was funny, he was warm, he was generous, he was thoughtful—all you can say is silly blamed things like that. My husband, David, is an actor, and Guy wrote a song called 'A New Pair of Shoes' for him to use as an audition piece."

This is the exemplary ghost that haunted Waterman, hovering over him as the embodiment of Ariel, an ideal to live up to. As he once said in a jesting comment that contained more than a kernel of truth: "I'm trying to be the person my dog thinks I am." Small wonder he loved dogs so much: the man drawn forth by their adoring fidelity and purity of heart was much the man he wished to be. Ariel's glamorous idealism was the aspect of his psyche he felt to be increasingly under siege in the decade of the 1980s, a time when he said "gloom about my sons" spread "a darkening shadow over the main currents of my life."

"Initially there was an incredible inclusiveness about Guy," said his friend John Dunn, the physician who helped bring his body down from Lafayette. "He had unbridled enthusiasm for life and for people. He was a great listener. He got people to talk about themselves. He would deflect questions about himself. The rigidity, the judgment, the control were applied very gradually."

Waterman's main preoccupation for most of the decade was the Herculean work of researching and writing *Forest and Crag,* an almost-nine-hundred-page history of hiking and mountaineering in the Northeast, and its companion volume, the climbing history *Yankee Rock and Ice.* Guy and Laura both worked on the project, and share credit as coauthors as they do on their two "ethics" books, but Guy was the driving force—the book a tribute to his formidable ability to organize vast amounts of data. The Watermans estimated it would take a few years to write *Forest and Crag.* It took ten.

The aches and pains of getting older—Waterman turned fifty in May 1982—drove home the degree to which his happiness was staked to the body and the physical exercise of sawing wood, hauling water, and outstripping thirty-five-year-olds on epic bushwhacks. He was still remarkably fit for a man of his age, and proud of his condition. He believed the loss of his ability to lead hard rock climbs was "more a failing of character than of physical strength." But leading *was* the pleasure of climbing for him, and when he couldn't lead, he didn't want to climb. Self-crippling perfectionism made no concessions to nature and the inevitable decline of the body. The desire not to traduce his standards came to mean more than enjoying the pleasures of climbing, just as his self-image—the fictive projection of how he wished to be—came to mean more than his actual self. The trap and pathos of the pattern is that it could only paint him further and further into a corner. In his memoirs, Waterman writes of his estrangement from climbing as if it were not a choice *he* made but something that happened to him, something he was powerless to alter, like the weather. "I should not leave the impression that I quit climbing, rock or ice, casually or out of boredom or preoccupation with more important things," he noted. "Climbing had been central to my emotional life. My gradual alienation from it caused deep pain. I always yearned to go back up there, still do. To be unable hurts, bad."

Waterman was fifty-seven when he closed out a quarter-century of roping up. His last technical rock climb, in October 1989, was the route Johnny had put up at Cannon, the now ironically named and emotionally freighted Consolation Prize. Haunted by memories, Waterman gave up going to the Gunks around that time as well. Seemingly petty frustrations soon spoiled the pleasure he took on steep ice and snow. His crampons wouldn't fit his boots. The points got unworkably short from being repeatedly sharpened with a file over the years, and the expense of a new pair didn't seem worth it. Enough, then. By the early 1990s, he was done with all forms of technical ice and snow climbing.

There was still joy and satisfaction for him in hiking the backcountry, especially in winter. During the 1980s, Waterman organized an annual group trip for which he corralled ten or twelve friends for a long weekend of camping and exploration. But what braced him most during the decade of his mounting disenchantment—what kept the disenchantment at bay—were long backcountry journeys he took alone in the White Mountains. These were considerable feats in their own right, for they were accomplished in dangerously cold and wet conditions, without companions to fall back on, and Waterman was often traveling off-trail, battling his solitary way through thickets of alder and spruce traps and deep slopes of unbroken snow.

The trips were also considerable for the way the agenda of a man answered the hunger of a boy: the fantasies of childhood dressed up as adult objectives, and mixed with enough suffering to make them seem not quite like games. Waterman was often on the brink of frostbite, or anxious to find water, or so chafed by loneliness the sight of a spruce hen or boreal chickadees would overwhelm him with love for life. Carrying two clocks (to have a spare in case one broke), he made sure to mind the time while immersed in the timeless landscapes of the wild. These were songs of experience he was singing: he delighted in having the savvy to assess the weather, in finding the best route and campsite, and if some nights he had to shiver in a soaked sleeping bag or get water by holding a canteen of snow inside his shirt to melt it, well, that was the price of taking "real" risks, and putting himself out there in the teeth of the mean season. And yet there *was* something irreducibly innocent about these winter passages, too. A grown man traveling alone with a child's menagerie of stuffed animals—Lion, Sheep, Mr. Rat, Racky the Raccoon, maybe the two koalas, and others. On some trips he wrote journal entries as letters to Laura, filling her in on what Sheep and Mr. Rat and other members of what he called "the peaceable kingdom" were up to, what they were saying, how they were feeling, where they slept, whether the fusillade of hail streaming sideways over an ice-clapped summit kept them lying low in the cozy shelter of "G's pack."

Winter in the White Mountains assured Waterman nothing was "dinky" about the range; he needn't apologize for his provincial obsessions when it was ten below and the wind was shrieking like a jet engine in the passes. He was proud of the mastery he developed: "I shall shamelessly boast by saying I don't think anyone knew the White Mountains so well as I did in those years, in winter, that is, on trail and off, and in the most extreme weather conditions. Talk about joy, pride, emotional riches!"

It was key to Waterman's pleasure that his trips were part of a bigger picture, a constantly evolving set of self-assigned goals.

One of the feats I aspired to in those days was to climb all the 4,000-footers of the White Mountains in winter. I climbed all of them in winter six times, two-thirds of them eight times, and one-third ten times, some much more. I then set out to climb each of them by off-trail routes, and each of them solo. Then I climbed by all four points of the compass, in winter, a project which made a fascinating focus for many adventurous trips into little-visited corners of the mountains.

Waterman kept upping the stakes. The pleasure of being in the mountains was the pleasure of fulfilling goals and seeing his competence reflected in his once again having outwitted death's "half-dreaded, half-invited angel." While he was partial to the maxim of philosophical mountaineers, "The summit's in the climb," the Zen-like sentiment wasn't something that enraptured the computational heart of Barra's Chief Statistician. He cared too much not to count, and kept track of his conquests as carefully as Don Juan.

Waterman finished the last of his all-points-of-the-compass winter ascents, on Mt. Moosilauke, in March 1987. He was accompanied that day by Laura and his friend Dan Allen, who had joined him on a number of winter adventures. (They had spent many hours working alongside each other on the Franconia Ridge Trail, Guy clipping on the right side of the trail, Dan on the left in recognition of their political differences.) But rather than the euphoria he expected to feel upon completing his great project, Waterman was overcome by a sense of loss, and felt rudderless the following winter. "This is not to say that I still did not love being up on any mountain, especially if the weather or conditions were challenging," he wrote in his memoirs. "But I found I badly missed having that big goal in front of me, giving shape to my individual trips. . . . I couldn't come up with equally challenging further objectives. And this depressed me. As with my loss of rock and ice climbing, I felt unspeakably impoverished by not being able to find once more the high-spirited adventure I had known in the mountains in winter for so long."

Had he chased goals in winter that had led him to a dead end or that couldn't point him toward any larger meaning or sense of purpose? What was the point of going into wilderness in any season? This was the question Waterman had fumbled in *Wilderness Ethics*. He had an unrivalled record passing the tests he'd taken up, but what was the point of the tests when the experience taught you only how to pass more tests? Certainly it was crucial to know how to survive in the elements, and certainly climbers often enacted what poets and professors only prattled on about. But in the end, even someone who has come back from the brink of death in the wild must answer the question: Survive for what? To do what? For what purpose? What are these flirtations with mortality really about? What is being celebrated? Or avoided? Is it all just pointless sport, like baseball but with the frisson of casualties to make it seem meaningful? Was it that Waterman had no faith in demands that could be placed on him by forces other than himself—family, for example—and absent such faith, found himself mired in the meaninglessness of his achievement, "unspeakably impoverished" as he put it, because he recognized the futility of further tests? Had he exhausted his range? It seemed that the logic that had carried him to the limits of the White Mountains could not take him beyond them. His profound bewilderment could not be lifted by greater goals and further trips. It required a different approach to wilderness itself. It required an understanding of nature that did not entail a disdain for the limitations of the body, a disdain that was fast becoming—if it was not already an expression of—the cancer of self-hatred.

So perhaps in this light the balance tips toward the idea that suicide is indeed a form of mistaken identity. The conclusion can be strengthened by looking ahead a moment to 1994, when Guy Waterman himself sketched a vision of a new life apart from his passion for the gauntlets of wilderness—when he seemed reconciled, ruefully to be sure, to the limitations of getting older and not estranged from the love of being, not helplessly sunk in some corner of Miltonic hell. The moment came two months before his sixty-second birthday, in a letter to his niece Jean Cooley, for whom he felt a genuine kinship. She shared his love of wilderness—she worked as a seasonal employee in national parks during the winters, and hiked in the mountains during the summers. Guy wanted to let Jean know one of Laura's knees had gotten badly out of line and that, as a result, big changes were looming in their outdoor life. He was still feeling his way into the changes, trying to envision the new future, perhaps trying to put the best face on his qualms about it. He outlined his and Laura's prospects, groping for conviction:

> It appears that if we restructure our lives in a major way, eliminating long mountain descents, we may be able to keep things bearable, maybe indefinitely, if lucky. So we are rethinking our lives, probably to reduce the role which mountains have played for so long. We have had a good quarter century together in the steep places; now for another good quarter century together on the less exacting terrain of our own twenty-seven acres and the limitless horizons of the mind. There is much we can fill our lives with here and in writing—Laura's fiction, Guy's baseball, our own collaborations, of which we have more than one book idea for the future—so it should be great. We'll always have rich memories of our mountain adventures, plus a good feeling that our presence in the hills continues through our books: both our histories, which people seem to enjoy, and our "ethics" books, which seem to be affecting a lot of folks' thinking.

> Hopeful visions of the years to come.

In truth, since Johnny's death the limitless horizons of Waterman's mind had been steadily contracting, and the theme that came to dominate his life in the 1980s, apart from the bracing punishment and exhilaration of solo winter journeys, was the disjunction of self and persona, the private man and his public face. Guy was greatly relieved to be done with *Forest and Crag.* The book, published in 1989 with a dedication to Johnny ("for whom these forests and these crags were a beginning"), was an unexpected success and added to the fame the Watermans had achieved in New England climbing and outdoors circles. They were asked to speak before groups. Articles about them appeared in regional newspapers and magazines. A long profile ran in the April 1991 issue of *Backpacker* magazine, where Laura had once been an associate editor.

The assistance Guy gave to Jonathan Waterman, the writer of the *Backpacker* article, pointed up the increasing disparity in Guy's life between how things seemed and the way they really were. What Guy felt was not something he wanted friends or even Laura to know about, much less the readers of *Backpacker.* What he wanted to say to the public he summarized in a letter to Jon Waterman: "Understand and believe in wilderness values! Don't support more backcountry development! Practice true commitment to self-reliance and adventure in the backcountry! Speak out against helicopters and radios and large parties in the woods and guaranteed search-and-rescue arrangements! Preserve the opportunities for solitude and genuine risk in wilderness!"

Jon Waterman had first met Guy in 1975 as a winter mountaineering student. Via letters, Jon's visits to Barra and hiking adventures together, the two Watermans had drawn close. The father-son resonance characteristic of Guy's relationships with a number of younger male climbers was especially intense between them: both men loved mountains, both were writers—Jon had read many pages of *Forest and Crag* in manuscript and made helpful editorial suggestions—and, of course, they shared the same last name. When Jon Waterman lived in Alaska in the early 1980s he had often received mail addressed to Guy's lost son Johnny.

For the article, Jon coaxed Guy into setting down some of his thoughts about his sons; in doing so, Guy gave a glimpse of his own dark state of mind. In a 1988 letter, for instance, speaking to what had persuaded him Johnny had committed suicide on Denali, Guy wrote:

I think if Johnny had really wanted to be attempting the almost impossible achievement—as he had on Hunter in 1978—it would have gone differently. There is too much evidence in his behavior on the Ruth during those last days that he had no intention of returning or even giving it a serious try. . . . I think I have some inkling of his mood, from my own lows. The only thing that brings me back is awareness of some nice things in life, and Johnny had found little or none of that. Also, no Laura.

Jon Waterman sent Guy a draft to preview. The piece closed with an anecdote about a summer evening when Jon had walked into Barra and Guy had come rushing from the garden with a lantern in hand, only to pull up short, crestfallen and flustered. As Jon Waterman told the story, Guy emerged sheepishly the next morning to apologize for the way he had greeted him the night before and to explain he had mistaken Jon for his son Bill.

Guy replied in January 1990, praising the draft of the profile. "It is *very* good and much more flattering for us than is good for us, or so Jonathan Edwards would feel, doubtless." But he took issue with the encounter described at the end, suggesting Jon delete it because it "didn't ring true."

"I really don't think I've ever come that close to mistaking anyone's arrival for one of my son's returning," he said in the letter. "If one of my sons did return, [he] would call 'Hey, Dad,' not 'Hey, Guy,' for one thing." Lest his objection leave Jon in the lurch, Guy proposed a substitute conclusion. "How about bringing the loss of sons back to the central theme of our wilderness values and fight to preserve wildness?" he said. And as an "old ghost writer," he roughed out how the paragraph concluding the profile of himself might go:

But Guy's normally well hidden preoccupation with his lost sons only emphasizes the central role which true wilderness values play in the lives of all these Watermans. Both sons were lost to the wilderness of Alaska, which can be a harsh, unforgiving god. Yet the Watermans return unceasingly to wilderness within the narrower, less brutal confines of their native New England. For both Laura and Guy, wilderness is at the core of existence. If, as Thoreau wrote, "in wildness is the preservation of the world," the mission of the Watermans over a century later remains "the preservation of wildness," at whatever the cost.

Did Waterman mean to imply that wilderness was so important his commitment to it could withstand the sacrifice of two sons—had, in effect, been *validated* by the death of his boys? As for returning unceasingly to the wilderness—wasn't that just what he was falling away from at the time, convinced there was no juice in the orange? Wasn't it the case that the pleasures of going into wilderness no longer intrigued him now that he had bagged every peak from all four points of the compass, alone and in winter, and lacked the overarching goals which had given meaning to his journeys? What he wished to show had nothing to do with what he felt. He was keeping up appearances. Let the persona who wore the tam-o'-shanter do the talking while the soul closed the shutters and withdrew. Let the tam persona proclaim undying commitment to wilderness values even as the man was retreating from the field with a sense of alienation and unspeakable poverty—retreating because ostensibly there was nothing left to *do*. But why was unappointed *being* not enough for Waterman? Why was it not enough simply to *be* among those mountains and ridges with the cloud shadows on them? Perhaps it had been once, and then having objectives and goals and something to *do* in the mountains got in the way, or became a way of not having to be, not having to stop and face himself, his being, the beings his life was bound to and impinged upon. How could a man whose life was as deeply allied to wild places, who had invested so much of himself in the mountains, become estranged from what he loved so intensely and knew so well? Well might he have asked of himself the anguished question he cried out to the shade of his lost son: *Was there nothing to go back to?*

The most remarkable thing about the whole business of Waterman's retreat from the field, his self-spiting exile from pleasures once the mainstay of his happiness, is how he oversold it, to himself mostly, but to his community as well. In his memoirs, which he knew his family and his friends would comb for clues to his suicide, he played up his estrangement from the mountains, as if to persuade himself such was really the case. Categorical exile became part of his persona, part of his defense of his desire to die, which might be hampered if he were still finding pleasure in the mountains. The fact is, he *did* go back to the mountains. Having wrapped up his rock and ice climbing career by the early 1990s, and then his career as a solitary winter traveler traversing the range, he made a long sled-hauling trip through the Hundred Mile Woods in Maine with his friend Dan Allen in 1991.

That year he also started working as a substitute caretaker for the Randolph Mountain Club. He slept in the club's stove-warmed hut on the shoulder of Mt. Adams known as Gray Knob, and made regular rounds to three other unheated cabins, including one half a mile away at King Ravine called Crag Camp, where his father and his oldest brother, Alan, had passed a night in July 1931. (They had left their names on a deerskin register, and Hawee had played songs on the cabin's foot-pumped organ. The stopover was part of a hike across the range Hawee had devised for his oldest son for fear Alan Jr. might contract polio if he went off to Boy Scout camp with his troop.)

By the winter of 1993–94, Guy was employed as a half-time caretaker at Gray Knob, working Wednesday to Wednesday stints every other week from the start of November through the end of May—his first salaried job since he'd composed speeches for moguls at General Electric. And it was work he loved: some days he had the strafing wind and rimed cairns and snowbound domes of the northern Presidential Range all to himself. When there were guests, he collected fees and answered questions. He seemed to many the very incarnation of the White Mountains, a genial if motley druid in his white beard and tam and clothes held together by duct tape and thread. "I went up one night," recalled Doug Mayer, "and there was a guest in the hut with Guy who had a lot of expensive gear on. He was wearing a one-piece Gore-Tex jumpsuit. We were cooking dinner and the fellow was saying 'It's a shame, with all the gear

you need you can't come up here for less than two thousand dollars.'
Meanwhile, Guy is sitting there in layers of wool and army surplus from
the 1950s—the sum total of everything he has on is less than thirty dollars.
Guy just caught my eye and smiled." Waterman's rounds at Gray Knob
regularly took him past a windswept overlook near a shelter known as the
Perch. Sometimes on icy winter evenings at sunset he would stop and
gaze beyond the outcrops of the Castellated Ridge and say goodnight to
Laura, somewhere out there to the west at Barra.

After concluding his duties at Gray Knob on the first of June 1994,
Waterman climbed Mt. Adams, then made his last trip out down Lowe's
Path. On his way home, he stopped at Mayer's house in Randolph and discovered forty people, including Laura, had gathered for a surprise party
in honor of his retirement. They gave him a gold sun dial in lieu of a
watch. Two days later, he received his first Social Security check.

So the curtain fell on his life as a Hard Man tempting the furies of the
season he loved most. In early January 1995, he headed up the Falling Waters trail but turned back because a crampon broke. At the end of the
month he bushwhacked up Crawford Dome with his friends Peter
Crane, Ned Therrien, and Mark Dindorf, who owned an inn in Bartlett
where Waterman had an open invitation to stay. Guy climbed Bartlett
Haystack alone the next day. And on the day after that, February 2, in the
company of his friends, he went up Mt. Saunders.

Except to die, he never went into the mountains in winter again.

He did continue to consort with the wild in milder months. He went
on autumn bushwhacks with Doug Mayer. He climbed Franconia Ridge
on April 1 to commune with Johnny's cairn. But these trips could not be
put toward some larger goal or official purpose. There was nothing about
them that could be counted, really, and so in some sad way that speaks to
the wintry estrangement in his heart, they didn't really count.

The idea of preserving wilderness at whatever cost has ominous un-
dertones in the mouth of a man soon to be hunting his half-dreaded angel.
The ghosted paragraph, which Jon Waterman did not incorporate in
his story, shows what confusion can ensue when self and persona are at

odds. (Only persona could propose *normally well hidden* to describe a preoccupation that, while seldom discussed, was as conspicuous as a Day-Glo parka to anyone who knew Guy well.) Jon Waterman did accede to the old man's wish and removed the anecdote of their evening encounter from his *Backpacker* article, but three years later, when he published *In the Shadow of Denali,* he concluded his chapter about the life of Johnny Waterman with the deleted scene of Guy mistaking him for one of his lost sons. The surrogate son saw it as owning the truth that loyalty had induced him to suppress; the surrogate father saw it as a misrepresentation of fact and a betrayal of trust. Their friendship did not survive.

How had he put it: *no Laura.* At some level, Guy understood Laura's love was all the difference, all that had saved him from Johnny's fate, and in many ways, acting on his understanding, he had looked after his wife. When Laura's knees went, Guy regraded the trails at Barra so it was easier for her to walk back down to the house from the outhouse and in and out to the car at the head of the road. Almost every night, having finished eating before her, he read aloud to Laura in his high shy singsong—269 books altogether; thirty-six more books read aloud than he read silently to himself. He sang to Laura. He wrote her letters from the mountains when he was off on his solo adventures. He was always missing her when they were apart. They were such a pair that when she was away once and he went down to Hanover to do some research at the Dartmouth College library, he used no more of the table in the special collections room than he would have had the two of them been sharing it as they normally did. And he reported in a note to Laura how odd and lonely it felt to push through the revolving door at the library without her in the compartment in front of him.

But there was real wilderness between them, territory of a self Laura knew nothing about and which Guy could not bear to show her. When Laura was packing up Barra after Guy's death, she found a letter tucked under some socks on a shelf of his clothes. It had been written two weeks before Guy's sixtieth birthday. That is: two weeks after the eleventh anniversary of Johnny's death, nineteen years since anybody had heard from Bill, and two pointed years *before* Guy would seek to reassure his niece with the prophecy of another good quarter century with Laura on the "less exacting terrain" of their homestead. April 1992. "Dearest Laura," it began:

I expect you may take this as a very selfish act. It is. I am getting out of a world which I find increasingly unbearable, but I leave you behind to cope by yourself, in a setting we designed for two. I am very very sorry.

But I don't think that you've found me a pleasure to be around lately. I hope that you may create a good life without me, and then may look back on earlier good times, times we created together, or enjoyed together, and maybe a few kindnesses I used to do for you once in a while. . .

Barra was a wonderful dream and we pulled it off, we made it work, we created something. Didn't we? We also stood for something in this world, though others often articulated it better than we.

But Laura, it's just too hard. It's just too sad. Everything fades, everything sours. Barra doesn't, but I can't shout out the rest of the world.

I don't know whether I can do this last thing. First, I am terrified that it will hurt. Secondly, I am egotistical to the last and keep wanting to see how people will react. The best answer to that is briefly, whatever people think or say they shall soon forget me as we all do everything. And anyway why should that be a consideration to me now.

Please remember me from when I was kinder to you, in days now long gone, not the poisoned spirit I have become.

I have tried to wait until some money sources came in, and also until the manuscripts for all our books were in reasonably good shape. I think you have as much financial means now as we've had in quite a while.

A note of explanation for a suicide apparently not attempted. Waterman's disenchantment was crystallizing around the affronts of age. He would be sixty soon. Sixty! It was the one number the Chief Statistician, the man with an extraordinary command of numbers, just couldn't factor. Against the backdrop of his emotional malaise, Waterman's anxiety over his inevitable physical decline began to make mountains out of what might seem the molehills of minor ailments. After his death, Laura also discovered a list he'd drawn up of seventeen physical complaints. Among the items: "1) An ingrown toe nail; 2) Knees which give or hurt on downhills or in certain movements; 3) Odd surface coldness on outer thighs and rear end; 4) Hemorrhoids; 5) Swollen prostate (I assume from difficulty peeing); 6) Dried-up right hand; 7) Teeth literally falling apart; 8) Distant eyesight is getting bad; 9) Fungus on feet; 10) Fallen arches; 11) Cut above ear." Certainly, none of these—or the six more—were a day at the beach, but neither were they the sort of woes anyone wouldn't be happy to have in lieu of a serious illness.

Jotting down thoughts in a tiny spiral-bound notebook the day after his birthday, Waterman explored the question of suicide. He seemed to be struggling not with the decision to end his life so much as with the moral legitimacy of his reasons.

Having turned sixty [he wrote in May 1992], I'm at a point of recognizing that the remaining years are limited from now on anyway. So is not each individual entitled to make a decision to conclude life when that makes sense? Before sixty, to end one's life may be viewed as destructive or a failure to face and solve problems. But after sixty, may a decision to conclude life simply be a sensible option to take? The trick is to get thoroughly in mind that life holds no further interest, that physical ailments are beginning to accumulate to the point of being a significant detriment to enjoying life; and that the pain of unavoidable conflicts and suppressed hostilities will persist from now on, so that there is less pain to leaving life than holding on to it. Oddly, the chief attraction to remaining on Earth for me now is curiosity to do more baseball research and writing, and to continue with the elaborate fantasy baseball which has occupied my leisure hours for so many years now. Otherwise, I'm prepared to accept sixty years as a sufficient lifetime; and my intermittent glories as a piano player, politician, father, homesteader, and mountain environmental advocate and activist as concluded.

Waterman's speculations turned to the timing and the technical question of how best to accomplish his death. He was hoping to wait around until the spring of 1993, or long enough into the year to see the publication of two new Waterman books: *Wilderness Ethics* and a companion volume to *Forest and Crag* called *Yankee Rock and Ice*. In his gloom was a spark of curiosity about how the books would look. "So it may be that after next sugar season in late April 1993 might be a good time to conclude." He was uncertain whether he had the nerve either to jump off the Whitney-Gilman Ridge at Cannon or leap from the top of the Pinnacle into Huntington Ravine. His resolve was weakened by the thought of the hardship recovering his body would cause for Laura. Nor did he much like the idea of destroying himself physically. What about starvation? His mother had stopped eating five months before she died. Dehydration? Would there be time for such methods if Laura took a ten-day climbing trip to the Gunks? "Suicides have a special language," the poet and suicide Anne Sexton once wrote. "Like carpenters, they want to know which tools. They never ask why build."

What turned Waterman away from dying in the spring of 1993? Clearly, he was depressed. A biomedical view might ascribe the change to a cyclical repositioning in his portfolio of neurotransmitters. Or maybe more light in the day for a Vermonter's beleaguered pineal gland. Or the mysterious ebb and flow of mood. Socially, perhaps he was pulled out of himself by his work as a caretaker at Gray Knob. His time and effort were valued by others. Psychologically, perhaps it might be the case that he found a way past the crisis, at least for a while, when he began to express some of his feelings in poems and eventually, in a qualified way, in his memoirs.

For the better part of the dozen years since Johnny's death, Waterman had been dwelling in what psychoanalyst and essayist Adam Phillips calls "the realm of the unspoken," a place that "comes to represent, among other things, the unwillingness to mourn, or to relinquish primary involvements." If mourning entails some motion, however painful, toward a new state, Waterman seemed truly stricken by his grief, unable to move, unable to generate the impetus to do the work of mourning. He was stuck, frozen in place—paralyzed by his refusal or inability to speak, to let go of his "primary involvement," or, in the end, to yield to simple curiosity. Depression was the mountain he could not climb. As Phillips notes in his book *On Flirtation,* the "desolate apathy of depression is less painful than the meanings it attempts to blank off [sic]. The possibility of meaning, the release of curiosity, is what depression works to deny." Whatever its chemical correlates, perhaps depression served Waterman's psyche as a buffer against feeling certain kinds of pain. Perhaps in Waterman's case the depression that usefully blanked out one set of painful meanings generated another set even more debilitating. Recall the verse from *Paradise Lost* so scalding to him after Johnny's death—*Nor from hell one step no more than from himself can fly by change of place*—and set it against his exhaustive place-changing journeys within the confines of his chosen range.

Waterman's memoirs, dominated by the voice of the persona, conceal the morbid shadows crowding his sixtieth year. Other than alluding to the moment of transitory despair on the Calvert Street Bridge in Washington in 1959, his autobiography makes no mention of his suicidal inclinations. But some new heart or change of mood, some depression-circumventing release of curiosity, can be inferred from the projects that began to preoccupy him as his mountain life fell by the way. What lured him back ranged from small curiosities, such as seeing how a book might turn out, to large passions—some reawakened, some blazing up for the first time.

The Arcadian pleasures of baseball, for instance, one of the great joys of his boyhood: Waterman looked askance at the modern game with its gargantuan salaries, labor disputes, and ear-shattering music between innings, but it is hard to imagine a man more immersed in the sport. He didn't need an actual live game to entertain him. For years, he had been playing complex fantasy baseball games in his head, tracking the results with his phenomenal memory and tiny, all-but-indecipherable notations packed like hieroglyphics on index cards. He would trigger the action by an elaborate code keyed to lines and back-counted letters in *Paradise Lost*. Even Tom Simon, the man of the soft lawyer's hands who noticed the way dice caromed off Guy's leathery paws when they played dice baseball together, didn't fully understand how the *Paradise Lost* system worked. But from what Guy had told him, and what evidence he found in the baseball files Waterman bequeathed to him, Guy had been steadily replaying virtually the entire history of the National League, every contest waged by eight teams starting in 1880. At the time of his death, he'd worked his way up to the 1930s, the decade he was born. He would run the games in his mind even while talking to Laura. And as he went so far as to specify, how it was all going to turn out was one of the curiosities keeping him alive.

Baseball also breached Waterman's isolation in more conventional ways. In December 1993, he and a platoon of other baseball scholars and historically minded fans organized a Vermont chapter of the Society for American Baseball Research. Tom Simon was elected the chapter president, Waterman its first secretary. Guy later served a term as vice president. Though the presidency was his for the asking, as in his Capitol Hill days he preferred to be the power behind the throne. Chapter meetings in Burlington gave him a chance not only to attend minor league games but also to join Laura, Tom Simon, and Tom's wife, Carolyn, at Burlington opera productions.

What also may have called him back was a project poignantly symbolic of his desire to make accommodations for family and friends at Barra. He and Laura had been gathering logs for the construction of the guest cabin, Twin Firs, since the late 1980s—three years of hauling trees by hand up to a site near two balsam firs and the Gabriel birch, the overmatched guardian at the gates of Barra. The yellow birch had fallen on hard times, and in 1993, Waterman had to chop it down. In its place, the cabin rose; work began in earnest in 1993. Waterman put uncountable hours into Twin Firs. All the labor was done by hand with axe, saw, peavey, broadaxe, draw shaves, brace and bit, framing chisels, and wooden mallets. Waterman carved more than seven hundred pegs with which to pin the logs together in a bewitchingly intricate arrangement of exterior and interior walls inset with shelves, ladders, bunks, benches, and nooks. Waterman recalled many times during the construction when things went wrong and he was "ready to touch a match to the whole thing and forget it." But Twin Firs enchanted children and rickety old grown-ups alike.

Other things might have called him back: the desire to make a carefully detailed map of Barra; to prepare the Nine-Year Plan for his sugar bush; to wander the precincts of his woods: Hop Hollow, Middle Earth, Pavilion Hill, Sandy Point, the Forest of Arden. To visit the grave of his dog Ralph, "the best of companions" as Waterman had called him in the dedication of *Backwoods Ethics*. The doughty tramper, reliable adversary of porcupines and unofficial member of the Four Thousand Footer Club, had spent his last three years at Barra and had finally given up the ghost in 1976, at age thirteen. Waterman had a new dog now, Elsa, a mutt with German shepherd and a dash of coyote in her lineage. Perhaps he was reluctant to abandon her.

And then there was the vastly larger matter of his remaining son, Jim. Father and son had rarely seen each other and had had little communication. In 1985, Jim had invited Guy out to Colorado for the back-to-back ceremonies of his graduation from the University of Colorado and his wedding. Guy had carved a chess set for Jim for a wedding present. Three years later, in June 1988, Guy, referring to the trip to Colorado, told Jon Waterman that "we seemed to have [had] a good time the last time I saw him." But he added that Jim did not write to him and that the two of them were not close. He tried to explain it. "When I took my vow of poverty, so to speak, and came to Vermont, I know Johnny and Jim both felt abandoned financially. Jim may have felt that my abandonment led directly to what happened to Johnny and maybe to Bill. Ever the realist of the three, he has made his own way in the world, with little help and no example from me."

In August 1989, Guy's sister Bobbie hosted a Waterman family reunion at her house in Durham, Connecticut. More than thirty family members showed up, pitching tents in the yard. They played volleyball, croquet, and the old Maine camp game "Pickee," which is easier to play than to explain. Some of the happy hours of the reunion were captured on video. Guy played his father's bagpipes, dressed in shorts, a blue denim shirt, and his tam-o'-shanter. In the evenings, he sat at the piano, the youngest of the five Waterman elders, and as his father had, accompanied the chorus of family voices singing "Beautiful Dreamer" and other songs. All the time, Guy was hoping son Jim would show up. At one point he heard someone pull into the driveway. "Guy went tearing out thinking it was Jim," Bobbie recalled. "When he saw that it wasn't, he went for a long walk."

"The closest I came to confronting Guy about what I thought were the errors in his philosophy was in some of the sadness he felt about Jim's distance from him," Dane Waterman told me. "I saw a similarity between Jim and his wife and their independence and distance from Guy, and I tried to say to Guy, 'Aren't you getting back what you gave out?'"

But Dane's uncle wouldn't take up the subject. The pain was too much or the habit of evasion was too ingrained, too closely allied in spirit to that yearning for escape which had first sent him to the mountains. "Guy was looking for salvation in nature because he had rejected it where it could be found," Dane's wife, Bernadette Waterman Ward, wrote to me. "He looked for it in climbing, too, and it saved him from drink. Physical activity makes it possible for a while not to look at the things that are catching up with you."

So perhaps the prospect of a reconciliation with his remaining son was important enough to bestow a stay of execution upon himself. Jim and Kathleen came to Barra for a visit in the fall of 1994, arriving on a Monday, the second week in October. They stayed for most of the week. They brought their nine-year-old wedding pictures, which Guy and Laura had never seen. Jim helped Guy work on Twin Firs. They prepared window frames and raised the first post of the south wall. Kathleen helped Laura make applesauce. To Laura, Kathleen seemed strong and calm and funny. Guy told Laura on the second night of the visit Jim had lots of good ideas for Twin Firs and the two of them worked well together. Guy and Jim began to talk, for the first time, about Johnny's death thirteen years before, and about Bill, gone now more than twenty years. Laura wrote in her diary:

G & J talked about early family life, J's place in it. He felt the other two [boys] had more of G's love—the divorce, his eventually living with G (and me) in Marlboro. The divorce was hard. I could say I'm sorry if I did anything that was hard on you. But I said my recollections are it was a good time for the three of us crowded into that tiny apartment with Ralph, going climbing, the Gunks life. J agreed. It was a powerful time. . . .

She came back to her diary later with a startling entry: *I had it all wrong.*

Jim, who could climb 5.10, had told Guy what he had once told Dane: that the only way he could have Guy as a father was by going hiking and climbing with him. Guy had always assumed that all his sons felt as he did about the joy of climbing and the balm of wilderness.

G took J's remarks [to mean he had been] a bad father, letting J down. So G thinks the other two [sons] must have felt this too. "Oh God, it's worse than I thought," he said. He feels such pain, such self-blame, such guilt—and nothing I can say, no number of hugs or tears on both our parts seems able to change this. "I let people down," he said. I can only say "I love you. You don't let me down." Then he went and played heart-wrenching blues. My eyes kept crying.

In his memoirs, which he drafted two years later, Waterman wrote:

We receive a Christmas package each year which appears to be generated entirely by [Jim's] wife Kathleen, and a card or letter, often around Father's Day, also just from Kathleen. So I have basically lost all three sons. I suspect that Jim cannot forgive my walking out on my financial responsibility for him, and may blame my actions for the frame of mind which Johnny fell into before he headed off to his death. Since I think any such feelings on Jim's part would be justified, I do not inquire.

Great souls suffer in silence," wrote Schiller, the crown prince of German Romanticism and a college discovery of Johnny Waterman. Paradoxically, great souls also reach for language when they wish to disparage its adequacy. Waterman did not inquire, but in the mid-1990s the realm of the unspoken began to ask after him, and words and feelings pushed through the earth of a man who was loath to dig into his emotions. In the poems Waterman took to writing a few years before he died, he seems to drop his guard and be willing to confront in verse form subjects he could not bring himself to talk about—guilt, negligence, the darkness eating away at him. Waterman was new to writing poems and had yet to master the technique. Now and then there's a perfect line—"old speeches penned for famous men"—but often his language founders on his theme. It is the old problem of trying to carry twenty gallons of feeling in a five-gallon jar, or sending a river down the bed of a creek. What often doesn't work as literary creation is nonetheless heartrending as personal history, the late confessions of a man trying to come in from the cold.

"You hunch there in the corner, gnawing on / the litter of your children's bones, while they / Murmur assurance, it's OK, OK," he wrote in a poem called "City."

In one sonnet he wrote in 1996, Waterman rued the "dark fiend that stole my sons" as if the malignity came from outside himself. But more and more in the poems he explored the idea the demons and fiends were projections of an interior darkness. A poem called "In Memoriam" unflinchingly took up the notion of his responsibility for what happened to his son Johnny. Its five stanzas trace the course of a young boy who leaps onto his father and clutches him, the father embracing him in turn. In school, the child pines in the corner, and the father remembers a parallel loneliness. As a mountain prodigy, the son ascends a "jagged fin of ice" and the admiring dad follows every move. When the son huddles against the gales with the "mountain lords . . . screaming madness in [his] senses," the father huddles beside him. And finally, when "a savage god" beckons to the son to "come through shadowed agony of poisoned dreams, exhausted anguish, finally—discarded hope" to find shelter in a "hollow Silence—your only peace at last," Waterman poses the question that was drawing him toward his own death:

"Did you not know / I was that savage god?"

Perhaps in the end, this was Waterman's anguish, this recognition that the dark fiend that stole his sons was his shadow projected, the face of his Caliban, and that all his virtues, his sensitivity, his deliberateness, his humor, his habit of thinking through issues, his carefully formulated principles, his pluralistic devotion to diverse points of view, his respect for privacy, had been in vain where his children were concerned. It bears repeating: what these anguished last poems lack in literary merit they make up for in biographical poignancy. Here, late in his life, were his written confessions, his true autobiography, each with an implicit request for absolution, each with an implicit acknowledgment that he did indeed live in a community and that his identity was not solely his own. Whether visited upon him or made in the factory of his mind, misfortune had stripped the mask of Ariel and exposed the fallacies of Waterman's doctrine. It was no longer possible for him to believe that the meaning of one's life comes from the autonomy and freedom of the individual rather than from the knots of the heart.

It was going on five years now since life had called Waterman back from oblivion. Since 1993, he had amassed a thick binder of baseball articles, poems, and short stories. A wonderfully idiosyncratic guest cabin stood where the Gabriel birch had once been. Despite his retreat from the field of his life's great adventures, his reputation as the gray eminence of the White Mountains, the bearded spirit of winter wilderness itself, was undiminished. His Social Security windfall enabled him to buy tickets to plays and operas—opera companies all over New England were liable to see Guy and Laura Waterman in the audience. Waterman had even developed an enthusiasm for Dartmouth women's ice hockey, and was now a rinkside fixture at the Rupert Thompson arena in Hanover, New Hampshire, always sitting in seat G1.

In late 1996, Waterman began composing his memoirs. He worked into the following year, devoting to writing time he would have previously spent climbing. In December 1997, he confided in a letter to his sister Bobbie: "I thought I'd have grandchildren for sure, having raised three sons, but struck out completely on that score. That hurts, that hurts." On the very same day, December 17, he wrote to Doug Mayer, to ask if Doug could bring a tape recorder out to Barra on one of his visits. For "various morbid reasons," Guy and Laura had been thinking about their funerals, and he wanted to record a selection of music that could be played at his service.

Over the winter, Guy returned to the typewriter, and by February 1998 *Prospero's Options* was complete—all but the final pages. The "various morbid reasons" were more pressing than Laura knew. Two weeks after the seventeenth anniversary of Johnny's death, Waterman stopped the log of daily activities he'd been keeping in a three-ring notebook almost since the start of life at Barra. The pages for the second half of April, and for all of May and June, were blank. Near the bottom of the page reserved for July, he had written only "NO MORE."

Was Waterman gravely ill, or suffering from some condition more serious than the seventeen ailments he had listed in 1992? His father had died of pancreatic cancer, and Guy was concerned enough about some abdominal pains he felt in the spring and summer of 1998 to complain to John Dunn. Both Dunn and his wife, Linda, who also was a physician, urged him to go for tests. He refused. "He didn't see any point in it," recalled Dunn. "If it were a malignancy, he wouldn't have treatment." Dunn kept an eye peeled for symptoms in Guy but didn't see any. "He didn't appear to be losing weight. He wasn't jaundiced, he didn't appear to be anemic. He had a vitamin B_{12} deficiency from his strict vegetarian diet, but his strength was good." Both John and Linda also broached the more delicate question of depression and the possibility of medication or psychotherapy, but Waterman wouldn't hear of it. Visiting him on his birthday weekend—Guy turned sixty-six on May 1—Dunn asked, "How are you doing?"

"I've had enough," Waterman said.

On May 27, Guy's brother Alan and his nephew Dane came for a visit at Barra. Earlier in the year, Guy had given them a manuscript copy of *Prospero's Options*. Alan noticed the text stopped at page 178, and the appendices began at page 183.

"Where are the last pages?" he asked.

"I haven't written them yet," Guy said.

Though they had not said anything to Guy at the time, the two-day visit in May disturbed Dane and Alan. It was not that Guy had sent away for literature from the Hemlock Society (Alan was a member himself), or that he alluded to his belief that he and his siblings would expire in reverse order of their birth as the eight brothers and sisters of Mary Mallon nearly had done. What they missed was the sense of an intimate connection with him. "My dad and I were both disappointed at how bright and superficial the visit was," Dane Waterman recalled. "Half the time was filled up with other people. It wasn't a phony mask Guy was wearing, it was a deflecting of things—of not wanting to get below the surface. . . . [W]e saw him only five weeks before July third."

In late spring, Guy's dog, Elsa, whose health had been deteriorating since mid-winter, was nearly immobile with arthritic hips and "very depressed." Waterman noted in a letter to Brad Snyder dated June 22: "We hope Elsa may enjoy one last nice weekend . . . then we'll ask the vet to come and ease her free of this world's travails. Wish there were a vet to do this for me when the time comes . . ."

On June 29, Elsa was put to sleep and was laid in the earth of Barra beside Ralph. On June 30, Waterman wrote a deceptively breezy poem called "The Way Down":

A fine climb we had, the sky shining bright above . . .
Marvelous views—
But what do we do from here? What do we do?

I get bored after a few minutes on top,
Restless, seek diversion . . .
A fine climb we had, but now we must descend
The long slope downward to the scrubby land below,
Long miles of tedious plodding . . .
The shadows darken, night grows near . . .
There is, of course, the high cliff, splendid, over
On the other side: the quick way down.
I think perhaps I'll go that way . . .

Sometime during the weeks since he'd turned sixty-six, Waterman had finished the final pages of *Prospero's Options,* but he did not show them to anyone, not his brother Alan, not his nephew Dane, not Laura. The closing lines depict a man irredeemably caught between the glory of his father and the ruin of his son. There was no escape from family in the end:

I know that the . . . high positive impulses of Hawee's have been prominent in me at times—wonderful tendencies. But the same demons which drove Johnny to destruction have always intervened—where, after all, did Johnny get them from? And though I've grown a protective covering of smiles and talk, I too am alienated from my fellow humanity and dwell in a private world of storm and darkness. Ariel versus Caliban. Prospero's options—the world was all before him, where to choose his place of rest. As I look at where I have come to, after sixty-six years of struggling, I see that Caliban has won.

On July 3, a Friday, Waterman got up early. He seemed very agitated to Laura. He had planned a long day hiking by himself in the White Mountains—something unusual for him to do in midsummer. Laura could feel his distress when she hugged him good-bye. She hoped his day on the heights would do him good. Soothe his spirits. Bring some peace. She had no idea he expected never to see her again. Whatever music had called him back five years earlier was gone.

9.

GOOD MORNING
MIDNIGHT

*

Pass to thy Rendezvous of Light
Pangless except for us—
Who slowly ford the Mystery
Which thou hast leaped across!

EMILY DICKINSON,
letter #868

Anyone who has been out overdue on a walk as darkness comes on knows that night doesn't fall. It rises out of the ground from under thick woods. It wells up beneath the dark trees, the thick-branched evergreens first, and, after milling around for some time in the dense forest, gradually steals out into the clearings, keeping close to the ground. Only gradually does it rise and envelop people and the works of people. It hugs the shores of lakes and rivers, then slowly ventures out over the black waters. The sky is where it reaches last. Long after the earth is under its spell, the sky still holds out in brightness, save that a single gleaming jewel of a star foretells the end of the light.

GUY WATERMAN, *Wilderness Ethics*

DEPARTING BARRA AT DAWN, Waterman drove east toward Franconia Notch in the light of the yawning day. He parked in the lot where Cannon climbers always park. His was the only car. He was alone, unobserved. So far so good. He hurried up the trail on the south side of Cannon, then scrambled down through the brush to the clearing of lichen-flecked rock atop the Whitney-Gilman Ridge. Here now at his feet was his "splendid high cliff," the longest ridge in the East, a classic arête first ascended in 1929, when its 5.7 crux was the frontier of difficulty. Climbing partners always knew when Guy was at the crux of Whitney-Gilman because he stopped singing. It was not yet eight A.M. He was alone with only an uninterrupted fall of soft air between himself and the granite boulders six hundred feet below. Exits are everywhere, said the stoic Seneca. One step, a few seconds. The quick way down.

But with life and death in the balance, he got hung up on the sort of tragicomic impediments that might foil a sad sack in a silent movie. He'd climbed the back side of Whitney-Gilman with a pint of Ben and Jerry's vanilla ice cream in his pack, and now he sat down to have his one final treat—a last bit of sweetness before concluding a life that had been straitened by so much homestead asceticism and self-denial.

Ice cream—the child's delight. As Waterman sank his spoon into the pint, he thought he heard the voices of climbers approaching on the talus below, and he found himself wolfing down what he wanted most to savor. When the voices faded, he wondered if he'd conjured them. Having bolted his treat, he felt vaguely ill. He thought he would sit for a while in the sun. The sun felt nice; he stripped off his shirt to let the heat warm his back. Even eyes dimmed with the prospect of death could see what a glorious day was unfolding over the Franconia Range. East across the valley stood Johnny's cairn; beyond it, the backlit silhouette of Franconia Ridge; down below, the trailhead where he had tumbled out of the car that rainy Saturday night thirty-five years before, knowing nothing more about these mountains than what was on his gas station map. No one knew them better now. How beautiful to watch the morning light tender the world, embracing all things equally . . .

Waterman shook off the reverie and began to unpack the signs he had prepared to inform whomever it might concern: the owner of this soon-to-be-abandoned pack had not fallen accidentally from the top of Whitney-Gilman; the keys to his green Subaru could be found in the dashboard tray; his wife might be notified in East Corinth, Vermont. When he had finished arranging the notices, he walked toward the edge of the cliff. And was shocked: he couldn't do it—he couldn't step over the edge. The exit was at hand, but something as palpable as a wall checked him in his tracks. The will that had carried him up the trail to the threshold of his death was suddenly powerless to get him across it.

Well, if he couldn't seize oblivion, maybe he could help oblivion seize him. He retreated from the east-facing precipice and lowered himself onto the overhanging rock atop the Black Dike, a dank, perpetually shadowed gully that divided the Whitney-Gilman Ridge from the main cliff. In winter, water freezing in the Black Dike forms a 600-foot ice climb considered one of the hardest in the East. It had been Guy and Laura's most triumphant winter ascent when they had gotten up its mixed ice and rock pitches in March 1975—Laura, the first woman to do the route. They had tumbled into each other's arms at the top, weeping with joy and relief. Even Johnny had been impressed.

Waterman scrambled down onto the face above the Dike, hoping the dangerously rotten rock would break out from under him and deliver the coup de grace. A foothold promptly sheared away. Despite himself, he lunged for a hold for his hands. He traversed the rock. It was no use. Three decades he'd been climbing under the principle the leader must not fall, drawing on reserves of strength and calculation to run the gauntlet of countless pitches. Everything in him was oriented to holding on, not letting go. He pulled himself back up and off the cliff above the Black Dike. He tried rocking back and forth at the edge, hoping his feet would slip, but again the defiance of gravity was too deeply ingrained. "You might as well live," Dorothy Parker once wrote. He put his signs away and went home.

What large themes resound in Waterman's inability to take a little step! The tenacity of life. The mystery of existence beyond the reach of a man's will. The necessity of confession and forgiveness as conditions of being. The primacy of our social nature and its lyrical message that we begin to die when we are unable to share ourselves. But are these the themes inevitably implied by Waterman's paralysis on the brink of oblivion or are they simply wishful inferences that might be drawn by those who loved him or who would idealize him for reasons of their own? How, in the end, is one to translate his hesitation? Was he tugged home by pangs of conscience or did he return by default? Did he go back to Barra to discharge the debts he owed his wife or to incur, however unwittingly, incalculable new ones?

Where we place the stress speaks less to Waterman's beliefs about human nature and his capacity for unselfish action than to our own. Perhaps, in the spirit of Ariel, he feared compounding the shame of dropped responsibilities by walking out on Laura as he had walked out on his sons. Perhaps he understood more than his corpse would be shattered were his body left for recovery teams to stretcher off the skirts of Cannon. In some

sense, his legacy, his life's work in defense of wild places, even the moral legitimacy of his decision to die, depended on not leaving his wife to fend for herself on a homestead set up for two. Perhaps it was not dread of the void that constrained him but the vision of an empty wood shed and a widow struggling by herself with a four-handed saw . . .

However, it is also possible Waterman's return to Barra was not Ariel's last stand but Caliban's most diabolical triumph. Couldn't it be argued that in desiring to confide in his wife what he wanted was her permission and assistance, and that he was seeking these under extortionate conditions that gave her little choice but to grant his wishes and participate in his plan? Couldn't it be argued that by coming back he was making her, in effect, an accessory in the death of the man he meant to kill? How considerate is a husband who destroys what his wife most loves? How could it be that in repudiating himself, and their partnership at Barra, he was not also repudiating her and their history of adventure in wild places? And if he'd come back not to change his mind, or be talked out of suicide by anything she might say, then wasn't the reason for his return just to make a show of being sensitive to her needs—the trivial practical needs as opposed to the fundamental ones? One of the results of his return was to put her in the morally perilous position of equating love for her husband with complying with his wish to die.

One might wonder if, in keeping with the suicide's apocalyptic self-contempt and perverse notions, such as "If you love me there must be something wrong with you, too," Waterman returned to punish Laura for loving someone as unlovable as he felt himself to be. Doubtless, nothing could be further from his conscious desire than to hurt the one person who loved him unconditionally, but that's the point: Caliban had always operated against Waterman's conscious desires; Caliban was the very emblem of forces in his psyche beyond his control. Waterman could return to soften the blow, but he was still going to deliver it. Certainly, he knew Laura knew after three decades together the futility of trying to change his mind when it was made up. He knew even if she had been in a position to offer pointed opposition to his plans, she wouldn't have been emotionally equipped to do so. She had often said she trusted Guy to make the right decisions for them both. He also knew he could most likely count on her to keep his secret, help him prevaricate with friends and family, help him lie outright if necessary. And when he had renounced his life, he could count on her to spin a loyal tale in the spirit of the tam.

So was it Caliban or Ariel who brought him home? Surely it was both, as it had always been both throughout his life, not one or the other, not the black and white of a stark and bookish dialectic but the gray ambiguity of a man's existence in the round, in the wholeness of his contradictions: shadow, persona, self, soul, all rolled into one.

Here he was now, coming up through the garden gate at the bottom of the hill. July 3, 6:15 in the evening. Laura was sitting on the porch with a surprise visitor. Mike Young, the doctor, their old climbing friend, had unexpectedly dropped by. He'd brought provisions for supper. Laura could see instantly that Guy's day in the mountains had not been much comfort to him. But Guy made an effort to mask his distress all through dinner as the three of them talked about Mike's plans to move back east after a long absence. When Mike went off to sleep in Twin Firs, Laura sat at the little table by the south windows of the cabin, intending to write a letter. Guy was pacing about. Finally, he came out with it:

"I tried to jump off Cannon today."

For all the clues he'd left—the poem about the quick way down, the taped funeral songs, the literature from the Hemlock Society—she was astonished. Even more terrifying—and this is what might tilt the inter-pretation of his return toward the darkness of Caliban rather than the light of Ariel—he had not come back to listen to entreaties. He said he wanted to try again later that week. Wednesday or Thursday maybe. She had about four days.

Laura Waterman recounted her reaction in the article she published two weeks after her husband's death in the Lebanon, New Hampshire, *Valley News*: "My first thought was, as I watched him pace as he was telling me: Am I married to a crazy man? But I knew I wasn't, and I re-alized how much I loved him, and that the most important thing was to go on loving him as hard as ever I could."

That weekend astonishment gave way to disbelief, disbelief to anger. Anger morphed into compassion, compassion into love and gratitude. At first, Laura was just shocked. They had talked about not wanting to suf-fer the humiliation of getting older, but why *now*, so soon? Guy was as vigorous as any sixty-six-year-old in New England. What was the hurry? She could scarcely believe what he was saying, but after Mike Young left on Saturday morning—not a word had they breathed to him of the crisis unfolding offstage—Guy showed Laura the signs he had made. He brought out the notes he'd written to send to family members. What more than anything pierced her disbelief and conveyed the depth of his deter-mination to die—more than the signs, more than the notes, more than exit poems, Hemlock Society pamphlets, and funeral music—was the number of index cards in his pocket. Normally, he carried half a dozen or so. But when he returned Friday night, Guy was down to a single card, and there was nothing written on it past July 3.

And when Laura saw the point of no return to which anguish had driven Guy, she was overwhelmed with gratitude that he had come back, and that he wouldn't take the fatal step without telling her. The joy of knowing he needed to tell her; he needed her. It was paradoxical that hap-piness should flow from the revelation of Guy's suicidal despair, but the crisis broke the stalemate between them. For the first time in ages, he told her he loved her, and said he wished he'd told her that more often.

In the catharsis of confession, Laura accepted Guy's intentions. She accepted that he could not be dissuaded; she accepted the inevitability of his death. She understood their partnership, their double dream, the first-person-plural voice in which they had narrated their lives for the last three decades, was coming apart. She would have to make a separate future; she would have to figure out what she wanted to do, how she wanted to go about her life without him.

Maybe another woman in another marriage would have reacted differently. Would not have been so supportive, would not have extended to her husband what Guy described as Laura's "great kindness"—the kindness of not challenging or interfering with his desire to die. Maybe in the face of his exclusive silence, his demons, his antipsychiatric bias, his penchant for hiding his feelings behind literary masks and curtains of Milton's dense verse, she might have found herself on the verge of homicidal exasperation and saved her husband the trouble of killing himself. Or at least given him a fast smack in the chops. Or walked out. Gotten help. Something. Anything. Told a friend, fetched a doctor. In the person of Mike Young, a friend and doctor had been bunked next door at Twin Firs on Friday night. But Laura kept the confidence Guy vouchsafed. Later she would take his self-romanticizing cue and write in the *Valley News*: "Friends have asked me, why did he not seek medical help? I cannot easily answer that question either, except to say it was not Guy's way. I believe he would not have wanted to dull the ache or appease the demons with medication. Medicate his demons? Guy Waterman had no wish to do so. Better to live with the full blast of his terrors than to soften those sharp edges."

Still, she slept badly Friday night, and even worse Saturday, wracking her brain to come up with some project that would keep Guy from leaving in the next few days. It was plain he didn't want to live, and she couldn't make him live. But he had come back—and part of the reason was to fulfill his obligation to help her arrange a future. Barra was a task for two; it wasn't fair for him to leave her alone there. What did she want to do? What could prolong their time together and secure her future?

Sometime in the small hours of Sunday morning, Laura came up with an idea. She could not imagine living at Barra without Guy, but she would like to stay in East Corinth. With his Social Security, their savings, some money she had inherited from her mother, perhaps they could find a piece of land and build a house within walking distance of the post office and general store in town. Perhaps Guy could stay around long enough to see her situated elsewhere. They talked about it. It seemed like a sound plan to them both. He admitted he was still looking for alternatives to jumping to his death. He liked the idea of waiting till winter, when he might employ a method he had read about in Derek Humphry's well-known Hemlock Society classic, *Final Exit*. Humphry wrote:

> Not so bizarre, and a method for which I have respect, is freezing to death on a mountain. It takes a certain sort of person to wish to die this way: determined, having knowledge of the mountains, and an enduring courage to carry it off. They must still be fit enough to make the journey. A few terminally ill persons I have known have quietly ascended their favorite mountain late in the day and made sure they were above the freezing line for that particular time of year. They used public transportation to get there so a parked car was not spotted. Then, wearing light clothing, they sat down in a secluded spot to await the end. Some have said that they intended to take a tranquilizer to hasten the sleep of death. From what we know of hypothermia, they would pass out as the cold reached a certain level and they would die within a few hours.

So it was settled. A last collaboration for the coauthors. The aesthetics of freezing on a mountain versus falling off a cliff were not lost on either of them, or on their friends, who could look back at the decision in light of details they learned after Guy's death. As Brad Snyder put it in a letter to me:

> I am impressed by how much Guy "grew" between July 1998 and when he died, in February 2000. Based on what I've read about

suicide, the Cannon jump would have been quite ordinary—sudden, violent toward himself, intentionally or unintentionally cruel toward Laura and all other relatives and friends. Specifically, I'm thinking of the solemn procession [of friends carrying Guy's body] down Lafayette versus its alternative—a rescue worker wearing rubber gloves and picking the bloody pulp off the rocks at the base of Cannon Cliff. I don't think I could have forgiven him for leaving Laura in the lurch in so many practical and emotional ways. Guy took that destructive impulse and, with characteristic planning and creativity, turned it into something relatively gentle, relatively constructive, relatively intelligent, relatively endurable. Guy got his way in the end, but in those nineteen months he did a lot for his survivors, especially Laura.

It was settled, and they could go back to their lives as if . . . as if nothing were different. They could take up their cozy routines, resume even their pleasures. The bargain they had struck in July meant Guy could attend the annual baseball research society meeting in Burlington in early August and, a few weeks later, celebrate his and Laura's twenty-sixth wedding anniversary. It meant they could go to the annual chicken-pie supper for the church in East Corinth, "a huge success," according to a column in a local newspaper, thanks in part to the blueberries the Watermans contributed. The bargain meant Guy would live to see the record harvest of 1998, which netted forty-three thousand blueberries. It meant they could celebrate Laura's birthday in October with one of Jean Therrien's chocolate cakes, and Guy could take another ride on Ned Therrien's tractor. They could see the new Dartmouth women's hockey season, and operas in Burlington. They could hail the first night the cold called for a fire in the Ashley. They could revel in the wonder of snow falling again on Barra, the deep peace and stillness of the season jelling in the woods.

In hindsight, John Dunn was struck by how Guy stopped complaining about his physical ailments after the summer of 1998. He wondered if the aches and pains eased up once Guy had confessed his intentions to

Laura. With the end in view, his ailments may have seemed less severe, or even resolved themselves, "healed" as it were by the prospect of his termination.

So many events in Waterman's life had seemed beyond his control; he could be sure now the last one would not be. Maybe that thought infused him with some strange enthusiasm—the paradox of life's delight igniting out of death. Maybe this was his liberation and rebirth, this sense of being able to live without the uncertainty of when and how he would die—of how long he would have to go on with the weight he was carrying. Johnny was renewed by each unbroken snow bridge that didn't send him to his death, his father by the knowledge that he would soon have death send for him. Who is to say this is not what he'd been born to do? Months after his death, I received a letter from Dane Waterman's wife, Bernadette Waterman Ward. She was replying to a letter in which I had wondered whether her uncle was a victim of his own ways and perhaps was making choices in the grip of a pathology, somehow not fully *himself*:

When you call him "a victim of his own ways," I agree—a sacrificial victim [she wrote]. He offered himself, body and soul, to an illusion, or if you like, a series of them. He offered his children and I think his wives, and the autonomy he was feeding remained voracious; but he *was* the author of the ways that consumed him, and you violate all that I know about his sense of the point of living at all, of being human, if you deny him that dignity. He did himself in, and he very emphatically did it himself.

Indeed, he would not need or ask for help when the day came to climb into the killing cold on Mt. Lafayette. The method he had chosen, as Derek Humphry noted in *Final Exit,* originated among the native peoples of the Arctic, and among the Japanese. One of the haunting little sidelights in the long, sad saga of Waterman and his sons is that in Japanese lore a father too infirm or ill to climb the mountain on which he wished to die could depend on his son to carry him up.

———

They found land just outside the village, six acres along the same branch of the Waits River that flowed through town. They chose a contractor, John Nininger, who specialized in building houses from enormous white pine logs, hand hewn and hand fitted. Guy threw himself into the design, poring over plans that called for a 1,200-square-foot story-and-a-half house with a porch, a gravel driveway, and a basement, not to mention a complement of amenities that would usher Laura into the modern world. He came up with the name Page Hollow though often in casual conversation he referred to the place as "Laura's house."

In January 1999, Laura went on a long trip to Australia with Carolyn Hanson. Tom Simon drove down to play dice baseball with Guy at Barra. Waterman also spent some of the time alone at the library at Dartmouth doing baseball research. He stayed a night with Tek and Sally Tomlinson in Orford, New Hampshire—Sally had been an old grade-school classmate of Laura's, and Tek, a tall, openhearted man unfettered by Yankee inhibitions, had become like a brother to Waterman. "Guy just longed for Laura when he was here without her," Tek recalled.

When Laura returned, bearing the gift of a wombat for the tribe of stuffed animals that lived in their bedding, the Watermans embarked on their final year of homesteading. The face of Barra was second nature to them now, and in a way nothing had changed. Nothing had changed, but everything was different. A clock was ticking in the once timeless cycle of the seasons. A strange dark sand was running in the hourglass of familiar chores; what had seemed solid about the order of the place was suddenly fragile and evanescent. It was like looking at the face of an old friend and seeing the bones beneath the skin.

Guy would wait one winter, but Laura knew he would not wait two. When there was nothing more for him to do on the house, he would go. At first, that day seemed far off in the future. Life resumed. Guy went out to take the daily temperatures, morning, midday, and evening. They dusted the Dickens, the Kipling, and the Scott as the schedule directed.

Determined to live in the here and now, Laura did not think about a scene she couldn't begin to imagine. But at odd moments it would hit her: this was the last time they would be dusting these books together. It was as if they were saying good-bye all the time, to everything they would never do together again. The sense of the present was heightened by the impending future, and all their ordinary actions, the mundane details of daily life—a pair of shucked-off winter boots, a flashlight with their teeth marks on the handle, Orion rising in the bedroom window, chickadees fussing in the new morning snow—were radiant with meaning.

To fill the void left by the end of their winter climbing trips, the Watermans had taken to volunteering at the library in East Corinth, three days a week from the week after Thanksgiving to the start of sugar season, in early March or so. They reorganized the entire card catalogue. They initiated an author-of-the-month program, writing short sketches of some thirty literary masters and their foremost works. They always arrived precisely at two in the afternoon. If Janine Moore, the librarian, was a minute late coming back from lunch, she could count on finding them in the foyer peeling off their heavy sweaters. They worked until just before dark. They were good customers of the library's copying machine. That season they were in the process of compiling their fifth and final book together, a collection of mountain stories and nonfiction pieces called *A Fine Kind of Madness.* As ever, they were nothing but modest about their own literary achievements. "I never knew they had written any books until I was working in the W's," Janine Moore said.

So the first winter passed. In early March Guy drove to Cooperstown, New York, to do research at the Baseball Hall of Fame. He pitched a tent in a campground. "The maintenance guys at the campground let him take ice cold showers," Tom Simon said. "Guy talked about it like it was a great thing they had done for him."

When he returned, the sap was flowing and it was time to snowshoe out to the sugar bush to hang the green buckets on their maples. Ozymandias, King Lear, Lady Walshingham, the champion Mad Dog. Twin Firs was full of friends and guests who'd come to help out. Everyone hauled the buckets laden with sap to the kettle boiling over the fire by the sugar shed. The sharp air rang with voices and the zippy wheeze of the bow saw and the rat-a-tat-tat of woodpeckers grubbing for bugs in the decrepit beech. When they were done, Laura looked back at the sugar shed and knew Guy would not be there next year, *this is the last time sugaring together* ... "Spring briefer than an apple-blossom's breath," Elinor Wylie wrote in the poem read at Waterman's funeral, and "summer, so much too beautiful to stay." It was the same with the garden later that month, and all through May: they did the planting and digging and mulching as they usually did, putting in the brussels sprouts and the tomato seedlings and the spinach and the arugula and the trellises for the peas, but now with the knowledge that it was all for the last time together.

Meanwhile, a short walk from the village, Page Hollow was progressing. In May, the foundation was poured. John Nininger and his crew would fit the logs of the house together in his company's yard in South Ryegate, Vermont, then transport them by truck to the house site. That summer, Tek and Sally Tomlinson came by to see how the work was coming. Tek donned a pair of gloves and helped Guy clear a trail along the river for Laura to walk to town. It was hot; Guy had stripped off his shirt. He was pulling poison ivy with a plastic bag wrapped around his hand.

Tek asked him what they would do when Page Hollow was finished, would they leave Barra and move in, or rent out the new house perhaps? He knew that in the spring of 1998 Guy had mentioned to Sally that he wanted out of Barra.

"Laura will live here after I'm gone," Waterman said. And then, at length: "I'm thinking of ending my life."

Tomlinson told me he had always been moved by the wounded light in Waterman's eyes. An unusually beautiful person is how he described Guy, a gallant man who had a way of getting into your depths but who never offered a complete picture of himself, a man who seemed permanently grief-stricken, inhibited by his upbringing, his modesty, his sense that the world should not be burdened with his tears.

"Look, Guy," Tek said, "I'll respect your decision, but there are certain things we are not capable of doing, and one of them is playing God.

If you go tomorrow, you'll take a bit of Laura with you. How is it you feel you can take away part of her life?"

"But I'm not," Waterman said. "She'll have a part of me."

The bag on Waterman's hand began to rip. He gave a little laugh. "What is this?" he said, which Tek took to mean, what trouble could poison ivy present a man who was planning to kill himself?

"We had this conversation continually," Tomlinson told me after Waterman's death. "I literally would beg him to reconsider his decision. I knew I was imposing my values on him and it could backfire, but he didn't seem to tire of it."

That summer Waterman began rehearsing with local cabaret singer Danuta Jacob. She had been looking for an accompanist, and approached Guy at the Old Church Community Theatre in Bradford, Vermont, where Laura and Guy had season tickets. Every Wednesday on her lunch hour, Danuta hiked into Barra or met Guy at the piano in the Corinth town hall. They would go over songs together, often ones Waterman remembered from his days with Scotty Lawrence and the Riverboat Trio in Washington, D.C.

"When we were working on our sets, one of the songs we played was 'Over the Rainbow,'" Danuta told me. "Guy said, 'Every time you sing that song, it reminds me of my son Johnny who went up into the mountains and never came down.' I said, 'Oh, I'm sorry.' And he said, 'No it's a good thing. Johnny was a very troubled person and never fit in, and the mountains were where he felt he belonged, and I believe that's why he went there to die.'"

They worked up three sets. Danuta felt so enthusiastic about the music they were making she said they ought to perform somewhere. Guy said he didn't like to go out at night. But there was a benefit concert scheduled for the coming January at the Corinth town hall to raise money for the Tabor Valley Players and the East Corinth Fourth of July Parade Committee. It was a good cause and a great place to introduce their act. Waterman agreed. They were eventually booked as the closing act of the cabaret for two performances, on the fifteenth and sixteenth of January, a Saturday and Sunday night.

In late November, Rebecca Oreskes and her husband, Brad Ray, stopped by Barra to visit; Guy had played the piano at their wedding. "It was the only time we were ever there when there wasn't a work project to do," Rebecca recalled. "It was a beautiful day under a cobalt sky. We walked in on the winter trail. There was snow on the ground. We were looking out over the garden, and Guy said, 'We've had wonderful times here, I wish it could go on forever, but it can't.' We stayed until it got dark. And at the end, Guy gave me a stronger hug than usual. I know now he was saying good-bye."

On December 10, Waterman hiked up the Old Bridle Path to scout where amid the pearly monotones of Mt. Lafayette he might find the best place for an unattended death. On the ascent, he dropped a black-and-white wool mitten Laura had knitted for him. While he was having a can of Spam for lunch at the Greenleaf Hut, a man named Dominick Takis hiked up. Waterman asked if he'd seen a mitten. Takis had come across it, and as best he could described the rock where he had set it down, out of the mud of the trail. He was struck by how much it seemed to pain the man to have lost a mitten his wife had made. Waterman had about a half hour head start on the way down. When Takis came along, he saw that Waterman had not found the mitten. He grabbed it, and with little idea what a speedster he was chasing, began to run down the trail, thinking he might catch the old fellow. Not a chance. He described the white-bearded guy to some people at the Appalachian Mountain Club office at Pinkham Notch; they mentioned a man named Guy. Two months later, in an AMC publication, Takis read about the death of Guy Waterman, author of *Wilderness Ethics* and other books. He went to the library, recognized the man on the back cover of *Ethics* as the fellow who'd lost the mitten, and took it upon himself to mail it back to Waterman's widow.

In mid-December, Laura went down to New Jersey to visit her friend Anne—Annie—Barry, whom she had known since they were in their early twenties and just starting careers in New York City. Barry had worked for many years as an assistant to Norman Mailer, and had published a book about life on Bellevue Hospital's psychiatric ward called

Bellevue Is a State of Mind. After many years of kidney trouble, she had re-gained her health and was teaching writing. She lived in Jersey City, New Jersey, with her husband, David Greenwood, an actor.

On the last night of Laura's visit, the two women went to a Chinese restaurant near Lincoln Center, in Manhattan. For a while, Laura had been mulling over whether to let Anne in on Guy's plans. Annie was her closest friend, and the person she would call first after Guy was gone. Guy had been dropping hints to close friends in Vermont, but his death would take Annie completely by surprise.

"I have to tell you something that's very tough," Laura said. "Guy is going to take his own life."

She said she didn't know when exactly. Guy wouldn't leave until Page Hollow was well along, but if he waited past mid-February the weather would not be reliably cold enough. So probably sometime in late winter, definitely before sugar season. Laura told Annie she wanted to write a book about her and Guy's life at Barra.

Annie asked her, what about Guy's remaining son, what about Jim? And Laura described the last time when Jim had visited Guy and tried to talk about the past. It was so upsetting, Guy had been depressed for a week. He'd said he never wanted to have a conversation like that again.

"Can I tell David about this?" Annie asked. "Can I write you about this?"

Laura said she didn't want Annie to mention that she'd told her about Guy's plans. She always showed her letters to Guy, and she didn't want to deceive him.

"Oh, so all the deception falls to me?" said Annie.

"Yes," Laura said.

"I can do it," Annie said, much to her chagrin afterwards. "You have enough on your plate."

When Annie told her husband, he was enraged. "She's an enabler!" David stormed around the house, hollering "I'm going up there. We'll both go up there and stop this stupid waste of a life!"

Repudiating what she quickly decided was her own collusion in a lie, Anne wrote Laura a letter on the sixteenth of December, confiding

David's reaction. She enclosed a copy of a book about male depression called *I Don't Want to Talk About It*. She implored Laura to come to New York and see a Fifth Avenue psychiatrist named Chris Fabian who had helped her; she pointed out that both of them, Laura and herself, were children of alcoholic parents, and their responses, their willingness to dissemble on someone else's behalf, to put a beamish face on a bad situation, were part of a classic pattern.

You said our friendship had reached a new level [she wrote to Laura]. Well maybe. Surely our complicity has reached a new level. Certainly I was trying to do everything you wanted. But sometimes being a friend is not the same thing as shutting down the brain and heart and going into agreement. Sometimes it's saying stuff your friend doesn't want to hear. Here are the ways I want to be your friend: I want you to have the information you need to best guide your own behavior, whatever you choose that to be. Right now you know what Guy wants, but do you know everything that's been learned in the last few years about depression? You may not know what none of us knew when I was a kid about the repercussions of suicide on family members. I say: do what you do, whatever you think best, but first inform yourself on your course of action. . . . If you still feel [in] over your head in helping Guy live (as opposed to helping him die), get help for yourself, not him . . . Don't have the money? I'll lend it to you. Can't get away? Can't leave Guy? Don't dare leave Guy? Well, what's the alternative? If you're right, and all is lost already, will it make it that much worse to get some help for yourself? . . . If you are right, that helping Guy do what he wants to do is the kindest and most loving course of action, [therapist Chris Fabian] will support you in this, and help you out with all the painful emotions to come in the next months. On the other hand, because Chris has experience with suicidal people, because he is a doctor . . . he may know some way to turn this seemingly inevitable chain of events around.

When Laura showed Guy what Annie had written, he was distressed. "I can't expect you not to have told anyone," he said to Laura, "but you picked the wrong person." He promised Laura that if either David or Annie set foot on the porch of Barra intent on stopping a wasteful death, he would go right out the window. He would have nothing to do with *I Don't Want to Talk About It.*

Laura replied ten days later, on December 26:

Thank you for your letter and for the book. Thank you for being such a good friend. I have showed both to Guy and we have talked. He doesn't want professional help. I don't feel I need it either right now.

Some cultures are comfortable with suicide, but in America keeping humans alive no matter how deteriorated in mind and body seems top priority. There is a shame to suicide in America that other countries don't feel. We have an Ethiopian friend who we've talked to about Johnny's death. He (Tek) felt some of the write-ups on Johnny were locked into this American way of viewing death and the shameful stigma associated with suicide. Remember the ancient Greeks? The Romans? Brutus falling on his sword? The Japanese who die with honor? The Eskimo elders who go out on the ice when they feel useless in mind and body?

Guy feels his time has come.

I'm not going to feel guilt after he's gone. He doesn't want me to. There is no need to. We have talked about this. I'm very grateful he's allowing me to be part of the process. He knows I will miss him beyond belief. But I don't feel he is abandoning me. In fact, together we are, as you know, preparing my next step. And he has made it clear that he is grateful I'm not hounding him into the shrink's office.

Death is a natural part of life. How we end our lives is important. Guy feels this deeply and has made a choice that I, too, believe is right for him. I can let him go because I love him. Because this is what he wants, I want it too.

Can you look at it this way? . . .

Months ago Guy and I considered telling close friends and family. We knew that by doing this it would give them a chance to say good-bye to Guy. But we decided against it, except in a few cases, since it puts people in the position of trying to talk him out of it, of telling him he needs counseling, etc. They would be doing this because they love him, of course. But he doesn't want to be "helped." He has told me this many times. We have talked with a few of our very closest friends, and we felt they understood that Guy might reach a decision to end his life some day. And we felt their acceptance.

I told you, Annie, because you are my dearest friend. Also, by telling you I had in mind making it easier for myself when I called you with the news that Guy was gone. I knew it would be very difficult for you to understand. In this way, I thought, you would have advance warning and I wanted you to have this—to make telling you the final news easier on *me*. My mistake was not talking this over with Guy. . . .

I fear I've put too much of a burden on you. I wasn't asking for help. I was asking for your understanding. I realize now the way we are approaching Guy's death—*his* next stage—seems shocking, unnatural, antilife, even un-American. While to us it feels normal, a logical step out of a life he is now ready to leave and that we have planned for. We are both leaving Barra . . . I am going to a new life to be lived nearby in our village. He is taking the giant step into oblivion. Eternity, to use Emily Dickinson's favorite word . . .

Annie thought Laura's arguments in defense of suicide were irrelevant to Guy's situation, and worse, betrayed the degree to which her own point of view was submerged in his. "I thought her letters were filled with Guy's crackpot rationale," she told me when I went to see her nearly a year after Waterman's death. "Your thoughts aren't you. If you have a thought *I'm going to kill myself,* that's not you. Here's a man who had a condition that could have been treated. If you had a broken arm, you'd get it treated. That pattern of not accepting help was really a tragedy. It was a tragedy that he didn't go to Alcoholics Anonymous. In AA the self-pity, the self-dramatization, and all the bs is not rewarded. You get no strokes for any crap. When your best manipulative devices are met with silence, you start to put two and two together. Here was a guy who had the life he wanted. He had all the joys of creation."

Laura wrote Annie one more time before Guy died, and then Annie did not hear from her until three weeks after his death, which she read about when she opened the Sunday *New York Times* on February 20. She burst into tears when she saw the headline: "Guy Waterman Dies at 67; Wrote Books About Hiking." She was disgusted by what she perceived as the romanticizing of Guy's death. Laura had sent her a bunch of tributes from the service in East Corinth, including an editorial from the Bradford, Vermont, *Journal Opinion*:

> Few of us get to live the lives we really want to lead. Even fewer of us end our lives in a meaningful, dare we say positive, way. Guy Waterman of East Corinth, a true Renaissance man, did just that. . . . Guy Waterman serves as a great lesson to all of us. Although the loss of a great man will be keenly felt by both his neighbors and his readers throughout the world, we can all take comfort in the fact that he passed away with the peace and dignity he showed throughout his life.

Even more infuriating to Barry were the last lines in the article Laura wrote in the Lebanon *Valley News,* which was published on the same Sunday as the obit in the *Times*: "Medicate his demons? Guy Waterman had no wish to do so. Better to live with the full blast of his terrors than to soften those sharp edges. He stayed with us as long as he could."

Well after Waterman's death, and after she had mended fences with Laura—in fact, had brought Laura much closer to the point of view Laura had rejected in December 1999—I received an email from Anne

Barry. She wanted to explain what was behind her anger. She reeled off the risk factors that had increased the likelihood of Guy's suicide—depression, alcoholism, age, family history of suicide. In many cases of depression, she said, treatment is perceived as a threat, and therefore resistance to treatment is built in:

I think I reacted so furiously to all the "He stayed with us as long as he could" talk because it was so easy—as I well knew having been briefly sucked in myself. And it was so ignorant given what we know about depression. . . . At the same time Barra also surrounded [Guy] with wilderness lovers and climbers who tend to tolerate death and romanticize risk, while simultaneously cutting him off from current information about depression, news about fairly simple new treatments, contact with others who have been depressed and successfully treated. Barra made it easy to isolate himself from human connection and possible confrontation about his view of himself and his place in the world.

I'm not saying for a minute these "explain" Guy's death, but every one is a risk factor, and every one played a part in urging him on to death. Absent any one or two or four of them, he still may well have died. But there they all were, and no one at all was able to see what was going on and confront the possibility, or in aggregate, the probability of his death.

But to look at it another way: there are many people with risk factors for suicide (though it's hard to name anyone with quite so many) who do not commit suicide, who somehow at least try treatment. What made Guy different? . . . Not, why did Guy die? (Because of some psychiatric/alcoholic/whatever model.) But, why did he, who was willing to be so unconventional in so many ways, so original, why didn't he fight the odds and live? His character, his idiosyncrasies and history (his previous run-ins with psychiatry, his stubbornness, his intelligence, his high aspirations for himself, his love of the wilderness, his love of Laura) all these, which might have turned to assets to support his will for living, he used to outwit his own drive to live. How come? I'm stumped by this question. . . .

Here at last was the millennium, the year Waterman loved to make jokes about. He explained to his brother Alan that a passage of upside-down handwriting in his letter could be blamed on a pen that was not Y2K compliant. However, Barra's outhouse was, he reassured visitors. Guy and Laura celebrated New Year's at the homestead with the gathering of friends that had become a tradition since the era of winter mountaineering classes had ended: Dan Allen and Natalie Davis, John Dunn and Linda Collins, Nancy Rich and Lee Manchester. The Birthday Group, they called themselves, for those in the party who all had birthdays around the same time in the spring. Dan Allen and Guy were actually born on the same day of the same year.

It was thirteen below zero on New Year's Eve. The group had a festive supper of soup and salad, and ice cream for dessert. Dan Allen recalled: "At one point I asked Guy, 'Didn't you as a young person always hope to get to the year 2000?' I had to ask twice; he didn't respond. He was probably so caught up in his plan."

As Guy liked to turn in by nine, everyone toasted the new century with glasses of tea at seven o'clock, which was midnight at the prime meridian, Greenwich Mean Time. Guy sat at the piano. Everyone gathered around, joined hands, and sang "Auld Lang Syne." None but Laura knew Guy was playing it for the final time.

A week later, Guy and Laura drove down to visit Guy's two sisters, Bobbie and Anne, in North Haven, Connecticut. Just as he had said to his brother Alan, Guy made a point of mentioning he thought the Waterman siblings would go in reverse order, much as the Mallons had gone. Bobbie and Anne were concerned about the hints Guy was dropping. "Guy was sitting there," Bobbie told me, "and I came out and put my arm around him, and said, 'When am I going to see you again?' He didn't answer."

Anne had brought a vacuum cleaner for Guy and Laura to use in their electrified new house. Back home in Bethesda, Maryland, she received a letter from Guy dated February 1: "Laura is pleased to have a modern vacuum cleaner. Don't know why we've let our vacuums remain so dirty for so long, but it will be good to clean them up. Isn't there some expression about Mother Nature abhorring a dirty vacuum?" That was the last word she would have from her brother.

The next weekend was the concert with Danuta Jacob. Two shows, both nights sold out. No one attending could have known what the evenings meant to Waterman. He had decided to use some of his Social Security funds to have the piano in the Corinth town hall professionally tuned. And after consulting with Danuta, who planned to wear a brown velvet dress, he went down to College Formals in Lebanon and rented a tuxedo.

The following weekend, on January 21, he and Laura drove to Burlington to attend a women's ice hockey game with Tom Simon and Carolyn Hanson. Dartmouth versus the University of Vermont. The two couples had a quick supper at a pizza joint. Guy happily recounted the concert he'd given with Danuta Jacob. What a joy to be back onstage performing with another musician, like he had when he was a teen jazz phenom with the Riverboat Trio.

"Wow, Guy, you've come full circle," Carolyn said.

After the game, the four of them went for ice cream. Guy slipped some of his to Carolyn's dog, Kensey.

The Watermans headed out early Monday morning.

"Every time they left, Guy would always pull out a card and check when we were next going to see each other, but this time he didn't," Tom Simon recalled.

Guy customarily hugged the Simons good-bye. This time, standing at the door, he embraced them both in a way that seemed especially heartfelt.

"I said, 'I'll see you in two weeks at the Flynn Theatre'—we had tickets to a show—but he didn't say anything," Tom recalled.

"He didn't pull out that card," Carolyn said.

On January 27, the raising of Page Hollow officially began as a large crane lowered a huge log onto the foundation and John Nininger began to fit the house together. The structure flew up. At Barra, the cord frames were brimming with wood. Since the summer, Waterman had been chopping and sawing and splitting red oak and maple, and now Laura had a supply of firewood that should carry her through March. Night temperatures in the region at the end of January were ranging from the low teens to zero, and diving well into minus figures in the White Mountains. With Page Hollow taking shape, Barra stocked with wood, and bitter cold settling in, the time had come.

Waterman felt free to go. There was nothing to hold him back.

Except that suddenly he was too sick to die. Some wily rear guard of the life force, some shift in the argument of being and nonbeing, or maybe just the immune-system-depressing stress of what was going on under the surface, the half-open secret, conspired to brew up a wicked case of the flu. Laura caught the bug two days later. The Watermans had almost never gotten sick in their twenty-seven years at Barra. Now, on the brink of good-bye, they dragged their bedding into the living room and lay down next to the heat of the Ashley. All the stuffed animals of the "Peaceable Kingdom" came with them.

Guy struggled up on Saturday, January 29, to go to Hanover with Rebecca Oreskes, Brad Ray, and Jon Martinson. Dartmouth women were skating against Princeton. The four of them started home near midnight. The others dropped Guy off in the parking lot in Bradford where he'd left his car. "Guy put on his wind pants," Jon Martinson recalled. "It was a very cold night, and he wasn't looking forward to the walk in to Barra. I commented to Brad and Rebecca that I'd never heard him complain before. We shook hands, and made arrangements to get together before I went on a trip I was going to take to Patagonia. That was the last time I saw him alive."

The effort to get to the game had drained Waterman. That Sunday he felt lousy, and Laura was even worse. Guy had promised to finish an index for a baseball book Tom Simon was editing called *Green Mountain Boys of Summer.* (Simon later dedicated the book to him.) He went woozily to his desk and flailed on with the list of names and page numbers. Sick as he still was on Monday, he sawed and split firewood, and shoveled the snow off the roof. One of the Watermans' construction mistakes when they built Barra in 1973 was not using rafters strong enough to support a lot of snow.

On the evening of Tuesday, February 1, Guy was playing the piano while Laura fixed supper. She was still debilitated by the flu. Though the small cabin was trembling with music she loved, Guy putting his all into her favorite songs from "Tennessee Waltz" to the hymn "Just a Closer Walk with Thee," the prospect of the music stopping forever was too painful. She asked her husband not to play any more.

Laura was still sick on Wednesday, but Guy felt better, and she was grateful to have him taking care of her—making tea, tending the fire, heating up some of the tomato-garlic soup he'd been given by Mo Nininger, the wife of the builder assembling Page Hollow. She knew without his even saying it that these were the last days, but she wasn't sure exactly when he would go. She understood the flu had been a blessing—a final dispensation of time together.

That day he told her he wanted to get out of her way.

They talked about what sort of obituary might be published. Maybe something in the local paper. He didn't expect much more than that. He'd had a whole folder of things that might be read at a funeral, but he'd thrown most of them away. If there was going to be anything from the Bible, please let it be only the verse from Ecclesiastes: "Vanity of vanities . . . all is vanity . . . one generation passeth away and another generation cometh: but the earth abideth forever . . . For in much wisdom is much grief: and he that increaseth knowledge increaseth sorrow . . ."

On Friday, February 4, the Watermans both went into town. They stopped at the post office. They did some work at the library. They wrote up some introductory bios for upcoming authors of the month and entered the library's latest acquisitions onto the shelf list, the master list, and the author cards in the card catalogue. On his way out of the library that afternoon, Guy rushed past Janine Moore's daughter, Daelynn, whom he normally would have scooped up into his arms. "At the time he said it was because he wasn't feeling well," Moore recalled. "I didn't think about it so much until later."

On toward evening, Guy told Laura, "I think I'm going to go in a couple of days."

She wrote in her journal the next day: *Is this our last day together? Neither of us knows.*

It was, as it turned out. Saturday, February 5, was their last full day together. Guy finished the index for *Green Mountain Boys of Summer.* All week he'd been writing notes, and he spent much of the day writing more. To Doug Mayer, the devoted young outdoorsman who had gotten him the part-time job as the Gray Knob caretaker and who had been such a game companion on his last bushwhacks, he wrote: "On a less cheery note, one of us wants to mention what perhaps he has hinted at in conversation over the past couple years. If you hear he's off to the mountains in killer weather, he hopes you may respect that it's his considered preference, and thus not sad news."

And to Tek Tomlinson:

Sorry to be taking this step as I was enjoying the developing friendship with you and Sally. I've discussed this *at length* with Laura. The prospects of aging, with all its discomforts, indignities, and limitations were even more than I cared to put up with. And there's much about this world that's too much for me. You've told me you come from a culture which respects a decision of this sort. I hope you can respect my decision. Please be a good friend to Laura, you and Sally. Thanks for your friendship.

To his old friend, contemporary, and rigorous editor Brad Snyder, who had helped plant the idea of Barra nearly thirty years earlier and before that helped guide Johnny up Denali:

Sorry to be leaving like this, but I've tried to explain my thinking about old age prospects and other shortcomings, for me, of this

life. Laura and I have discussed this at length. She'd *much rather*
I'd stay, but respects my preference. Of course, it isn't a question
of going or staying—just [of] when and how to go. Above tree
line in the wind seems appropriate—I'll be joining Johnny, to
whom I was always closer akin than anyone realized. In her new
house, once adjusted, Laura will do fine. Thanks for your friendship over many, many years. I know Laura will depend on your
continued friendship. *Thanks*—and good luck with your own
late years—Guy

Here in the note to Snyder was the saddest sort of faith—faith
not that a father and son would be reunited in the next world but
that they would always be paired in this one by the likeness of their
deaths.

Sometime Saturday he composed a schedule on a yellow index card:
"Leave Barra 8 A.M. Old Bridle Path trailhead 1 P.M. Dead Ass Bend 2:15
P.M. Summit 5 P.M." Sunset on Sunday, February 6, was 4:58 P.M. Waterman would arrive at the top of Layfayette as the sun went down. He told
Laura where the authorities should be able to find his body. They agreed
she would wait at least until Friday to begin notifying their friends. She
had suggested it might expedite things if he took some alcohol to drink,
and he agreed and had bought some whiskey. She watched him decant it
into one of his two canteens. He would take aspirin too, to acidify his
blood, impairing the brain's ability to regulate body temperature and has-
tening the loss of consciousness. She asked him how she would be able to
replenish the cabin's supply of kerosene. He said someone would be able
to help her.

She cooked potatoes and onions for dinner that night. He told her the
voices in his head would soon be still. She felt very weak. Her stomach
had been hurting for days. She took a bath in the cattle trough. He helped
her wash her hair.

On Sunday morning, she fixed the breakfast they normally had: steel-
cut oats, wheat germ, maple syrup. He gave her the final pages of his
memoir, which he had sequestered until just this moment. He asked her

not to read them until he was gone. He told her if the weather wasn't cold enough, he would put up in a motel, or possibly even have to come back.

She watched him pack. Almost everything went into the top pocket of his backpack. Three pencils, two pens, two canteens—one filled with water, and one with watered whiskey. Four flashlights, two tins of salmon, a can opener, two clocks, and two items he had always carried in his pack no matter where he went: the ivory-handled knife his son Bill had sent him from Alaska and a medal his son Johnny had gotten on a climbing trip to Russia. Also, from their bed: Killy the snow leopard and Ben the Bengal tiger—two members of the Peaceable Kingdom to watch over his final resting place.

He told her that after he left she should make bread.

He asked her not to come out onto the porch when he went outside to put on his snowshoes.

He zipped his faded blue wind jacket. He slipped his arms through the straps of the battered blue pack.

He put his arms around her. They held each other. He was crying. She could feel the dampness on her face. The matter of his being was shrinking like an island in a rising river, and she tried to engrave upon her memory the heft of his shoulders and the smell of his skin.

He said he would always be with her.

He told her to be brave.

And then he went out to the porch. Dutifully, Laura stayed inside. He stood by the worn bench he'd fashioned from the log of an ash tree, the spot where he often lingered to listen to the hermit thrush or watch the wind scuffle in the evergreens. She went to the bedroom and watched through the window as he gazed at their woods. He took the snowshoes off the wall and clomped down the steps. Good-bye porch, good-bye bench. He set the snowshoes down and stooped to fasten them to his boots—the plastic double boots Mike Young had given him in the hope some new equipment would reawaken the old man's desire to go into the mountains again.

At the window, Laura could see he had forgotten his father's ice axe.

"Guy!" she shouted, and ran out onto the porch.

She handed him the axe. She stood rooted there, no shoes, no coat in the zero-degree air. There she stayed as he thanked her, then set off, shuffling down the hill, paying out a line of tracks behind him. He turned at the bottom and raised his arm. A last wave. She waved back. And then the forest took him in, and he was gone.

Laura went inside and saw it was eight o'clock exactly. She got out the whole wheat flour, the rye flour, a little white flour, some wheat germ, some powdered milk and maple syrup and yeast, and began to make bread.

Later in the morning, Laura opened the file Guy had left for her. There was a note on a clean piece of paper, his hand in black ink:

Laura,

The one impossible note to write is this. Many of my other notes are inadequate but there's no way I can write one to you. Thanks for showing me the greatest love I've ever known. You have been a miracle in my life. I just want you to know I always appreciated what you gave me. So much of my life fell short but with you together we built something here, didn't we?

Every day you see what we built you see me. One part of me will never leave one part of you. But you will build your own life from now on, and I know that you will do it well. I love you. Forever, Guy.

She read the final three pages of his memoir, and found the tightness in her stomach easing. The pages spoke of his fear of getting old, of his regret at the diminishing influence of their books, and of how he wished he could have done better and made more of a difference. He wrote of how the last years of his life had passed numbly. He had put on the face of the genial host and wit but his real feelings had been off limits even to his most intimate friends, he said. And he spoke of his family, his father, Johnny, how they embodied the quarrel in himself. "Ariel versus Caliban," he wrote. "As I look at where I have come to, after sixty-six years of struggling, I see that Caliban has won."

Still later that morning Laura worked on a short story that had been vexing her for months—a piece of fiction based on her family and a young girl on the brink of adulthood, a girl such as Laura had once been. The girl has a crush on one of her formidable father's academic colleagues, a charismatically handsome and doomed young man named Bill Farrell. At the climactic moment of the story, at one of her parents' riotous parties, Bill Farrell offers the girl the olive in his empty martini glass. She bites it, and tastes all the fatal glamour of grown-up life. It was an Eden story, of course, with the olive as the apple, but Laura had been struggling to get it right—to clarify what it was really about. At last that morning, she felt she knew. She felt that Guy had given her a gift of insight. Guy had freed her to see what she was trying to say.

In the afternoon, she followed his progress in her mind—knowing where he would be as each hour passed. When she went out to the shed to saw wood she could see his tracks still crisply registered in the snow. The afternoon wore on, and dusk began to filter up out of the forest and steal into the garden. Laura lit the lamps. She wrote in her journal: *Did he start up? I hope he did. I hope he's up there now—even though that is so hard to think of: the cold and the wind. Alone, growing weaker. Did he use the whiskey?*

Stars that night, beautiful and severe. Orion rising in the bedroom window. And somewhere out there under the same sky, her husband hovering between worlds . . .

On Monday, with each hour that Laura did not hear Guy's footsteps on the porch, she was more certain he was dead. She worked feverishly on the tale of Bill Farrell and the end of a young girl's innocence. *The story grows stronger before my eyes—and I am happy. This is Guy's gift to me, which I couldn't have felt so strongly if he were alive. So he is with me—as he said he would be—and always will be.*

Laura carried her secret into town, amazed at how normal everything seemed, life ambling along. At the post office, she tried not say too much to the polite queries about how she and Guy were doing. She was fine, she said. She went over to the library to give Janine Moore an envelope Guy had asked her to deliver. It contained forty-five cents—money Waterman owed for using the copy machine. One of the bits of business he did not wish to leave outstanding. At the library Laura made copies of the last pages of Guy's memoir. "After sixty-six years of struggling I see that Caliban has won." She crossed out "sixty-six" and wrote "sixty-seven."

So that first day passed. *All the animals in the bedroom are sad. We slept close together last night and missed Guy. It could be several days before he is discovered.* She had agreed to wait at least until the end of the week. Tuesday came and went. She wrote, she sawed wood, she fixed things to eat and passed another night with Sheep and Mr. Rat and the koalas. Impossible to believe it was only two days ago: it seemed like centuries. Barra was the Gabriel birch reborn. She felt protected and far away, comforted by its solitude, its worn and familiar folds. Days of sun had softened the bite of the snowshoe tracks trailing into the woods.

Laura had been sure someone would have reported Guy's death by Thursday, but Thursday dawned and no one had. The weekend was looming. She would have to break the news, lest strangers come upon him. She put on her snowshoes and shuffled through the woods, then marched down the plowed road into town, across the Tabor Valley branch of the Waits River onto Main Street and then down to the white Congregational Church and the parsonage, where the Reverend Holly Noble lived. It was nine in the morning. She stood at the door of the reverend's home. When she knocked, the double life she had been living for the last year and a half would be over. It would finally be over. She stood at the door, hovering between worlds.

When he remembered his father's axe, Laura was there on the porch handing it to him. No coat, no shoes. He took the long shaft in his hands. Etched near the head were his father's initials: ATW. He thanked her. And then he went down the hill. At the bottom where the clearing ended at a stand of pines, he turned back, and waved—good-bye house, good-bye love—and then plunged on, shuffling over the blankets of snow, past the graves of Ralph and Elsa, past the sugar shed and the leafless maples he knew by name. His life was vested in every contour of the land, and now he was quitting it all, walking out, never to come back, never to set foot upon any of this beloved ground again.

He had made the drive countless times. He preferred the back roads—Route 5 to Wells River, then into New Hampshire on Route 10 and 302 to Littleton. In the early days, he'd driven with the heat off and the windows open on freezing winter nights. "Helps us acclimatize!" he cried to Mike Young. Today he stopped for newspapers—the Boston *Globe* for the weather forecast, the *Valley News* for the women's hockey scores. He went all the way over to Crawford Notch to check the Mt. Washington Summit Observatory forecast at the AMC hostel. And then he looped back into Franconia Notch.

It was a beautiful winter day, wildly windy and see-forever clear. Eight degrees that morning in Benton, west of the Franconia Range; five degrees in the town of Bethlehem, north of the mountains. And, of course, the conditions in the valleys did not begin to approach those in the mountains. The mean February-sixth temperature recorded at Mt. Washington was three below zero, with winds averaging seventy-eight miles an hour, and gusting to one hundred and thirty.

Waterman parked the Subaru in the lot across from the trailhead of the Old Bridle Path. He left his snowshoes in the car. The car keys he tucked in his breast pocket, along with the yellow schedule card—"5 P.M.: Summit"—and his glasses. He was nearsighted.

Hundreds of times he'd climbed the Old Bridle Path. The snow was broken out, a track through leafless birch and ragged mountain ash, and then, higher up, a defile through the dark stands of red spruce and balsam fir. Near the halfway point, the trail opened on a series of white rock ledges with panoramic views across Walker Ravine. Mt. Lincoln rose to the south; hidden on its flanks was Johnny's cairn.

Around two in the afternoon, a hiker named Marty Sample who had been on the summit of Lafayette at midday was about twenty minutes below the Greenleaf Hut, heading down. He passed an old man going up. They exchanged nods and continued on. Sample remembered thinking it was awfully late in the day to be heading up, especially for such an old fellow, in moldy-looking gear, with hardly any equipment in his pack and a long pole of an ice axe. Seemed like he knew what he was doing, though. Probably planning to turn around at the hut. What Sample remembered most was the ice axe. "It was at least a hundred centimeters," he told me over the phone. I asked how after a glancing encounter he was able to estimate its length so closely, and he told me he worked as an equipment buyer for Eastern Mountain Sports and had a professional interest in the fine points of ice axes. The eye sees what the mind knows.

Around 4,200 feet, Waterman reached the frozen bed of Eagle Lake and the boarded-up Greenleaf Hut. His father and his sister Anne had scribbled names in the hut's log in the 1940s. As winter climbers routinely do, Waterman stopped long enough to strap on crampons, and then ventured on into the hammering west wind. The icy white dome of Lafayette rose more than a thousand feet above him. He picked his way across the glassy open slopes where the only trees were wind-hounded dwarf evergreens that lay close to the ground.

From cairn to cairn, up to the summit, gaunt against a darkening sky. Waterman did not need his clocks to know what time it was. Slanting sundown light was pouring over the Presidential Range to the east. One of the most gorgeous sunsets of the winter was unfolding—an alpenglow of deep rose and tangerine igniting the distant peaks. At his feet, darkness was pooling in the great basin of the Pemigewasset Wilderness. He had first stood here in a driving rain thirty-five years before. Did he linger at the edge of the tumbling void to pitch Bill's knife and Johnny's medal into that wilderness of mountains and ridges which had not brought them home and now could never bring them back? Neither medal nor knife was found in the pack carried down by the friends who trundled Waterman's body off the mountain.

Down from the summit on the trail north, not ten minutes' clattering on the glassy rime along the line of the ridge. Just off the trail he stepped into the alcove of gray rocks he had scouted in December. Come spring, the ground underfoot would be a soft patch of moss and grass and tiny blueberries. He thrust the ice axe into the snow and sat down under his father's initials, facing north-northwest, the direction in which his sons had vanished, and so set out the line of his family, his father behind him, his sons ahead.

Inside a plastic bag in Waterman's breast pocket was a map of Barra, a map he had taken scrupulous pains to draw to scale and fill with the details of his woods, his stream, the orchards, the garden, the buildings, the trails, almost the very dance of life he and Laura had choreographed on their patch of earth. On the back, he'd written a message:

Please: 1. Do not take special efforts to save life. Death is intended. 2. Return pack and VT Subaru (green) in southbound parking lot to Laura Waterman, East Corinth, VT 05040. Thank you. Guy Waterman

Perhaps now he removed the map to look at it once more, or perhaps he took it out because he was stirred to record the words that had come swimming into his thoughts, six lines he wrote out in pencil. They were from *Paradise Lost,* Book II, the words of the fallen angel Belial who is lamenting the "sad cure" that is the destruction of life. He asks:

> *. . . for who would lose,*
> *Though full of pain, this intellectual being,*
> *Those thoughts that wander through eternity*
> *To perish rather, swallow'd up and lost*
> *In the wide womb of uncreated Night*
> *Devoid of sense and motion?*

The temperature would be sixteen below zero that night on Mt. Washington, and inconceivably more frigid in the winds that were gusting past at a hundred miles per hour. It was a matter of hours now, and perhaps much less than that. The fierce wind and heavy sweat of ascending would have precipitately wicked away what warmth Waterman had. He probably did not need the handful of aspirin he swallowed to acidify his blood, or the watered whiskey he drank to dilate his veins and hasten the loss of heat. As the medical examiner of New Hampshire later speculated, it could have been only a matter of minutes before the end.

Involuntary shivering begins when the body temperature drops below ninety-five degrees. Contractions start at the neck and spread down to the pectoral and abdominal muscles, and then out to the legs and arms, doubling and tripling the body's oxygen consumption. Below ninety-three degrees, the blood rushes to the organs at the core, shivering stops, drowsiness and apathy set in. "This is the Hour of Lead," Emily Dickinson once wrote. "Remembered, if outlived, / As Freezing persons, recollect the Snow— / First—Chill—then Stupor—then the letting go—"

Perhaps Waterman brought his arms up to his body and assumed the position in which he was found: reclining on his side, arms against his chest, hard as marble. Below body temperatures of ninety degrees, the heart begins to balk. The eyes dilate. The breath grows shallow. And then, ineluctably, with a kind of magisterial indifference, the curtain descends.

When the map of Barra with the penciled verse was returned to Laura by the party of friends who retrieved her husband's body, she imagined she could see in Guy's shaky hand something of his spirit holding out in brightness as he waited on his mountain for his long-sought night to rise.

Let the last vignette of Waterman be not of a lone figure in the snow but of the communal man he was three weeks earlier, standing among friends and admirers at his final performance. A concert he could not have looked forward to more; a turnout that could not have made him happier. Two shows, and not a ticket left for either one. He had asked Janine Moore if he could change into his rented tuxedo in the East Corinth library, and on the night of the first show, January 15, he came in well ahead of time, like it was his first day on the job. "It took him forty-five minutes to put the tux on," Moore recalled. "He was pulling on his sleeves and fiddling with the collar. He wouldn't pick up my daughter, Daelynn, which he normally did, because he didn't want to her to wrinkle the tux."

After months of rehearsing, Waterman and Jacob had refined a four-song set. They would start with the Gershwin standard "Our Love Is Here to Stay," and roll into "I Had Someone Else Before I Had You and I'll Have Someone After You're Gone"—with Guy taking a big rafter-rocking solo. Then they would torch things up with the classic "Body and Soul," and finally wrap their debut with a galloping rendition of "A Good Man Is Hard to Find." All songs Guy had been playing for more than half a century.

Laura went to the Saturday night show but found the prospect of watching Guy play for the last time in public more than she could bear, and she skipped the Sunday night performance. As it happened, when I went to visit Danuta Jacob in late March 2000, seven weeks after Water-man's death, she had just gotten a copy of the videotape of their final show at the Corinth town hall. We were sitting in the living room of her house in Piermont, New Hampshire. She slid the cassette into the VCR.

And there they were: the chanteuse standing on a small riser, in her long brown velvet dress, the piano player in his rented tux, hunched over the newly tuned upright, his back to the audience.

Waterman's diminutive form hardly seemed big enough for the music he was wringing from the keys. When Danuta finished "Our Love Is Here to Stay," Guy turned and applauded her, holding his hands down by his waist. On "I Had Someone Else Before I Had You" he was so eager to get to his solo Danuta had to hustle through the verse. When at last his moment came, his limelight stomp had the crowd whooping and holler-ing by the end. But again, after the splashy finish of the song, he clapped for her in that modest way, arms by his waist, hands never too ostenta-tiously far apart. The whole set was over before they knew it—four songs, and they were done by 9:30, and the emcee was sighing and saying what a wonderful night it had been and would everybody come back again next year. A photographer grabbed a few pictures. Someone in the crowd sug-gested Danuta and her self-effacing accompanist should try out for a tal-ent contest they'd heard about on National Public Radio. A few days later, Danuta received a letter from Guy:

I just want to say that for fifty years I treasured the hope and dream of accompanying a female vocalist, one who would captivate the crowd. My imagination always placed this in some dim-lit upscale cocktail lounge in Washington, D.C., or New York or maybe Baltimore or Boston. Time: two A.M. I would never have believed that I got to live this hope and dream, long after I thought it was gone, in small-town northern New England, in a bare town meeting hall, before nine P.M.

"I was looking at it as our debut," Danuta said sadly. "But he was looking at it as his grand finale. I can only guess that what was going on that night was a celebration of things never completed for him. Maybe he wanted the world to see that side of him one last time."

She dabbed her eyes. On the tape, she and Guy had just finished "A Good Man Is Hard to Find." The audience was clapping, and Danuta was trying to coax Guy onto the stage to acknowledge the ovation. She almost had to tug him up there. It was poignant to see his hatless head and the bashful happiness that flashed across his face when he turned to receive the balm of the crowd's acclaim. It was as if he couldn't believe he had done anything to deserve it. But then maybe he had. The uncertainty made him awkward and boyish. Or perhaps it was just the novel texture of the rented tux, and knowing he was up past his bedtime, and that he had to change and make the long hike home to the cabin in the woods, and that this was good-bye, this was it, this was the end, this was the end that counted. The sweet noise of the night was dying away, and with no further ceremony, he slipped from the stage.

ACKNOWLEDGMENTS

✳

MANY PEOPLE HELPED ME explore the intricacies of Guy Waterman's life and death, none more intently than his widow, Laura, who, as I hope the text makes plain, bravely opened her life up to a stranger when that wasn't the easiest thing to do. I admire her courage, her willingness to examine her own actions, and the license she gave me to come to my own conclusions. She helped me locate many of her husband's papers, tracked down facts and dates, shared her own diaries and letters, and even put me up for the night during my visits with her in Vermont. Over the last two years, she has written me dozens of letters about her and her husband's life in the mountains and on their homestead in Vermont. This book would be much impoverished without her help. She and some of her husband's close friends have started the Guy Waterman Alpine Stewardship Fund to raise money for the care and preservation of the White Mountain trails that flourished under his stewardship. The Fund is a worthy and important cause for anyone who cares about the condition of the backcountry. Contributions can be mailed to: The Guy Waterman Alpine Stewardship Fund, P.O. Box 1064, East Corinth, Vermont, 05040. The Web address is: www.watermanfund.org.

Other members of Waterman family also helped me greatly, including Guy's brother Alan T. Waterman Jr., his sister Anne Waterman Cooley, and his sister Barbara Waterman Carney, who died in the spring of 2001, six months after I interviewed her. (She was the sort of person who'd mail you back the umbrella you left in her kitchen.) My thanks also to family members Donna Waterman, Tim Carney, Laura Cooley, Jean Cooley, and especially Dane Waterman and Bernadette Waterman Ward, who wrote me a number of letters, and introduced me to moral and spiritual perspectives that enriched my understanding of their uncle.

The story told here had an earlier incarnation as a magazine article that appeared in the June 2000 issue of *Men's Journal*. I am indebted to then-editor Mark Bryant, who assigned me the piece, helped shape it for print, and made sure the magazine's hawk-eyed accountants covered all my expenses except for the speeding ticket I got in New Hampshire trying to get to an interview on time. Also at *Men's Journal* I was helped a lot by the research and fact-checking of Tom Foster, the assistance of Taylor Plimpton, and the editorial guidance of Dan Ferrara. I'm grateful to Sid Evans and David Willey for reprinting the piece in a collection of *Men's Journal* articles called *Wild Stories,* and to Jann Wenner, the ringmaster of all this indoor and outdoor activity.

I have been greatly helped by the work of other journalists too, notably Rob Buchanan, who published an affecting piece about Waterman in *Outside;* Kate Millet, who wrote substantial portraits in *Yankee* and *Climbing* magazines; and Helen O'Neill of the Associated Press, whose feature on Waterman appeared in newspapers all over the country. I have relied heavily on Glenn Randall's gripping and regrettably out-of-print book *Breaking Point,* and also the ranger and author Jon Waterman's lyrical book *In the Shadow of Denali.* Both writers also generously gave me the benefits of their insights, as did Jon Krakauer, who wrote about Guy Waterman's son John in *Into the Wild.*

In Alaska, I am grateful for the help extended by Steve Williams,

Nancy Gordon, Tom Kizzia, Joel Gay, Dermot Cole, Bob Bell, Nan El-liot, James Brady, Roger Robinson, Dave Buchanan, Carla Browning, Gerry Flodin, Doug Buchanan, Carl Tobin, and especially Chena Koponen Newman, who took it upon herself to track down some facts that had eluded me for months.

In New England, I am especially grateful to John Dunn, Jon Martinson, and Doug Mayer, and to Mike Young, whom I met first many years ago when we were guinea pigs in a high-altitude physiology study in Canada's Yukon Territory. Thanks also to Rebecca Oreskes, Peter Crane, Mike Pelchat, Ned Therrien, Dan Allen and Natalie Davis, Louis Cornell, Danuta Jacob, Jim Lawrence, Marty Sample, Bonnie Christie, Janine Moore, David Roberts, Charles S. Houston, Tom Simon and Carolyn Hanson, Tek and Sally Tomlinson, John Saltmarsh, the late Thomas Johnston, Scott Himstead, Helen Whybrow, Dr. Richard Monroe, and Dr. Thomas Andrew.

Anne Barry in New Jersey and Brad Snyder in Colorado both sent me large collections of correspondence they had exchanged over the years with Guy and Laura Waterman, and were particularly insightful in their observations of Guy Waterman's life and character.

Elsewhere, at various points in the country and abroad, thanks to: Elizabeth Norman, Lori Leslie, Lance Leslie, Bob LaGuardia, Dean Rau, Jay Kerr, Kate Bull, the late Richard Stimson, Oscar Gottscho, Barbara Belmont, Alice Reed Morrison, Peter Morrison, Louise Hammond, Donald Nivers, John Daniels, Susan Staples, Christopher Braunholtz, Warren Robinson, Pete Metcalf, Henry Florschutz, and Keith LaBudde.

The title of this book comes from Emily Dickinson's poem #425, a stanza marvelously impacted with her inimitable dashes: "Good Morning—Midnight— / I'm coming home— / Day got tired of me— / How could I—of him?"

Thanks to my agent, Kris Dahl at ICM, who helped me file a new flight plan and convert a book about dreams into a book about wilderness, families, and self-inflicted death. At Riverhead, my thanks to the poetically attuned Lindsay Sagnette, Alex Morris, and Elizabeth Wagner, the resident black belt of English usage. Most of all, thanks to my editor, Julie

Grau, who instantly divined the larger possibilities of this story and dived into the manuscript with her singular passion, sensitivity, and skill. I have had three great editors in my life; she's one of them.

And finally, there is my own family, much on my mind as I thought about Guy Waterman and his family. I thank my mother, my brother, my sisters, and especially my father, who, a former editor and writer himself, was the first reader to have a look at this book, and the first to suggest cuts and revisions. "I know you don't want typo corrections," he wrote to me, "but I have to pass on a vital one in the first chapter. The 'Old Bridal Path' should be the Old Bridle Path—repeat, Bridle—unless New Hampshire weddings are particularly rugged affairs." Much of this book's smooth sailing at Riverhead is due to my dad's keen disdain for "sonorous twaddle."

And then there is my wife, Kate Betts, whose love, raucous laughter, and high style, not to mention newfound interest in cooking, kept my life from unraveling as this book was gestating. As she goes, so go I. More and more, we find the old bridal path leading us to the wonder of a little boy: our son, Oliver, who now is three. I wait for the day he will tell us what family means. I expect it may have something to do with flamboyant shorebirds, because when he was two, he came over to the computer one day and watched me for a while, his head barely clearing the edge of the table.

"What are you doing, Daddy?" he said.

"I'm writing a book, Ollie."

Nothing about this activity impressed him, but then he said, "Is there a flamingo in that book?"

Suddenly it seemed there should be, and I promised him that I would try to slip one in. Here's a flamingo for you, Ollie. Clear skies, fair winds for you both.

CREDITS AND PERMISSIONS

✳

Lyrics from "Lake Charles" by Lucinda Williams. Used by permission.

About the Author

✳

A former staff writer for *The Washington Post,* Chip Brown has written for *The New York Times Magazine, The New Yorker, Harper's, Esquire, Outside, Men's Journal, Vanity Fair, Vogue,* and *Condé Nast Traveler,* among other magazines. He has won numerous awards for his journalism, including a National Magazine Award for feature writing. He lives in New York City with his wife, Kate Betts, and their son, Oliver.